N EIGHTEEN HOLES

AQUA

M. HOLMER

AROUND
THE
WORLD
IN
EIGHTEEN
HOLES

AROUND THE WORLD IN EIGHTEEN HOLES

TOM CALLAHAN AND DAVE KINDRED

D O U B L E D A Y
New York   London   Toronto   Sydney   Auckland

PUBLISHED BY DOUBLEDAY
a division of Bantam Doubleday Dell Publishing Group, Inc.
1540 Broadway, New York, New York 10036

DOUBLEDAY and the portrayal of an anchor with a dolphin
are trademarks of Doubleday, a division of
Bantam Doubleday Dell Publishing Group, Inc.

Book design by Bonni and Martin Berman

Every effort has been made to locate current copyright holders for material excerpted
in this book. Please send any information regarding copyright material to the
publisher.

Library of Congress Cataloging-in-Publication Data
Callahan, Tom.
    Around the world in eighteen holes / Tom Callahan and Dave
Kindred. — 1st ed.
        p.   cm.
    1. Golf courses — Miscellanea.   2. Golf courses — Humor.
3. Kindred, Dave.   4. Callahan, Tom.   I. Kindred, Dave.   II. Title.
GV975.C37   1994
796.352′06′8 — dc20   93-51075
                                                                        CIP

ISBN 0-385-47315-X
Copyright © 1994 by Tom Callahan and Dave Kindred
All Rights Reserved
Printed in the United States of America
June 1994

1   3   5   7   9   10   8   6   4   2

First Edition

For a lot of old sportswriters, dead and dying, especially Si Burick,

Jack Murphy and Red Smith.

And for Marilyn Maxwell.

       T. C.

For Jeff and his world champion twins, Jared and Jacob.

       D. K.

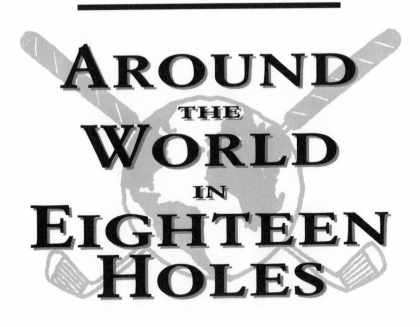

AROUND THE WORLD IN EIGHTEEN HOLES

CONTENTS

Contents

FOREWORD
LOOSENING UP

WE WOULD GO around the world playing golf. We would find eighteen diabolical holes in eighteen diabolical places and string those holes together to make a golf course. We would call it the Royal & Diabolical Global Golf Club. It would be a par 72. The length would be 37,319 miles.

We would go from the Arctic Circle past the Equator to the Tropic of Capricorn. We would stop in Scotland, Russia and China. We would play at midnight in Iceland and under Kathmandu's mad-dog noonday sun. In twenty countries on four continents, we would hit thousands of golf balls. Some would land in the Atlantic, Pacific and Indian oceans as well as the Baltic Sea, the river Eden and in an unmentionable spot on a golf course built in the shape of the French architect's mistress. We would play through monkeys and madmen, crocodiles and corpses. If we were not Phileas Fogg and Passepartout going around the world in eighty days, we would be Indiana Jones and Walter Mitty carrying 9-irons.

For however long it took, Tom Callahan and I would do what most everyone wants to do. We would run away from home. We would leave troubles behind. We would take out no garbage no more. We would be who we wanted to be. We would laugh all the way to the next tee, a pair of fugitive 14-handicappers with golf swings built from paper clips, prayers and spare parts. We would go to places we had never heard of and meet people we had never imagined. "In every parting," Goethe said, "there is a latent germ of madness." Exactly.

We revealed the plan to our friend, the Louisville sportswriter Billy Reed. The poor guy. Billy started laughing and couldn't stop. He had heard of sportswriter scams before. He had perpetrated one or two him-self. But this—this was beyond the pale. This was massive. All eaten up with envy, Billy finally said, "You guys have really done it now. This is the mother of all boondoggles."

To which Tom replied, "We prefer to think of it as a calling from God."

Anyone who wants to understand golf's appeal should first memorize everything Dan Jenkins ever wrote. Like Ben Hogan and Byron Nelson before him, Dan once was runner-up in the Fort Worth city tournament. Then he found out what he could really do. He could explain golf and America in eleven words, those being: "Golf is a mental disorder like gambling or women or politics."

The nineteenth-century Canadian philosopher Arnold Haultain wrote, "Golf is a Gargantuan jugglery, a prodigious prestidigitation, a Titanic thimble-rigging, a mighty legerdemain." The nineteenth-century Missouri philosopher Mark Twain needed fewer syllables: "Golf is a good walk spoiled."

Writers, thinkers, players and other fools have had at it. Golf is a ruin-ous disease. An ideal diversion. A pleasing madness. It is self-torture, dis-guised as a game. Golf is the most useless outdoor game ever devised to waste the time and try the spirit of man. Churchill said it was like chasing a quinine pill. Chesterton called it an expensive way to shoot marbles. It is a game of failures, a game of sorrows, an infernal fatheaded silly ass of a game.

(Here we reprise two hundred years of epithets and euphemisms in paragraphs stuffed as full as Ky Laffoon's car in the 1930s when the quirky pro piled his clothes in the back seat and made the trunk a general store carrying his clubs and shoes, shotguns and shells, flashlights and food-stuffs. Laffoon explained: "You never know when you might have to take off somewhere. You may get into a spat with your little lady. You may want to check an address at night. You can get hungry. You might see some quail in a field.")

Bernard Darwin said golf is not a funeral, though both can be very sad affairs. It is an X-ray of the soul. A young man's vice and an old man's penance. A game for deposed Latin-American dictators in plaid pants. Bourgeois desperation. The best game in the world at which to be bad. It is hell with the lawn mowed.

The game has been golve, gowf, gouf, colf, golff, gouffe, gowlfe, goffe, gauffe and goff. It is cow-pasture pool, aerial croquet and pedestrian polo. It is geography compounded by psychology explained best by phrenology. Alistair Cooke said golf is guaranteed to produce nervous exhaustion and despair leading to severe mental illness and, in some cases, petulance. Bernard Shaw called it a typical capitalist lunacy of upper-class Edwardian England. We have Vardoned, baseballed and interlocked the V's of our sweaty hands onto cleeks, spoons, mid-irons, mashies and niblicks, baffies, brassies and Big Berthas. These weapons have been hurled against gutties, featheries, bounding billies, Hummadingers, Jetflights, Podos and a pharmacy full of the cursed dimpled pellets which Chick Evans called "pills of quicksilver."

Never forgetting that backward it's flog.

It delivers misery. A. J. Balfour said we should play golf as children because it "punishes with eternal mediocrity those who too long defer devoting themselves to its service." Anyone arriving late may wind up with a swing that P. G. Wodehouse gave his creation Archibald Mealding: "a blend of hockey, Swedish drill and buck-and-wing dancing." In which case Edgar A. Guest has reminded us:

> Through time all other griefs may cure,
>   All other hurts may mend,
> The miseries of golf endure:
>   To them there is no end.

Jimmy Demaret, a great player, said, "Golf courses are the Demaret answer to the world's problems. When I get out on that green carpet called a fairway and manage to poke the ball right down the middle, my surroundings look like a touch of heaven on earth."

And again Bernard Darwin of the *Times of London*: "I can look back gratefully on many agreeable hours spent—or even wasted—in playing. I think not only of quiet corners of many courses, but of many fields where the grass was so long that almost every stroke required a search; I think of a mountain top in Wales and a plain in Macedonia; of innumerable floors on which I have tried to hit the table legs; I recall rain and wind and mud and the shadows of evening falling, so that the lights came twin-kling out in the houses round the links, and the ball's destiny was a matter of pure conjecture. Remembering all these things, I can say that I may have been an unprofitable practicer of the game, but at any rate I have been a happy one."

Calvin Coolidge and Mother Jones decried golf as senseless and elitist. In 1942 the curmudgeon H. L. Mencken used the game as a symbol of upwardly mobile pretense among newspaper reporters: "They undoubt-edly get a great deal more money than we did in 1900. I well recall my horror when I heard, for the first time, of a journalist who had laid in a pair of what were then called bicycle pants and taken to golf; it was as if I had encountered a studhorse with his hair done up in frizzes, and pink bowknots peeking out of them."

I believe all of them, Callahan and Jenkins and Churchill, the poet and Demaret and Mencken. Every opinion about golf, each theory, the insults, the love notes and all the aphorisms however contradictory, whether told under oath or under the influence—they are all absolutely and utterly true because golf is what you make it.

Michael Murphy's fictional hero Shivas Irons made it "an odyssey . . . from hole to hole, adventure after adventure, comic and tragic, spellin' out the human drama." It can be the love affair described by Shivas's friend Agatha: "Oh, golf is for smellin' heather and cut grass and walkin' fast across the countryside and feelin' the wind and watchin' the sun go down and seein' yer friends hit good shots and hittin' some yerself. It's love and it's feelin' the splendor o' this good world."

And here came two middle-aged sportswriters making golf an accom-plice as they went over the wall. For twenty years in ringside seats at the sports circus, Tom and I had been friends as newspaper columnists and magazine writers. There was no need to walk away from the show. But there comes a time. Things happen. Even a reasonable man can't figure out the reason for anything any more. At middle age, just when he knew some of the answers, the world throws all new questions at him.

So he turns to his buddy Callahan and says, "Let's bust outta this joint." And Callahan says, with a wink, "The sooner the better."

With the vaguest notion of what we hoped to learn by taking it on the lam, we knew only that we needed to go somewhere. Maybe the answers would be found in the going. Because we had done our talking for twenty years on golf courses while waiting for Muhammad Ali to rope a dope, or waiting for Pete Rose to get the 4,192nd hit, or waiting for Joe Montana to do another Joe Montana thing—because the golf course had been our refuge from the clamor, we packed our golf clubs and headed for the airport.

The impulse to leave is an old one. As a boy, I often climbed through a bedroom window and onto the front porch roof. From there I would pull myself onto the steeply pitched roof of the house Dad built by the railroad tracks in Atlanta, Illinois. Telescope stuffed in a back pocket, knees and elbows scratching against the grainy shingles, I squirmed up that mighty mountain of a roof. For hours I would sit by the chimney and study distant places through the looking glass. There were days a boy could see all the way to McLean, the next town north, three miles up U.S. 66.

I wanted to know what was out there.

Some nights, I wanted to jump onto the train passing our house. A Baltimore & Ohio freight would shake my bed with its sudden thunder. About ten o'clock the train would be at my window and then gone, moving in the darkness. I could hear its whistle at the depot crossing just before it left the city limits headed to a destination unknown to me. My father said the B & O went to Chicago.

"Where's Chicago?" I said.

He said, "The Cubs play there."

On the B & O nights, I thought it would be good to grab ahold of the passing train and swing up into a boxcar, the way cowboys did in movies. It wasn't that I wanted to go to Chicago, wherever that was. I just wanted to be someplace else, a place far away, even farther away than my telescope could take me. I liked to be in motion.

Many a summer later, an itinerant typist by then, I came to be with Callahan in Northern Ireland on the very top of the island at a lovely place named Portrush.

We stood on the tee of the par-3 fourteenth hole at Royal Portrush Golf Club. That hole's name is Calamity Corner. The name suggests the perils that threaten anyone who tees it up on the Antrim coastline. At 211 yards, Calamity's length is forbidding. Yet that's the least of the problem. Miss the shot to the left and it's lost over sand dunes deposited there a thousand years ago by the roaring Irish Sea; miss to the right and the ball clatters into a chasm dark with tangled gorse, that chasm named War Hollow. The only safe haven is the green itself, a bump of land so small

in the distance that it reminded me of Tom Wolfe's *Right Stuff* line about
fighter jocks learning to land on aircraft carriers: "It's like trying to land
a brick on a skillet."

At once beautiful to the eye and frightening to the imagination, a hole
like Calamity is physical evidence of golf's paradoxical seductive powers.
We take a walk on God's green acres hoping to gain some sweet reward by
putting ourselves at risk of calamity. There is this curiosity about golfers as
well: we're not sure pain is all that bad a deal. The golf architect Pete Dye
has said of his treacherous courses: "People will drive two hours and
they'll pass perfectly fine golf courses in order to get to one that is so hard
they can't play it. It's the golfer's character. He loves the pain."

That day in Northern Ireland, Callahan and I had braced ourselves with
two fingers of Bushmill's Irish whiskey at the turn, the elixir poured by a
wizened character who seemed to have lived in the tin hut behind the
tenth tee for a century or so.

"A nice day it is for golf," the old man said. A sea breeze howled and
rain came sideways on this nice golf day as we contemplated Calamity's
catastrophic possibilities.

"Piece of cake," Tom said.

"Nothin' to it," I said.

Photographs made that day of Tom down in War Hollow searching for
his Calamity tee shot have the feel of photos showing a man lost in a crater
of the moon. He is seen clinging to the chasm's upper side. He is seen
bent over in the gorse looking for his misguided ball. He is seen as a tiny
thing with the slimmest hope of survival in such a hostile environment.

While Callahan climbed from the chasm, I waited on the green because
I had hit a 5-wood that flew high in the sea breeze, landed safely and
rolled to within two feet of the cup. From that distance I often two-putt,
as I did, making par on one of the world's great tests of golf.

Immediately I heard myself saying, "Tom, what we ought to do is go
around the world playing diabolical holes. Eighteen holes like Calamity.
Be fun, wouldn't it?"

At that moment, the beleaguered victim of Calamity shared none of my
adventurer's delight. Tom's eyes were afire and tendrils of smoke rose
from his piratical red beard. He seemed ready to take up a gentler game,
perhaps international assassination. Rather than intrude on his introspec-
tive moment, I kept silent. I even put aside my proposal to go around the

world. I figured it was only one of those foolish things a guy says when he is on life's back nine.

Still, the urge to run, to get lost, to find a new way, is strong in anyone having a bad year. My newspaper folded; my son, with his twin boys, moved a thousand miles away; I couldn't write a note to the milkman. Then one day at an antique sale, I saw a wooden-block puzzle which, put together piece by piece, came to reveal a child's verse:

Ride, ride the carousel,
Reach for the golden ring.
Never to finish,
But to begin again.
Life is a circular thing.

Well, if a murmur floating over an Iowa cornfield can conjure Shoeless Joe Jackson, a child's puzzle can whisper: Around the world . . . now.

So in the summer of 1992 I brought it up to Tom again. We sat at an outdoor café in Barcelona during the Olympic Games. We had been to a thousand places doing our stuff and maybe we would go to a thousand more. But maybe not, either. We were contract writers, largely on our own schedules. We could, if we wanted, dream up the mother of all boondoggles.

Over a beer Tom said, "Around the world, eh?"

"Life is a circular thing," I said.

Soon enough, the good folks at Doubleday publishing and *Golf Digest* magazine bought in. And in the summer of 1993, Tom and I would tee it up on the Royal & Diabolical—but not before negotiating the stakes.

Being a high-rolling Midwesterner, I said, "So, a dollar a side, a dollar the eighteen?"

Tom grew up in the caddyshacks around Baltimore. "Not money," he said. "Let's figure out something better than money, something grander."

So it was agreed. We would ride, ride the carousel. We began thinking of our old friend Calamity.

The Itinerary

Sentimentally, Northern Ireland was the logical place to start. (The word "logical" will scarcely be needed again.) But after Calamity, where?

Catastrophe? Spinning the globe got too dizzying. A calendar was taken off the wall and a map was unfolded on the floor. We became explorers looking for a new way to get from here to there.

We knew only one thing for sure. On summer's longest day, we had to be in Iceland. That's when they play the Arctic Open. So after Calamity we would go west and north to Iceland, to that stark and beautiful land first touched by Vikings a thousand years ago.

As for the rest of the itinerary, it just grew. It grew from both whimsy and practicality. We needed 18 holes and we needed to get from Atlanta back to Atlanta. We wanted a trip backwards, touching places we had been, and we wanted the trip forward, to wherever that might lead us.

Golfers crossing the Atlantic commit a mortal sin by passing up a stop at St. Andrews. Not about to risk such a thing, we would leave Iceland and go directly to the Old Course and the Road Hole, a piece of land at once royal and diabolical.

Letters to golf associations asking for advice as to interesting courses in their countries produced this from Bernard Cartier of the Fédération Française de Golf: "Golf de La Salle in Mâcon. This golf course designed by the French architect Robert Berthet reproduces in most of the holes the different parts of a female body." This we had to see. From St. Andrews, then, we were drawn to France and if en route to France, why not buy tickets to ride on the Orient Express?

Belgium beckoned, not for the golf of it but on a personal mission to a little town near Brussels where a man lived for a while in 1944.

To Sweden from there, for no good reason other than we had never been there. I thought we should visit Stockholm so we would know the lay of the land in case the Nobel Prize people wanted us to show up for the 1994 award in literature. You never know. Besides, Callahan kept saying things like, "Blondes!"

The symbolic journey backward took us to Moscow. During the 1991 U. S. Open, public relations representatives handed the press a sophisticated brochure on the glories of golf at the Moscow Country Club. We knew Russia had changed. But golf?

We needed Africa. Twenty years before, we had been in Zaire with Muhammad Ali and George Foreman. We could do Kinshasa one more time. On second thought, we'd heard about machine-gun welcomes at the Zaire border. We decided on Johannesburg, and what a trip from Moscow to South Africa. You fly from the debris of an empire fallen. You fly into the brightness of middle Europe, stopping for a while at Zurich's dazzling airport. Then you fly south, over the Sahara, over the heart of dark Africa and into a country bloodied by violence. The excuse for the trip was golf alongside crocodiles. The real reason was to hear the voice of a man shaped by apartheid's past and future.

Out of Moscow and South Africa, where?

We looked at our map.

"Let's just get to Johannesburg," Callahan said, "and from there let's find an island."

That was our front nine: Northern Ireland, Iceland, Scotland, France, Belgium, Sweden, Russia, South Africa and an island to be named later.

The 10th hole: We flew over the Indian Ocean and over India and almost to Tibet, stopping at . . . KATHMANDU! Indiana Jones had gone there; or at least his alter ego, the actor Harrison Ford, had. We talked to a charter airline pilot who had flown Ford around the world. The pilot said, "The problem with Kathmandu is smoke from firewood that hangs in the valley there. The day we flew in, it was so hazy you couldn't see the Himalayas even. A couple years ago, a Pakistani airliner burrowed in there short of the runway. It's a high-speed landing because of the mountains and you can't see much until you get right on it. It gets somewhat hairy."

From Kathmandu, we had two thoughts: 1) Terrorists had blown up the Bombay airport shortly before our departure from Atlanta. 2) Terrorists also had blown up the New Delhi airport. These events helped us decide to make our one India stop in Calcutta.

Looking for a place to play in Asia, we did the 20th century equivalent of putting notes in bottles. We sent messages on the Prodigy computer network. One reply: "Haven't played the Saigon G.C. since '72. There was a resident alligator on the ninth hole. If you went into the trees looking for a ball, he would chase you in a beeline to the pond. I assume the resident sniper left when the war stopped. Gin and tonics (malaria prevention) were called for before going out, but not too many or you couldn't outwit or outrun the alligator. You didn't dally the first five or six holes, either. Sniper fire will do that for you. You could slow down after that because the sniper was terrible at longer ranges. Sure separated the golf talkers from the golf lovers."

No Vietnam for us. Thailand instead. From there to Singapore and on to China, there to walk on the street where a boy faced down an army's tanks.

And then to Japan, a nation of golf zealots. Another note on the Prodigy network: "At Atami, Japan, many years ago, you had to avoid holes scattered throughout the course. They were five inches by five inches. They were air vents to underground defense caverns. Your ball would drop to unknown depths." Would we find mystery in Japan?

Homeward bound, we would have to stop at Pebble Beach, a wonder of the world. And the piney cathedral of Augusta National Golf Club would be the only possible 18th hole. But months before we drove down Magnolia Lane onto Augusta's grounds, we looked at a map on the floor and Callahan said, "After Pebble and before Augusta, where then?" We found the answer to that question only by making the trip. It was an answer we'll remember always.

So, too, will we remember the first day of the journey. To Northern Ireland. To Royal Portrush Golf Club. To that beautiful place where, two years before, we had been befriended by one of the club's old captains, an architect named Roy Crawford. We wanted him to join us on the first leg of this escapade. We would begin, then, by making a telephone call to Roy.

CHAPTER 1

ROYAL
PORTRUSH

Portrush, Northern Ireland

"Jailer, Tell Roy We Bogeyed Calamity"

"Hello, Mrs. Crawford?"

"Yes."

"This is Tom Callahan calling from America. Is Roy there?"

"No."

"Do you expect him?"

"No."

"Oh. Is there another number I might try?"

"I could give him a message."

"Great. Please tell him Dave Kindred and I are returning to Ulster in a week. A couple of years ago, Roy steered us around Royal Portrush and we're hoping he can join us there again next Sunday or Monday."

"I'll tell him."

G O A R O U N D the world. Play diabolical holes. In the manner of John Cheever, Kindred was proposing we make a river out of all the backyard pools just so we could swim it purposelessly. "If we could find eighteen holes like this one," he said, "we could keep this conversation going." At forty-seven or fifty-two, utterly no reason can make a surprising lot of sense.

The conversation, unsurprisingly, was about the business. It's always about the business. Your story reminds me of my story reminds you of your story reminds me of my story. We're forever retelling our stories in almost exactly the same words. Red Smith, who spoke as beautifully as he wrote, rarely changed a syllable. But you didn't mind. That is, we didn't mind. Wives and other outsiders occasionally minded. They weren't really in the family.

"I'm bored!" Mary Nack suddenly announced one night in a Washington restaurant. It must have been a fine restaurant. David Brinkley was sitting at the next table. Mary's husband Bill, the voice of horse racing and grace for *Sports Illustrated,* was getting to the payoff of an animated anecdote my wife, Angie, had heard only about twelve times before. Everything stopped. Brinkley dropped his spoon.

"God, Mary, you're so right," I said finally. "Sportswriters must be the most boring people on earth. Let's start over and have a real conversation for once, involving all four of us. What should we talk about? You go ahead and kick us off." She got one word out before I shouted, "I'm bored!" Shortly, they were divorced. Shortly, I will be too.

Angie is a lovely girl—pardon me for still thinking in those terms—and an amazing sport. While I was at the Super Bowl, the Olympics, spring training, the Final Four, the Masters, the Kentucky Derby, the Preakness, the Belmont Stakes, the Indianapolis 500, the NBA playoffs, the U. S. Open (golf), Wimbledon, Henley-on-Thames, the U. S. Open (tennis), the British Open, the PGA, the baseball playoffs, the World Series, the World Cup, the football playoffs, the Rose, Orange, Cotton, Sugar, Gator, Fiesta, Holiday or Blockbuster Bowl, the great yacht race in Fremantle and the big fight in Zaire, she was raising two children alone.

The job she did, and I didn't, may be best illustrated by an exchange we had at the only parental function I can ever recall attending: a high school Mass and awards ceremony six or eight years ago. Tom was introduced as the president of his junior class. "Is Tom president of the class?" I whispered to Ang, who replied understandingly, "You jerk."

For the length of the eighties, when I wrote the sports for *Time* magazine, I kept at least one foot along with a few other body parts in New

York City. Still, we had been together a nominal—in fact, phenomenal—twenty-six years. They can't say we weren't serious. Two days after our twenty-sixth anniversary, I left on this longest and most eccentric of all the journeys of my life. As well as Angela and I understand each other, it still surprised me that, while neither of us said so in so many words, both of us knew I wouldn't be back.

The first time Dave and I went to Northern Ireland, we imagined tail gunners on golf carts but encountered a surprising peacefulness, surpassing gentleness, at County Down, Ardglass, Balmoral, Clandeboye and Warrenpoint, where the club president, Tom McAteer, raced from two fairways over to extend greetings. "Are you the Yanks?" he called. A silver-haired hummingbird, McAteer fluttered with stories of his one trip to the States, the year the Brooklyn Dodgers won the World Series. "You see," he said with a twinkle, "we all keep time by that."

Both as witnesses to normalcy and testimony to it, visitors are cherished in Northern Ireland. They are merely welcomed to the Republic.

This time, flying from Atlanta to Shannon to Dublin, we rented a car and had the agent point us toward Belfast. She said to follow the yellow road on the map. "The road isn't literally yellow, is it?" Dave puzzled. I think he was kidding. Throughout the trip, our mutual ineptness in the area of directions would range from mildly pathetic to perfectly pitiful.

Young shoulders slung with automatic weapons mark the Irish borders clearly enough. The smiles bobbing between the flak jackets and the helmets fit the soldiers better than their hardware. "Are you guys getting younger or am I getting older?" I asked the first boy who stopped us. "I don't know, sir," he said sweetly. "I don't want to offend you."

Kneeling beside the car, propping his elbows on Dave's open window, he smoothed the map and attempted to straighten our course. All the same, we were lost again in five minutes, stumbling into the border community of Clones, where nine holes materialized like Brigadoon.

"Isn't this Barry McGuigan's hometown?" Dave asked the woman who collected our greens fees. "Sure," she said. "He's away in London." One imagined that, for any given instant, she could pinpoint the whereabouts of every son and daughter of Clones. "His brother's on the golf course right now. The fourth hole, or thereabouts."

Dave and I shook hands, hit swooping drives and, though calling it a practice round, began the long game.

You may never have heard of Barry McGuigan, but he was the feather-weight champion of the world, a great and savage little boxer with enough going on inside his head to realize when there was less. He lost his title to a last-minute substitute on a 100-degree day in Las Vegas, "a cod of a town," in his mother's perfect phrase. "You know, I lost brain cells in that fight," McGuigan whispered a few days later, out of his wife's hearing. He may be the only fighter who ever enunciated it. "I've heard about this my whole life," he said. "Now I know what it is."

When McGuigan was an amateur tough, Belfast and Dublin embraced him equally. From hill to hamlet, all over the Irelands, he was trundled like a carnival attraction, an obsolete whale on a flatcar. "They'd always put me on last," he said, "and I'd knock guys dead as Hector. Although I shouldn't say that, because I did kill a man in the ring, a Nigerian who went by the name of Young Ali. Both of our wives were pregnant at the time. He never knew it, but he had a son too. I still see that wee man in my dreams."

A Catholic married to a Protestant, McGuigan lived so close to the boundary that he found it convenient to order his telephone from North-ern Ireland and his electricity from the Republic. "It's a fookin' joke," he said. When I wondered if he'd seen much of the troubles, he laughed wearily. "You mean, besides men with plastic bags over their heads and pitchforks in their hearts?"

In the clubhouse after the nine—a dim, beery cave—the regulars drew us into their circle, clicked our glasses and pumped us about the journey. "Are they naturally friendly people," Dave murmured aside, "or are we complete curiosities?"

"After here, where?" inquired one of them, a Catholic priest.

"We're going to Iceland," Dave told him, "to play in the Arctic Open."

"Well," he said. "You might as well."

At dusk, we pressed on to Belfast, where another soldier, a veteran for a change, commanded the roadblock. "Look at this," he said in the exasperated tone of a school crossing guard, "an American in Belfast with his seat belt undone."

"Everything okay?" Dave asked.

"We're holding our own," the soldier said. "We'll beat them someday. If your friend would just buckle in, everything would be battened down for the night."

None of the restaurants he recommended showed up on the black road. Just below Portrush, in the community of Coleraine, an inn appeared, a picture postcard: Bushtown House. The kitchen was closed but a pretty girl in a country apron said she'd see what was left: "chicken Maryland." It was delicious. The bellman hauling our bags up two flights wouldn't accept a tip. "Amazingly enough," he said sheepishly, "I own the place." Speaking of sheep, they were there for the counting outside our windows.

Royal Portrush is the most sparkling golf course in the Irelands and, Dave and I think, maybe the world. The usual tastes and textures of the sea are carried to grand extremes: from a wind you can relax into without keeling over to a calm that can blow you away. In a clatter of birdsong, magpies compete with larks. Foxes dance in the fairways. The rough consists largely of thigh-high hay thatched with thorny-fisted wildflowers (the yellow ones smell like almonds) and nineteen varieties of orchids.

Portrush is the only course in Northern Ireland to host a British Open (1951). It also nurtured one of the champions, Fred Daly (1947). In Wilma Erskine, a young Katharine Hepburn in jeans and tennis shoes ("You've missed my dreaded plaid skirt"), it boasts the sole female secretary of a royal golf course in the world.

She was the one, two years ago, who introduced us to Roy Crawford, a retired architect who screeched up to the first tee in the only motorized cart permitted on the premises, a concession to a powerful personality attached to a swollen knee. If Crawford didn't inspire this whimsy, he was in on it anyway. The first outline was hatched over his bottle of Black Bush.

Awaking at fifty-five in the same spot where he was born, Roy ached to escape monotony and winter. We understood. He had it in his heart, for some reason, that Hilton Head, South Carolina, was the place to go. "I've a few loose ends to tie up," he said, referring to a parcel of real estate downtown. "But soon I'll be ready to get away."

"From the troubles?" I asked.

"No, from the cold. The troubles are exaggerated."

I tried to call Roy the week before we arrived. His wife had sounded odd on the telephone. (Maybe Angie does now to people calling for me.) Dave tried again that Sunday morning. This time an adolescent male voice would say only "He's away."

"Well, he would be, wouldn't he?" Norman Gallagher said a half hour later. "He's in Crumlin Road Prison in Belfast."

We were stunned. "What?" Dave finally said.

"For supplying funds to terrorists," said the Portrush manager, "and for blowing up a hotel."

The headquarters of the *Chronicle* in the heart of Coleraine's business district is a newspaper set from a period play, complete with counter and flap, an antique wooden cashbox and a turn-of-the-century safe. "This is a printing office," proclaims a sampler on the wall, "crossroads of civilization, armoury of fearless truth. Friend, you stand on sacred ground."

A young woman with a mouth full of wire, thirty-two years old but impersonating a teenager in her braces, strummed through slabs of back issues, singing, "Bombings, bombings. It's all I've heard since I was nine."

Having to close up then, she suggested we return the following morning. But, the next instant, she came racing down the sidewalk waving a sheaf of paper, shouting: "There you are! I found it!"

The headline was a jolt:

HOTEL OWNER LINKED TO MURDER

A Portrush businessman accused of paying the UVF to burn down his hotel may have been implicated in a murder, it was alleged in the High Court in Belfast yesterday.

The court heard details of a tape which was sent anonymously to police with the voice of the former owner of the Northern Counties Hotel, Roy Crawford, on it.

Also identified on the tape, it was claimed, was Samuel Rice, who was murdered in east Belfast last September.

Crawford (57), of Ballymacrea Road, who was refused bail, is accused of burning the hotel, destroyed in a fire in March 1990, six months after he paid £385,000 for it.

He is further charged with giving the UVF £46,000 and for making a false insurance claim for £3,000,000 after the fire. . . .

Crawford, the lawyer claimed, had admitted one of the voices on the tape was his, and further admitted that he passed on Mr. Rice's details to a member of the UVF.

This man said it was believed Mr. Rice had been pocketing some of the arson contract money for himself. Crawford was told Mr. Rice had been murdered for using UVF money to buy drugs and that a third man on the tape had been knee-capped. . . .

Knee-capped? UVF, we found out, stands for Ulster Volunteer Force, a Protestant paramilitary organization somewhat less celebrated than the Irish Republican Army. "If his crime was merely greed," explained one of the reporters for the *Coleraine Chronicle,* "the greater offense would be making money available to terrorists. Of course, the bad guys are all terrorists of some stripe. It's pretty hard to find an arsonist around here who isn't affiliated with one side or the other."

We waited for Crumlin Road's visiting hour in Belfast's Front Page saloon. "Do newspaper guys hang out here?" Dave made light conversation with the barmaid, a robust chestnut with a long face reminiscent of Secretariat's but hair perhaps half a shade lighter.

"Sometimes the *Belfast Telegram* people do," she said with a yawn, "depending on the day of the month, and whether they have any money left."

"Dave and I are newspapermen," I volunteered.

"That'll be three pounds," she said.

The families of the Crumlin remanded queue up beside a sickly yellow fence across from a pink Hall of Justice. The children are all in their Sunday bests. As Holly Golightly observed at Sing Sing, you'd think there were going to be ice cream. Mothers didn't have to admonish children not to touch anything. Basically, "The Crum" is an untouchable box of razor wire, although the interior voices weren't jagged in the least.

"Is he expecting you?" asked the fourth unofficious official in a stream of them.

"No," I confessed.

"But, you see, he's permitted just three visits a week and only his wife is on the list."

"We're friends from America and just heard about the charges. We're only here for two days and thought we'd take a chance."

"I'll pass you through, if you really want me to. We can call him out. But it'll cost her a visit. Do you want that?"

"No, of course not. But may we leave him a message?"

"Next door. Not in writing, but next door."

Next door, a woman who declined to take business cards politely took notes. Clumsily, we asked her to wish him well, to tell him the trip had begun and the first hole was Calamity.

The Diabolical's First Hole
211 Yards, Par 3

Because our first was Portrush's fourteenth, we considered one through thirteen a warmup. "But you'll be needing a warmup to the warmup," figured Norman Gallagher, the club manager, who led us to Sam Moore's locker.

Our British colleague, Peter Dobereiner, had mentioned a locker at Portrush that was worth looking into. "The doctor's locker," Peter called it, "a penny a small go." And here it was.

"Moore's not technically a doctor," Gallagher said, "but he has a medical turn of mind." Inside the cabinet, an intricate network of surgical tubing was hooked up to an old-fashioned intravenous bottle emblazoned with an official red cross. It dispensed a rusty solution of whiskey, Drambuie and ginger, a penny a small go. "You better take two," advised Gallagher. "The rough is murder now. We've had so much rain. We need the burning off."

Murder was an exaggeration, though the sound of that word again resonated around the walls like the echo of a kettledrum. It was more like manslaughter. In fact, the rough didn't kill you at all. It merely untied your shoelaces and bit off the aglets. "You know what I love about this course?" Dave said dryly, lifting one pants leg to daub at a pincushion of polka dots. "You can lose a ball on every shot."

We played alternately great and awful on the front, a trend that would continue for weeks. On a moderate par 3, we hit 6- and 7-irons inside ten feet and Dave made his putt for our only birdie. Strolling along behind

was a black and white oystercatcher with a bent orange beak, systemati-
cally unreplacing all of our divots in search of grubs. When we came to
Calamity Corner, he helicoptered backward half a fairway in a spasm of
dread, wheeled around and walked away.

A breeze came up—against us, naturally—tossing a sand spray. Calamity is on the dune line. Where we had employed 5-woods and 3-irons in
still conditions, we both selected drivers this time. The shot was 211 yards
into now a real wind. Bud Chapman's surreal art could have been inspired
by Calamity. The effect was of shooting at an island in a cloud. If you're
short, long or left, it's just inconvenient. If you're right, forget it.

Dave led off. Bewitched by this hole for two years, he took the club
away twice as easily as he had ever been able to do it in a daydream.
Proving his virtue, he hit a drive farther than he can and almost straighter
than one can be hit. The ball pushed its way up and over the wall of wind
and parachuted onto the left side of the green some thirty-five feet beyond
the hole.

My tee shot wasn't quite as poetic. "When it's breezy," I reminded my
muscles, "swing easy." But, on the way down, they forgot two things: it
wasn't a truncheon in my hand and the ball wasn't a snake. I thudded a
low, hard hook that, improved by the wind and saved by the terrain,
rocked to rest undeservedly just left of the green. I chipped ham-handedly
to about eight feet and pulled the putt: a bogey 4.

Still infused with romance, Dave was certain he would make his thirty-
five-footer and all but did. At the last instant, the ball leaned over sideways
to avoid the drop and, scarcely pausing to thank God for the fun and the
escape, rolled on. In dejection, Dave underhit the five-footer coming back,
a considerable upset. Kindred missing a five-footer is an unlikelihood
roughly on the order of me making one.

Three-putt bogey. A pair of 4s. Except for the spots on Dave's legs,
no blood.

As we hacked on undramatically, we thought of Roy in jail in Belfast.

"I think he's innocent," I said with some chagrin. "Does that surprise
you?"

"You reacting uncynically to something?" Dave smiled. "What's surprising about that?"

"Seriously, I don't believe he did it."

"How can we possibly know, one way or the other?"

"By the golf. We played golf with him. Don't you know a man a little after you've played golf with him? More than a little. For one thing—the biggest thing—you have a sense of whether he's honest or not. With himself, I mean. On the front side, I was remembering the balls Roy lost that stayed lost, and the times he'd head off into the gorse with an 8-iron only to come back for a wedge. I wonder if there's ever been a thief who didn't tee it up in the rough."

"So, do you turn into a sentimentalist whenever you leave the States, or is it just here?"

"Just here."

"Well, Callahans probably can't help that."

"The first time I came to Ireland—you'll be shocked to know—I got lost on the road for a while and kept crossing the border back and forth. Different batteries of soldiers kept waving me along. Clerics, babies, grandmothers with groceries, Bishop Sheen, Mother Teresa—everybody else on the highway—was pulled over and frisked. It was God damn insulting. At a glance, they knew me: a lost American in a Hertz rent-a-car grinding the gears idiotically with his left hand.

"Eventually, I came to a gray, forbidding little house that said 'Customs House' on its side, and 'No Photography.' A bulb-nosed sentry stepped out of the box and asked in a bored voice: 'Anything to declare?'

" 'Just one thing,' I said.

" 'What?'

" 'I'M A FOOKIN' IRISHMAN!'

"God, what a great laugh he had. 'God bless you,' he said. 'Go through.'

"By the way, what are you? What's 'Kindred'?"

"A fookin' Englishman."

"Oh, Lord."

"English or Irish, we're doing nobody any good. The horror comes from both sides. I felt just as sad in Dublin as in Belfast. Look at this. We come to play golf with Roy and we wind up at a prison."

"Well, God bless, Roy, and goodbye, Portrush. We'll be off to Iceland now."

"We might as well."

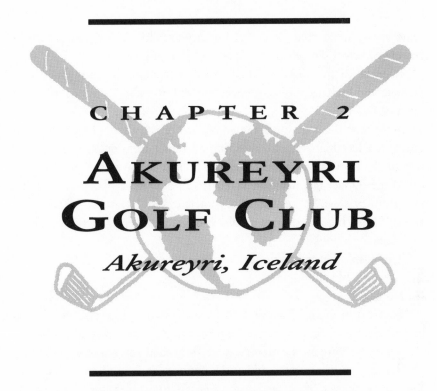

CHAPTER 2
AKUREYRI
GOLF CLUB
Akureyri, Iceland

Where the Widow Louise Wins the Chocolate Monkey

IF THE IRISH priest in Clones harbored a cheery dubiousness about two Yanks claiming they were headed for Iceland, he would have been astonished by our route.

From Belfast to Dublin, the best road goes directly south. Instead, we drove into the countryside. We had to see the Maze, the infamous Northern Ireland prison where, to judge by the name, labyrinthine terrors are visited upon convicts who blow up hotels in the name of God.

"Traveling south on the motorway out of Belfast," an Irish journalist once wrote, "two sights catch the eye." The first is Milltown cemetery spreading in stony silence away from the road. As for the second . . . "You slowly become aware of a high, flat wall, broken here and there by towers, running through the middle of unworked fields off to the right of the road. At night it is bathed in orange sodium light, accentuating its air of remoteness. What could it be? A military airfield? A scientific research center? Slowly it dawns on you: it is the Maze prison.

"Recruits to the IRA are taught in their training lectures that their involvement in the republican movement will probably lead them to Milltown or the Maze."

Just outside the little town named Maze, we saw a wall of steel painted green, ten feet high, blank, solid, impenetrable from either the civilian side or the convict's. My Irish friend, Thomas Christopher Callahan, recalled the hunger-fast death of IRA hero Bobby Sands. Then Tom mentioned the prisoner strikes staged in protest of cruel treatment. Finally, he asked, "How big an advance would you need, Dave, to spend a year in the Maze for a book?"

"There isn't that much money."

"A million? Five million?"

"No way."

"First day in there," Tom said, "you take a two-by-four and whack the biggest, meanest, ugliest guy on the property. After that, you'd be okay."

By then we were on the motorway south headed a hundred miles to the Dublin airport where we could catch the week's only flight to Iceland. With three hours to do it, such a drive posed no problem for tourists who (1) could read a map, (2) could follow road signs and (3) would ask directions if lost.

We soon were lost because we always have been incapable of (1) and (2) while reluctant in the extreme to resort to (3), as Mr. Callahan ex-

plained during a U-turn: "It's unmanly to ask directions. Women ask directions. Real men wander."

"If we miss this plane to Iceland, there's not another one until next week," I said. "We miss it and we miss the Arctic Open."

"We'll make it. Just keep wandering."

We wandered. We made it. We made it only after a madcap car ride down Irish country roads that caused me to transcribe these shaky notes:

"Leaving Northern Ireland. Drove 75 mph on hilly little roads except when we went 5 mph through a dozen villages. Trapped behind every farm vehicle known to man, one a manure spreader carrying a load so fresh, so aromatic, so farm-y, it brought tears to my eyes.

"Drove past a hotel bombed by the IRA. Huge fire, timbers charred, roof gone. Police doing press conference by roadside.

"Going 60 toward a roundabout near Dublin when Callahan says, 'Look out for that horse.' HORSE? We skid to a stop. A spotted pony pulling a sulky passes in front of our bumper. A pony! And sulky! Be a nice headline: USA SPORTSWRITERS DIE IN FREAK ACCIDENT; IRISH PONY SURVIVES.

"The movie should animate these car rides. A boxy little yellow car on a twisty road showing tractors and bomb bursts and a pony flying off the car fender. Car on two wheels, doing 360-degree spins, double Salchows, bootlegger turns, with Callahan hanging out his door.

"Had no time to return the rental car properly. Skidded up to the airport. Imposed on an Irish cop to let me leave it there. Told him the rental-car people said it was okay, they'd come get it.

"Took keys to the rental people. Told them where the car was. Told them a cop was watching it until they got there.

"Made the plane by a minute. Aer Lingus jet from Dublin to Glasgow to meet Icelandair's flight 435 to Reykjavik. I'm sweating and Callahan is comfy and carefree in his seat. He says, 'Just think. One more little town, we don't make it. If the airport's on the other side of Dublin, we don't make it. One more horse and sulky, we don't make it. But we made it. We could have had a sandwich along the way. God is good; God will provide.'

"If only I had a two-by-four . . ."

As the Clones priest might have guessed, logic had nothing to do with it. We knew no more about Iceland than this: the Arctic Open is played at midnight on a golf course thrown up by volcanoes a thousand years ago. It is fifty miles from the Arctic Circle. Temperatures there have reached 85 below zero. As late as May in the little fishing port of Akureyri, snow can pile up three feet high.

"Here we are in Iceland, on top of the world, and everybody below us is asleep," Tom said, bewitched by the geography of the thing. "They're sleeping and we're freezing. What more could be perfecter?"

"Maybe a volcano will erupt while we're here."

"You know, Dave, I'd lava it," Tom said.

From Dublin we had flown east to Glasgow and then 836 miles northwest across the Atlantic Ocean to Reykjavik, the Iceland capital and the first of many places that we had never seen and would never see again. If we knew Reykjavik at all, it was as a meeting place of enemies who can't agree to meet anywhere else. The reclusive genius, Bobby Fischer, played Boris Spassky for the world chess championship there in 1972. Presidents Nixon and Bush flew in to meet Pompidou and Gorbachev.

In the thirty-one flights of our journey, we would see an array of astonishments. We would see snowy big-shouldered mountains filling up Switzerland; the Himalayas ringing Kathmandu's green valley; the rising sun afire on the South African horizon; a rainbow touching a sea of cottony clouds above Bangkok's jungly mountains; a watercolorist's idea of a dreamy sky over Singapore. All of that—but nothing more astonishing than our first recognition of Iceland.

As flight 435 began its descent at 10:30 P.M. on a midsummer night, Tom turned in his window seat. "Wake up," he said. "We're landing on the moon."

Touched with the light of the midnight sun, the southwest coast of this remote island suggested a truth we had never imagined. We saw no trees, no flowers, no houses and no evidence of man on an abrupt, jagged and hostile landscape black with lava fields. That, we expected. We didn't expect so barren a place to be so beautiful.

"It's the moon with snow," I said.

"And pots of gold," Tom said.

We saw snowy mountains and lakes, ponds and waterfalls and rivers running to the sea, all of it painted gold by the midnight light. Occasionally, when the plane tilted just so, as if the pilot were an artist seeking new light, the Icelandic moonscape changed colors. Gold became copper became silver. Only land and water and light, the Iceland we saw in midsummer 1993 must have been the Iceland first seen in the ninth century by Norsemen who sailed across the North Atlantic. They, too, followed the midnight sun to this forbidding island and surely they explored the great field of snow inland from the southern coast.

"A glacier?" I said to the young woman in the next seat.

She wrote its name in my notebook. *Myrdalsjokull.* Her haste to help me might have been a defense against exasperation. Better to educate the American tourist than to have him be another of those people mistaking foolishness for fact. Kristin Jonsdottir, fifteen, returning home from a week's vacation riding horses in Scotland (she wanted to be a veterinarian), laughed at what some people think: "They think everybody in Iceland lives in an ice house. And they think it snows all the time. They get us mixed up with Greenland and Eskimos. We don't have any Eskimos and we don't have any polar bears, either."

Kristin's parents also grew up in Iceland. Smiling, she raised her left arm and made a muscle. She said, "We Vikings."

An indomitable lot, those Vikings must be. Their island is fire and ice. Its two hundred volcanoes include Hekla, known in the Middle Ages as the abode of the damned. It erupted for most of 1947, its column of ash

going 100,000 feet high. The 1783 fissure eruption of Lakagigar produced the biggest lava flow in history; it covered 218 square miles and caused famine that killed tens of thousands of people. On the average, an Icelandic volcano erupts every fifth year.

No shortage of volcanic ash, then, and it once contributed to characteristics that made Akureyri Golf Club unique. The club used the fluffy black stuff in its bunkers. Balls could sink into the powdery ash without a trace. Now the bunkers are filled with beach-shell sand, into which no ball can disappear but from which escape is problematic. Some dirt, some sand and a jillion little seashells are stirred into a gumbo the consistency of cement at the pouring stage.

We first saw the golf course from its dirt-road entrance as we bumped along in a van driven by Kristjan Grant, a white-haired, broad-shouldered, fifty-six-year-old Viking who throws himself into a geothermally heated pool every morning at seven o'clock.

"Into the hot pot!" he cried out, crying out being Kristjan's normal speech pattern. "Is good for joints! You want hot pot?"

I looked at Tom. Tom looked at me. We not Vikings.

"Maybe, someday," one of us said. "How about golf, Kristjan? Do you play?"

"Four years ago, I start golf. Golf EVERY day! I CRAZY!"

Two years earlier, during a visit to his sister in Erie, Ohio, Grant had bought a golf cart for $500 and shipped it to Iceland. Last we saw of him, he bounded into his golf cart and roared away, dust flying, clubs clattering in the back.

Akureyri's eighteen holes are goat-hilly things laid sideways across the foot of a mountain range rising alongside a fiord. Seldom does a golfer take a dozen steps without being asked to climb a ridge or pass around a volcanic fissure splitting the fairway. Grass is an adventure as well, suffering through Iceland's long and dark winters of hip-deep snow and arctic cold. Even in midsummer Akureyri's fairways were haggard and the greens so hairy and spongy that a six-foot putt required a strongman's hammering. Yet, for some agronomical reason, every putt, no matter how firmly struck, came to a Velcro-y stop by the hole.

We loved the place from the minute Hot Pot Grant unloaded us near the pro shop door. There on the door's window was Anthony Ravielli's line drawing of the young Ben Hogan striking a shot, the Hogan company logo. The Akureyri pro, a British immigrant named David Barnwell, was the single Hogan distributor in Iceland.

All that way to the top of the world and there was Ben Hogan. I thought of 1967 when a kid sportswriter first went to the Masters. The kid had two objectives: he wanted to see Red Smith, the best sportswriter ever, and he wanted to see Ben Hogan.

There was Hogan on the practice tee, stern and silent. The kid noticed the great man's hands. They were thick and strong, the hands of a workingman. They had been shaped by his work to a certain hard beauty. Then the kid knew what he saw. He saw what he had seen at home. Hogan's hands were a carpenter's hands. They were my father's hands, and there on the practice tee in 1967 I wanted to tell Dad that. He had died four years earlier. I promised myself I would write about it someday.

For the Arctic Open's first round, Tom's tee time was 11:10 P.M. and mine was twenty minutes later. We would finish at four in the morning. Such hours were possible because in late June in Akureyri, near the top of the world, the sun goes down for only a few minutes. As we hit practice balls, the setting/rising sun burned orange atop a mountain ridge by the fiord.

"It's like heaven," said the pro Barnwell. "The sun goes down and comes up almost simultaneously. The temperature drops and rises with the sun. When the sun comes back up, it can go from 40 degrees to 60 in a minute. It's like a hiss of heat."

Two over par through four holes, I hit a tee shot at the fifth hole which refused to become airborne. It bounced and rolled and bounced, altogether a disheartening sight made the more discouraging when the ball disappeared into a volcanic fissure.

On land built by volcanoes, a fissure is a crack in the earth. The better part of valor would have been to declare the ball unplayable. But I had come to Iceland in search of golf's joy/misery. I had come half hoping to be crushed by a glacier if not lost in a volcano.

So I descended into the riven earth and dealt the ball a succession of fierce blows. Each moved the smirking Titleist six inches this way, three that. After tapping in a putt (much later), I asked the scorer, "How do you count to ten in Icelandic?"

He wrote it out: *einn, tveir, prir, fjorir, fimm, sex, sjo, atta, niu, tiu.*
"Gimme a *tiu.*"

Went to bed at *fimm* in the morning after a first-round 92 that, odd as it sounds, put me in the top quarter of the field, tied with someone named Callahan.

As cocktail parties go, the Arctic Open's was memorable for its hors d'oeuvres of shark meat and a wine neither red nor white but an iridescent blue.

To a waiter offering these goodies, Tom said, "I have an agreement with sharks. If they won't eat me, I won't eat them. And give me a beer. Keep the mouthwash."

Akureyri's city council chairman greeted the hundred golfers with an invitation: "Here in Iceland we believe that, if you strip naked and roll yourself in the dew under the midnight sun, it cures at least eighteen diseases. So, please, feel free to do so. We in Akureyri will not stop you."

The Arctic Open, second night, 2:25 A.M.

Cold, maybe 45 degrees.

Dark and raining.

Akureyri must be the only place on earth where you can hit a tee shot at two in the morning while Icelandic ponies, full of horse sense, lie asleep in pastures a few feet away.

I was miserably happy. Couldn't play a lick. Had no depth perception. Almost couldn't see the ball at my feet in the slight light of the summer night. But I heard a happy sound from my playing partner, a lanky Icelander named Sigurdur Ringstad.

Wearing a neck warmer and ski gloves, sucking on a cough tablet, Sigurdur said with a smile, "Is amazink?"

"What?" I said.

"Golf in Iceland, amazink, yes?"

"Very amazink."

That second night, I shot an amazinkly bad 95. Even with *sjo* at the par-3 eighteenth hole, the Callahan character moved past me with an 89. Neither of us won any silver.

Coming in out of the chill and dark and rain, I warmed my hands around a cup of coffee while sitting across from a Tugboat Annie character, a short, stout, strong old woman in a dark windbreaker, turtleneck and knit cap tugged down to her eyebrows. I told my new pal, Louise Wakeman, "This is like playing golf in a refrigerator with a fifteen-watt bulb."

"In a *defrosting* refrigerator," she said.

The irrepressible Louise had mounted her own defense against the Icelandic summer. It took the shape of a whiskey glass filled to three fingers with scotch. At age sixty-eight, she sought out the adventure in Akureyri because she refused to believe widowhood is a disabling condition.

Louise's husband of forty years died in 1985 and the next spring she took up golf because it was something she could do alone. She played at the Airways Golf & Country Club near her home in East Hartland, Connecticut. She also tended a half-acre flower and vegetable garden, cut her grass by hand with a push mower and chain-sawed fallen trees on her two-and-a-half-acre lot. ("The good Lord knocks 'em down and I cut 'em up for firewood. The Devil's going to take me on the spot without looking at my résumé. He'll say, 'That lady knows how to make a fire!' ")

After those chores, Louise was on the golf course most mornings at 6:20 A.M. What luscious lunacy. As a wife and mother of four, Louise Wakeman never put a hand on a golf club; as a widow, she couldn't get enough of the game. She practiced chip shots in her backyard, depending on her German shepherd, Nipper Digger, to catch them in his mouth and bring them to her for another round.

"One day, I play good enough," she said. "The next day, okay. Another time, it's a riot. I'll never change; I'm just an old apple with a worm in it. My husband's probably up there laughing at me. But really, every widow ought to take up golf. It's how I kept my sanity. It takes your mind off your loneliness. That little white ball takes over. I don't bowl, I don't play cards. Golf is it. Out on the course, I can forget even what day it is."

I also had things to forget. On June 12, 1991, Frank Deford called me at the U. S. Open golf tournament. He said, "We're closing."

Though we had done good work at *The National,* the editor's words were no surprise. The Mexican billionaire Emilio Azcarraga put his losses at $150 million. On a starry night in New York two years earlier, he had thrown a party on his 150-foot yacht. I asked Azcarraga why he thought a sports newspaper would make it. Spectacular successes around the world, such a paper had never been tried in the United States. The man called El Tigre in recognition of his business ferocity said, "I am fifty-eight years old. I am too old to fail."

Frank promised "the best-written, best-edited, best-looking newspaper in the history of newspapers." Instead, some nights we couldn't print the thing at all. (The high-dollar technology went on the fritz if it rained in Detroit.) Our business people lied to our advertisers about how many papers we sold. Maybe that was because our circulation people lied to our business people.

It didn't help my mood a year after closing to read *Forbes* magazine on "The World's Richest Latin-American," our man Emilio. The magazine said *The National*'s failure helped raise Azcarraga's net worth to $2.8 billion: ". . . the fiasco was a blessing in disguise to the Mexican mogul. Upset with his management, his minority partners in Televisa, Romulo O'Farrill and Miguel Aleman—son of the former president—agreed to sell out to him."

So Azcarraga's dance with *The National* riled his partners. They sold out to him. Almost simultaneously, he took his radio/TV empire public; its 309 million shares were valued at $3.4 billion. He owned sixty-five percent of those shares. In rapid order, he bought half of Chile's only private TV network and began deals in Venezuela, Argentina and Brazil. He raised his ad rates fifteen percent.

The National's demise can be simply explained. We launched an expensive enterprise in a hostile economic climate and did it badly. Too many major decisions were imprudent, and this is not hindsight; we felt the foolishness even as we perpetrated it. For one thing, what was the rush? The Gannett people planned *USA Today* for three years; yet Azcarraga demanded *The National* be up and running in six months. Dumb at best, suicidal at worst.

Whatever happened, *The National*'s closing left me at loose ends. The paper honored its deal with me, paying my full five-year contract. Reassuring as the money was, I no longer had the job I loved. I was proud to be a newspaper reporter. As Red Smith said, "I'm just a working stiff trying to write better than I can." For thirty-four years, since my junior year in high school, newspapers had given me a space to fill. But with Deford's phone call, that ended.

"We have applied for membership in the European Economic Community," said a slight English engineer who introduced himself as the Secretary of State of the great nation of Jabuga. David Beaumont was thirty-four years old and sometimes mistook himself for Elton John.

"After establishing the state of Jabuga," Beaumont said, "we thought, naturally enough, of invading Iceland. So here we are in Akureyri," where on the second night of the Arctic Open he strode to the first tee, announced, "I am very horny," and pulled from a grocery sack a horned Viking cap, plunked the horns on his head and hit a tee shot into the midnight gloaming.

As the nation's residents describe it, the People's Democratic Republic of Jabuga is contained in a vacation house sitting on one eighth of an acre of land. Anyone leaving through the front door has emigrated from Jabuga to Spain.

The population of Jabuga is seven and will not exceed seven and will become fewer than seven because no women are allowed in.

The presidency is decided by seventy-two holes of golf contested by those of the seven Jabugans who make it out the door each morning after the beery night before.

What's true is always better than anything you could make up. A man made up Jabuga and we laughed. But on Akureyri's clubhouse wall there was a real golf glove framed and autographed: Jack Nicklaus's glove, alongside a photo of Nicklaus in fishing gear with the inscription "All the best for 'hot' golf." So there we were, a half inch under the Arctic Circle having a midnight beer with Jabugans, when joined, sort of, by the best golfer who ever lived. Amazink, yes?

In the summer of 1992, Nicklaus, on the nearby Laxa River in pursuit of salmon, stopped by Akureyri and hit a hundred balls down the first fairway. "He was very nice to put on a little clinic," David Barnwell said. "I asked if we could make him an honorary member. 'Sure, I'd love it.' Those were his exact words. 'Sure, I'd love it.' "

With us at the bar was Beaumont's accomplice, the immediate past President of Jabuga, the Honorable Philip Mitchell, a retailing executive for an English store advertising itself as the bra supplier for two and a half of every three English women. "Which means," Mitchell said, "that five of every six cups in England are ours."

The trip to Akureyri appealed to Mitchell for reasons that appealed to Tom and me. "I'm pushing fifty and so I do silly things. My wife, friends and family think I'm crazy to come in the middle of summer to one of the coldest countries on earth to play golf at midnight. Then, later this summer, I'll go ride a bicycle four hundred kilometers through the desert of Israel.

"When my wife gives me a bit of stick about Jabuga or Iceland or the bicycle ride, I simply tell her, 'Life's too short to not do what you want to do.' It's like that American movie, *City Slickers,* where those fellows go looking for their smiles. Yes. Go find your smile."

Even one good shot among the dozens of foozles can do wonders for a wanderer's mood. "Eighteen holes of crap," Mitchell said, "and if you hit one good shot, you'll come back." His fellow Jabugan, the horned Beaumont, believed golf collars its victims either way: "After a good round, you can't wait to get on the course again. A bad round, you need to get out and put it right."

True as these reckonings were, they only partly explained a fellow's presence at the Arctic Open. Philip Mitchell explained it fully: "I have always wanted to have a daiquiri in Akureyri."

Louise Wakeman has made other trips. She went across the United States by train a few years ago. "I had a girlfriend with cancer whose doctor said she had six months to live. I told her, 'Get out of that bed and let's play golf.'

"Every time we played, if we said a naughty word, we'd kick a quarter into a kitty and say, 'Oops, another quarter for Amtrak.' We planned to take the train cross-country when we got enough money.

"We finally did it. Took two weeks on the train. From Springfield, Massachusetts, to Seattle to Vancouver through the Rockies to Banff and Edmonton to Montreal and back home. Played golf all along the way. She was sillier than me.

"We kept her alive two and a half years."

For Louise, the message was plain. Live life. If you're going to do anything foolish, don't wait for a better day. "So when I read about the Arctic Open, I said, 'That's for me.' My friends tell me I'm nuts. But, honey, they'd all like to be here, too, only they don't have the guts to do it."

Each day of the Arctic Open, Louise shot matching 152s. "I'll probably win the booby prize, a chocolate monkey, maybe," she said. Then she asked about Tom and me. "What's next for you guys?"

"We're going from here to St. Andrews," I said. "When are you headed home?"

She had heard about another Iceland course. It sat in the crater of an extinct volcano. Louise would go there on her way home. What more could be perfecter? Tom and I fly to golf's Mecca while the widow Louise takes her chocolate monkey to the first tee in a volcano.

The Diabolical's Second Hole
518 Yards, Par 5

At 3:17 A.M., with Icelandic ponies sleeping a club's length behind us, we hit tee shots on Akureyri's 518-yard seventeenth hole. The moderate length was deceptive because the hole ran uphill toward the mountains. On this midsummer morning, a cold wind came down from the snowy mountains. I soon developed a new rule of life: never play uphill into a wind that five minutes ago crossed the North Pole.

The idea on the seventeenth was to hit a big drive over the crest of a high ridge crossing the fairway, then keep a second shot between the lava-rock fields. On the fairway's right side, flat black rock lay under Akureyri's scraggly grass. On the left, purple and yellow flowers grew in the dark rubble of an outcropping that created a cliff twenty-five feet above the pasture next door. Abandon hope, all ye who jerk a 3-wood left.

The approach to the green was complicated by illusions. After two long uphill shots, the third was downhill to a flat green sitting level with the horizon—but the third shot had to be made from a fairway tilting severely right to left. It was a hook lie for a shot that must not be missed to the left because anything left, catching a precipitous slope, might not stop rolling until it reached Greenland.

Understanding the strategy necessary to play a diabolical hole is seldom the problem for a 14-handicapper. The problem comes with execution, as John McKay has said. During a twenty-six-game losing streak, the original Tampa Bay Buccaneers football coach was asked, "What do you think of your team's execution?" McKay said, "I'm in favor of it."

On this Diabolical, my tee shot was struck with a driver. After which, from the short side of the high ridge, I hit my driver again. Still two hundred yards away, by the lava rocks, I hit a third driver. Driver-driver-driver, each a serious lick. They just never seemed to leave the vicinity.

Callahan worked with a driver, 3-wood and 6-iron to produce a thirty-foot putt that stopped four inches short. An easy par while I two-putted from the fringe for a par. We were even after two holes.

CHAPTER 3
THE OLD COURSE
St. Andrews, Scotland

A Wee Wander With Tip and Old Tom

NO ONE IS exactly sure where or when golf was invented, although the Romans, the Dutch, the Chinese and a few others over the years have been willing to accept partial responsibility, reasoning that any grassy place with shepherds and crooks might have done it. After all, what is more inevitable than a man lifting a club to vent some hideous rage on the most innocent object in his path?

The consensus is that it came from Scotland. So, whatever their ancestry, golfers are disposed to imagine that, in some essential way, they did too. As for the location of the Scottish maternity ward, there is no question. It's St. Andrews. So Dave and I felt obligated to stop off at the Old Course, to genuflect in the bracken and be confirmed by the broom.

Our hole, naturally, would be the Road Hole, the par-4 seventeenth. St. Andrews's other plucked strings—the Swilken Burn, the Principal's Nose, the Beardies, the Coffins, Granny Clarke's Wynd, the Valley of

Sin—were only passing landmarks to us. While it is considered a crime against nature to plot a route to St. Andrews any less circuitous than by way of Turnberry, Troon, Prestwick and Muirfield, we broke the law and went directly to the old university town with its gray turrets and ruined spires by the North Sea.

Finding the bed-and-breakfasts brimming with tourists, we searched awhile before eventually securing two singles a block apart—to my landlord's peculiar relief. He explained:

"We recently had a pair of Americans share a double here—a Mr. McDonald and a Mr. Campbell. They arrived as great friends. Stupid me, I mentioned how refreshing it was to see Campbells and McDonalds getting on so nicely. As it happened, they had never heard of the Highland feud. Regrettably, my wife and I filled them in. The tension at their table grew by the day until the dining room became as quiet as a library and the rest of our guests couldn't eat fast enough. By the time they left, the great friends despised each other."

I laughed at his tale but it turned out to be a kind of premonition.

Dave and I reconvened to walk the narrow lanes of bookstores and pubs, to reacquaint ourselves with this misty precinct that has handed itself over so comprehensively to golf. From British Opens past, we thought we knew St. Andrews a little, but neither of us remembered a calliope playing. Had our eyesight sharpened over the last few years, or had all of the bright little stores turned into souvenir cuteshops with "niblicks" in their names?

Most distressingly of all, a front-page story in the local paper reiterated our landlords' warnings not to leave golf clubs in the car, even in the trunk. An overlapping crime wave had gripped St. Andrews; gloves were disappearing from back pockets.

Outside Tom Morris's Golf Shop on the perimeter of the Old Course stood a life-sized cardboard cutout of bearded Old Tom, with whom visitors were posing for arcade photos in a lemon light. A local artist has made an ancillary career out of portraying Tom at public and private occasions wearing a £600 beard.

It was a comfort to cross the street and step onto the eighteenth hole, and to remember that all golf courses have eighteen holes only because this one does. Dusk was falling and many people were abroad on the moor—the entire citizenry, it seemed—for what is termed "a wee wander," a tradition of the night. Dogs were romping the fairway, showing

reasonable restraint in respect to the grounds. In the distance, the Ladies'
Putting Society was packing up. None of the ladies wore golfing outfits.
They were dressed for church, or at least for tea. The Ladies' Putting
Course is situated near enough to the Old Course to appear to bubble up
out of it. The keeper of the enormous green, a Mrs. Nicholl, mows the
rolling lawn herself and sets the devilish pins. NO STILETTO HEELS, a
sign says.

St. Andrews had not lost all its charm.

My den of iniquity growing up was a caddy house. Others picked up
life, and the facts thereof, in pool halls or bowling alleys. During the
1950s, drugstores were also lively centers of low conversation. But my
particular black hole was a part wood and part sheet metal caddy house
grafted to the tailbone of a pro shop. Far from the hijinks of Bill Murray
and Chevy Chase, it was a one-room schoolhouse.

Full of philosophy, irresponsibility and alcohol, the instructors were
lost men with compact identities such as Jockey or Howser or One-Armed
Duke. They hadn't always lived alone. An unusually well-barbered speci-
men called Smitty kept two ancient fielder's mitts and a mildewed Raw-
lings baseball lodged in a cranny of the propane tank out back. Chained
and locked bicycles weren't safe in that yard, but no one disturbed the
props Smitty pulled out near the end of the day to pretend he still had
sons.

"Excuse me," Tip Anderson said, tilting back a sixteen-ounce can of
McEwan's Export lager, "I'm just having my breakfast."

When we had asked for Tip at the starter's shed, a marshal astride a
motorbike at first just laughed and said, "My, you do believe in fairies,
don't you?" But then he directed us to go back into St. Andrews's
cramped caddy quarters, and this time to peek around a corner into an
alcove, where we found Arnold Palmer's old friend drinking his breakfast.

"Oh yes, Arnie and I first joined up in 1960," Anderson said. "Whew,
where's it all gone, eh? I was twenty-eight. I'm sixty-one next Tuesday."

He looked every bit of sixty-one: tall, slender and white-headed under
a cap with a full bill that suggested a fisherman before a golfer. He wore

a tan jacket with the military cut of a television correspondent. His nose was a veiny purple masterpiece.

Still, it was possible to picture Tip at fifteen, the eager apprentice heading out. "My father was a caddy before me," he said. "He was 'Tip' too; that is, he wasn't 'Jim' either. I was an observant kid; I listened. They don't listen, these boys. That's the way in all trades now, all over the world, I suppose."

His father caddied for Walter Hagen and Henry Cotton but never won an Open. It was young Tip who bagged the bag of a lifetime. "I was a 3-handicap myself in those days," he said. "You know, we didn't use yardages back then. We eyeballed it. Well, it was funny, but I was precisely two clubs shorter than Arnie. My 3-iron was his 5 practically to the inch. It just worked out. We got along grand."

They started off shakily, though. "I remember, it was the Centenary

Open, 1960, and of course it was here at St. Andrews. He was the U. S. Open and the U. S. Masters champion. The first practice round was a disaster. Palmer shot 87. Mind you, the wind was blowing about fifty miles an hour. We were playing with Roberto DeVicenzo and Arnie was full of temper and wanted to quit mid-round. 'C'mon, stop your crying,' I told him, 'you've come all the way to St. Andrews to win the Open.' He took that from me. What a grand man he is.

"Well, we got beat one shot for that Open by Kel Nagle, who used nine fewer putts. But we won the next two at Royal Birkdale and Royal Troon—ah, I've never seen golf like that at Troon—and, two years after, Tony Lema and 1 beat Nicklaus by five shots back here. So I had three firsts and a second in five years. They can't take that away from you. As I keep telling Arnie, I've won three Opens. He's won only two."

When Lema died suddenly in a plane crash, Tip began to die gradually on the ground. "Lema, lovely Tony," he whispered. "All that champagne down the drain."

So why had we come to St. Andrews? he wanted to know. Tip understood the reasons as well as anyone, but he wished to hear us state them.

"Yes, golfers have no choice but to come here," he agreed when we were through. "That's why I haven't had to move scarcely a foot my whole life. Everyone comes to me. Back to Old Tom and Young Tom Morris, Henry Cotton and Bobby Jones, Palmer and Nicklaus, Watson and Faldo, all the great players save one have wandered St. Andrews, all the players period save one."

When neither Dave nor I could guess the one, he told us:

"Hogan, of course." (Hogan again.) "Ben doesn't go places, you know. He never follows the rest."

We knew Hogan's solitary British Open was at Carnoustie in 1953, and he won it (as he had the Masters and U. S. Open that year, choosing to skip the PGA). To Scots, he forever became "the Wee Icemon." But could it be true the Wee Icemon has never seen St. Andrews?

"Oh, he saw it from the air," according to Tip. "Leaving Carnoustie for the airport, he told the helicopter pilot, 'You better swing by and let me have a look at St. Andrews.' After just a glance, he said, 'Okay, let's go.' "

Shaking the empty beer can, breathing a hollow sigh, the old caddy muttered, "I could have gone to Carnoustie that year; I should have done that. You know, he was the only Open winner to improve his score every day. I might have gone to see Hogan. That's my regret."

It was Dave then who insisted we drive to Carnoustie. He's the sentimentalist. A gliding apparition in a ghostly linen cap was becoming a third party in the hunt.

Dave received a letter from Hogan once, a rare event. I got a smile out of him another time, the only time I ever saw him. Hogan's nowhere to be found in golf and yet he's everywhere you go. Then, one morning, like a table with uneven legs, he came bobbling into the old green press barn at Augusta National to inquire blithely: "Is there anything I can do for you gentlemen?" The clump of writers loitering there would have been less astonished to look up and see Judge Crater.

You might as well know that, at a golf tournament, the press headquarters, be it a tent or a pavilion, is the sportswriters' equivalent of Shangri-la. Not only because of the foodstuffs and other complimentary comforts piled up there, but in the real sense that, if anyone ever roamed very far from the portal, he would oxidize like the hag in *Lost Horizon*.

It must have been 1977. Hogan is eighty-one now and he was sixty-four then. I remember this because, word had it, he had just shot a 64 at Shady Oaks near his Fort Worth home. If by that time (as Sam Snead liked to say) you could smoke a whole cigarette waiting for Ben to take the putter back, the rest of his game remained a wonder.

Always the absent champion at the Masters Champions dinner, Hogan had returned to Augusta only out of respect for Clifford Roberts, the massah of the plantation, who for everyone's sins (but mostly his own) had shot himself to death on the golf course that off-season. Hogan, who wouldn't stay for the tournament, had a purpose in dropping by the barn. TV people weren't discouraging rumors he was considering participating in a legends tournament. "I want you gentlemen to know," Hogan said summarily, "that my game is not fit for public display."

At the mention of the Shady Oaks 64, he just shrugged.

"Mr. Hogan," I asked, "have you ever shot a perfect round of golf?"

"The perfect round of golf," he explained with that tight smile, "would be an 18. I almost dreamed it once. I had seventeen holes in one and lipped out at the last. I was mad as hell."

For many days, someone had been running ahead of us writing "shanks" on everything. "Shanks and Morton," it said on a porcelain urinal in Belfast as well as a hotel washbasin in Akureyri. A Glasgow baggage cart was labeled "Shanks and McEwen." Our latest rent-a-car was signed over by a bloodcurdling female whose nameplate identified her as Emily Crookshanks. By the time we reached Carnoustie, I was squirting every other iron shot sideways off the hosel perfectly perpendicularly to the right. Sympathetically, Dave began topping his woods. Between us, we made one, whole, well-adjusted player.

Ten miles across the water, thirty miles by car through dazzling fields of bright yellow rape, Carnoustie was a sort of antidote to St. Andrews. No trappings, just a golf course, the toughest test in Scotland. In fact, it had so little golfing atmosphere that the absence of an atmosphere constituted an atmosphere. Lacking the space for a tented village and the spirit of a midway, Carnoustie has fallen out of the modern Open rotation and back into the arms of Scottish punters such as Willie Paul of Dunbar.

Paul and Robin Reiner were our playing partners on a historically placid day, the easiest Carnoustie day Reiner could recall. A friend of Dave's, David Boyd, had called it "the most masculine golf course in the world. It's got hair on its chest, and under the hair there's a tattoo that says, GODDAMMIT." We toasted the gentle conditions with swigs of the national soft drink, "Irn-Bru," which tastes like bubble gum. "Later comes the Belhaven light ale," promised Willie. "It's life-saving stuff. Practically flows out of the spigots in Dunbar."

As we reached the par-5 sixth hole (524 yards), Hogan rejoined us. "Here's Hogan's Alley," Reiner said, "the most famous hole on the course, where all four rounds he drove it in the same perfect place. My grandfather gave me a golf ball that belonged to Hogan, a Titleist bearing his identifying mark, the thumbnail dug into the number. When I was fifteen, I'm mortified to say, I traded it at Simpson's Golf Shop for three new ones."

Dave aimed for a sliver on the left between a bunker and a fence and was surprised to find his ball out of bounds. I hit a large drive past the bunker and, as shankers will, an even longer 3-wood onto the green. Willie Paul read a four-foot break into the eight-foot putt, and he was about right. But the eagle stayed on the lip (putting me in mind of an oyster-catcher I once knew in Portrush).

"This should be our hole," I told Dave.

"The Road Hole's going to be our hole," he said tersely.

"Some amalgam of this hole and the Road Hole would be ideal."

"Kiss my 3-wood."

A word on temperament. Golf is considered a boon to both physical and mental health, although almost no one ever looks or feels better after a round. While intended to be a display of self-control, fundamentally it reveals temper. Implied in the game's sociability are honor, forthrightness, friendship, kindness, courtesy, generosity and understanding. Yet nearly nowhere are frailties of character laid so bare as on a golf course. Golfers are at least as prone as policemen to develop fatalistic cynicisms regarding their fellow men.

In the early days of the trip, when I couldn't miss a drive or hit an iron and Dave couldn't miss a pitch or find a fairway (a circumstance that eventually would reverse itself), we lapsed into alternating spells of self-loathing, mine considerably darker than his. I brood, pout and curse. He just throws an occasional club, while declining, under the Bobby Knight system of justice, to count the repeaters.

One Derby week, we were playing with Indiana's fulminating basketball coach and the tragic Kentucky legend Ralph Beard. "You're not very passionate," I chided Knight. "You've only thrown four clubs." "Three," he snarled. "I threw that (adjectival) sand wedge twice." True enough, he had thrown it, retrieved it and thrown it again.

Dave often describes Knight as someone who gets all the little things wrong and all the big things right. But, in extending his hand to Beard, Bobby got a little thing very right. Virtually nobody remembers what a tremendous backcourtman Beard was. (Just Bob Cousy and anyone else who ever tried to keep up with him.) At full throttle, Beard's sneakers reportedly gave off perfect little puffs of smoke, like the model locomotives of Lionel trains. Ralph was a first-team All-Pro the only year he was permitted to play in the NBA, before the college gambling scandal of '51 played itself out into a lot of lonely little shoeboxes full of cash.

Beard took the money. He didn't fix the games. There is no proof of this except to know him.

On the golf course, still fit and fast in his early sixties, Beard doesn't care a whit about his own game. He is completely involved in yours. He isn't rooting only for his partner; he's pulling for the opponents too. It's as if, sitting in the stands all those years watching others play the sport he loved and lost, Beard learned how to take pleasure in their pleasure. He's the least bitter and most generous golfer I've ever met.

When, at the crest of our dueling funks, Dave came over to me and said, "Let's both stop grinding so hard," I thought of Ralph Beard. The golf became fun again and—do you know something else?—the shanks were gone for good. (Well, almost for good.) We finished the round laughing.

Dave was relating the Carnoustie experience of the *St. Petersburg Times* sports columnist Hubert Mizell, whose caddy informed him for the third time in about an hour: "This next hole is damnably hard."

"When do we get to the easy ones?" Hubert asked.

The Scotsman replied in a tangy brogue: "When ye get to St. Andrews."

The Diabolical's Third Hole
461 Yards, Par 4

The Road Hole could just as aptly have been dubbed the Roof Hole. At least as distinctive as the narrow road backstopping the green is a wide building blocking the tee. Depending on the direction of the wind, or the premonition of the caddy, a player takes his line from the appropriate letter spelling out "The Old Course Hotel" along a facing wall. He aims for the sky above, say, the capital O and starts whistling.

Tom Watson lost his Scottish Slam at the Road Hole in 1984. Having won the Open at Carnoustie (1975), Turnberry (1977), Muirfield (1980) and Troon (1982), Watson looked ready to complete the kilt at St. Andrews, especially after a pushed drive the last day ended up perfectly placed on the right edge of the seventeenth fairway. Ah, but a 2-iron struck from there put him on the road hard against the little stone barrier. He did wonderfully to skull the ball within twenty feet and two-putt for bogey. But from a hole ahead came the unmistakable hosannahs of a Seve Ballesteros birdie, and that was that. In his concise postmortem, Watson said, "I hit the wrong shot with the wrong club at the wrong time."

I had the honor. Dave had been making the better swings, but I had

been luckier, holing a hundred-foot putt at the eighth for a 2. We had the
company of Canadians, huge hitters but deliberate players, whose ten-
dency to gaze about and sigh orgasmically had brought the motorcycle
cop down on us three times before we were able to recoup the three-and-
a-half-hour pace St. Andrews demands.

Shooting at the O, I drove high and straight—far too, I thought, until
I got up to my ball on the left margin of the fairway to find one of the
Canadians' low left-to-right snake killers had run twenty yards past. Dave
had jerked his drive left of the rough almost through the adjoining fairway,
but hit a good 5-wood back onto the proper hole a hundred and fifty
yards from the green. I was at least two hundred yards out.

The yawning bunker fronting the green is known colloquially as the
Sands of Nakajima, commemorating an extensive excavation job by
Tommy Nakajima during one Open. It's a trap that can get you coming
or going. That droll angel, Henry Longhurst, was good at forecasting for
television which putts from the back of the green would roll (and roll) into
the bunker. "Ah well," he'd say when proved correct, "there you are."

Both of us made too sure of missing the sand: I pushed a 5-wood right;
Dave pulled a 5-iron left. After I lifted a sand wedge across the bunker to
the front fringe, Dave tried a putter from well off the green and stubbed
it. "It was the wrong shot with the wrong club at the wrong time," he
said. Chipping on, he two-putted for 7. Just a turn short with my first
putt, I tapped in for a 5. The Irish were one up.

Meanwhile, the longer of the Canadians, having achieved the bunker in
two, did something breathtaking. Forced by his lie to blast out of the sand
backward, he caught a bit too much of the ball and hit a 180-yard line
drive back up the fairway to more or less his previous position. "Ah well,
Henry," I thought, "there you are."

For emphasis, our partners rattled a few balls off the houses at eighteen
that help form a funnel of welcome to the finish line. The residents seem
always to be waiting in their front yards harumphing like Nigel Bruce.

"I guess you're used to ducking," I called to one of them.

"Quite," he said, sipping on a rugged pipe, "although it is rather customary to yell, 'Fore.' "

Behind the last green and the first tee sits an off-white mansion, the
headquarters of the Royal & Ancient, where George Wilson had invited
us for a post-round port. After twenty years with the R & A, the ultimate
caretakers of golf, his eyes can still shine from discovery. "We found some-

thing just the other day," he said excitedly. "In 1945, in the flush of peace, all the war heroes from Eisenhower to Bomber Harris were invited into the club. Only Churchill turned us down. We found his letter, Mountbatten's letter, all the return letters, in a cupboard here. Extraordinary."

Dave said he wasn't surprised Churchill demurred, recalling Sir Winston's juicy description of golf: "A curious sport whose object is to put a very small ball in a very small hole with implements ill designed for the purpose."

Stepping away from the past, Wilson referred to the new clubhouse and driving range on St. Andrews's drawing board. He sounded enthusiastic. "You can't change shoes in the car park forever," he said.

"Why not?" I wanted to know.

"St. Andrews can't rely on a seventeenth-century mystique forever."

"Why can't it?"

"St. Andrews has to move with the times or risk losing out."

I'll never get it. "There have been a lot of changes over the years," I said slowly, "every one of which I've opposed. Now even St. Andrews is turning into Coney Island."

Wilson laughed merrily, saying: "A few great little shops have been lost to souvenir stands, I'll grant you that much. But the aura's still there and it always will be. When you walk out of this building, look out over the course toward the estuary and tell me you don't feel it."

He was right. But gazing along the grounds as the wee wandering was starting up again, I pictured Carnoustie too. I'm afraid I prefer Carnoustie. I thought of the ninth hole and the train that rattled by just as Hogan was putting in 1953. "Did that train bother you, Mr. Hogan?" he was asked afterward. "What train?" he said.

"Well," Dave said, "we've got a train to catch."

"What train?"

"The Orient Express."

CHAPTER 4

GOLFS DU CHÂTEAU DE LA SALLE

Mâcon, France, Via the Orient Express

Where a Dogleg Is a Womanleg, Obviously Nicole's

ONCE AGAIN, Dave and I flat abandoned a car, this time according to the rental agent's specific instructions. She said to back it up against a certain wall around a hidden corner down a secret hill from Edinburgh's Waverly Station, and to stick the keys unobtrusively in the tailpipe. All preambles to the Orient Express ought to include some similar note of intrigue.

We jumped the InterCity train to London. As the Orient Express wasn't pulling out until just before noon the following day, we decided to kill an English evening at the theater. Dave had never seen *Les Miz*.

I've seen everything at least twice. Stages have half a hold on me still. At the age of sixteen, when I was six feet two and could pass for seventeen, I spent a summer in summer stock carrying spears and rounding out crowd scenes for the likes of Dorothy Collins, Lee Remick, Vivian Blaine, Howard Keel, John Raitt and George Gobel. I was among a troupe of stagehands exaggeratedly referred to as "apprentice actors," although Martha Raye (loudly reprising Lucille Ball's role in *Wildcat*) actually insisted on a special curtain call for the young women and men she lovingly termed "the apprenti." Our honest functions were setting trees and striking lampposts, or doing anything else the director directed, which is how I came to make love to Marilyn Maxwell at the Park Towson Hotel.

She was attempting Judy Holliday's part in *Bells Are Ringing* opposite a young Broadway understudy named Hal Linden, who would grow up to be television's Barney Miller. During the original New York run, Linden had sat around waiting for Sydney Chaplin to cough. Given his chance finally, he was brilliant. While she had a sweet enough voice, Marilyn was overmatched.

She had a sweet enough everything. At the overture each night, at least to a sixteen-year-old, she looked stunningly beautiful. Stubbornly she eschewed a wig in favor of her own honey-blond hair. But this was summertime, in Baltimore, in a tent, in the round, and by intermission her head was a mop. Of course she declined to wear her glasses anywhere near the stage, although without them during the changes she was as blind as Mrs. Magoo. In addition, by the end of the first week, her shin splints from bumping up and down the aisles and cascading into the scenery had been aggravated to a point where I was directed to set the lamppost and strike Marilyn Maxwell. She was a mess and I loved her.

Neglecting to mention I didn't have a driver's license, I was appointed to drive Marilyn home each night to her hotel, a better one than the rest of the company occupied. Literally I carried her in my arms to bed and, until the final night of the run, chastely sat and listened to her continuing dissertation on middle age.

After playing the "other woman" in a lot of B movies and touring a few war fronts with Bob Hope, she had landed what she imagined to be the lead role in the television series "Bus Stop." But all they seemed to want her to do was pour coffee. They were wasting her talent and time. To the boy sitting uncomfortably on the end of her bed, she advised savoring the romantic processes of beginning and building because the phase that follows, the maintaining, the upkeeping, can be a bitter time for desperate thoughts of lives squandered and dreams betrayed. We made love. Luckily, she knew how. This time, I was the one bumping into the scenery.

A few years ago at the Super Bowl, Dave asked me to sub for him in a pro-am, and I arrived at the first tee to find one of my partners proffering his hand. It was Hal Linden.

"Mr. Kindred, I presume," he said.

"I'm Callahan, his understudy."

He laughed.

"Dave's sort of my Sydney Chaplin," I went on.

He stopped laughing. "How do you know that?"

"Doesn't everybody know that? By the way, what do you hear from Sid Raymond?" I asked, pulling an old actor out of my hat.

"You've got to tell me where we met."

"Oh, I'm an old actor myself," I said, standing a ball up on a tee and staring into the distance. "I delivered the flowers to Marilyn Maxwell in the second act."

The Venice Simplon Orient Express was scheduled to pull out at 11:22 A.M. and the wheels commenced to turn on the stroke of 11:22.

The mahogany was deep and rich. The brass was polished. The vases were stacked with cut flowers perfectly setting off the velvet cushions and pewter lamp fixtures. The staff, from the conductor to the chef de train,

was impeccable. The food was delectable. (Typical fare: Cream of Watercress Soup, Poached Scotch Salmon with Mayonnaise and Mediterranean Prawns, Iceberg Salad with Cucumber Batons, Baby Sweetcorn, Mange-Tout and Cherry Tomatoes With Special VS-O-E Dressing, New Potatoes in Minted Butter, Summer Pudding and Coffee From Colombia.) With two exceptions, the passengers were turned out in formal splendor, practically painted in oil. Everything was just right except us.

Dave was wearing his perennial brown sports jacket that matches none of his ensembles but most of mine. I was featuring my all-purpose light blue blazer that complements few of my colors but the majority of his. Come to life, we were the famous pair of Bass Weejuns in the fabled world of tuxedos, and everybody aboard presumed we were . . . involved.

It did no good to whistle manly tunes and drink beer from the bottle as first and second honeymooners all around us slurped champagne from slippers and smooched up and down each other's brocaded arms. The French porter who made up our berths still beheld us pitiably.

Claiming the upper, Dave related a thrilling episode from a baseball road trip back in his whiz kid days with Illinois Wesleyan. En route by train to the big Mississippi Southern game, he had made the mistake of grabbing the lower bunk and was flooded out in the middle of the night by a beer-sopped teammate from above. Finishing his bottle with a belch, thereby releasing the loose water from every shower head in Europe, Dave flopped backward into the top bunk like Dick Fosbury. I slept somewhat fitfully. An inebriated woman in the next compartment kept singing the "Popeye" song. "I'm Popeye the sailor man, boop-boop." Whatever her partner was doing to inspire her increasingly enthusiastic boop-boops, I didn't care to know.

We awoke without incident to breakfast alongside the Rokoffs, June and David, a computer executive and her lawyer husband, from Boston. (They were not Popeye and Olive Oyl.) I opened the conversation the way I had been opening conversations for a while: "Pardon me, have either of you ever almost made an eagle on the sixth hole at Carnoustie?"

"What?" they exclaimed together.

"The other day . . ."

"Never mind him," Dave said. "What brings you two to the Orient Express?"

It turned out they represented something of the sentiment we were after or at least about. David Rokoff hadn't actually read Lou Holtz's memoirs, but he had heard about Holtz's list of one hundred life's wishes, a tabulation of small hopes and grand desires that could even include coaching the football team at Notre Dame. "Holtz recommends writing everything down, and he's right," Rokoff said. "If you don't start writing down your fantasies, you'll never do them, ever."

"Venice was from my list," June said. "We were there years ago and I wanted to go back."

"The Orient Express," her husband chimed in, "was from mine. So we're taking the train to Venice."

We told them where we had been and where we were going, and that the next stop was Burgundy, France, the wine country, where we had heard there was a golf course designed in the shape of a woman. When we had finished, their lists of dreams had grown by one.

"This conversation," sighed Mr. Rokoff, "is getting expensive."

At Golfs du Château de La Salle, near the town of Mâcon, we encountered the most unlikely thing imaginable: a friendly Frenchman. Patrick

De La Chesnais's general cheerfulness may have something to do with being married to the American television actress Stephanie Powers, but the happy way he welcomed us and insisted on showing us every cathedral and garden in Burgundy was more profound than a momentary mood. "I love my country," he said. "I love to share it."

Robert Berthet, the artist who had designed De La Chesnais's golf course—sculpted it, really—in the shadow of a magnificent old château, traveled from Paris to play with us. If Patrick was the picture of a dashing Gaul and polo-playing entrepreneur, Robert could have been sent from central casting to portray the artist at forty-one. Rangy and disjointed, he was an assembly of pipe cleaners connected exclusively at right angles. The shorts he wore emphasized his boniness. Behind tinted spectacles, he had the lost and faraway look of a man capable of spending five minutes rolling up his left sleeve only to put his right arm into the fishbowl. Topping the effect was a shock of orange hair that sprouted obstinately in every direction.

But the moment he took a club in his soft hands he was transformed. All of the ragged parts were marshaled into one easy, athletic slouch. He was a player. In fact, he had played the European tour from 1976 to 1979, until his mind wandered; rather, while his mind was wandering. His sister has won international tournaments. His brother is the coach of the French national team.

"France is slow coming to golf," Berthet explained. "Seventy percent of the country's players are beginners. Only one percent have a single-digit handicap."

"It's not in our knowledge, it's not in our culture," De La Chesnais said. "French people think it's not a sport. That's why I have no carts here. It's a sport. You have to walk. It's a discovery. We must get people to feel it, to know that golf is always a beautiful place."

This was an exceedingly beautiful place. When we first heard of a golf course modeled on a woman, we imagined jigsaw pieces that, put together, formed a portrait. But this was subtler than that, and sweeter.

"I had the idea a long time ago, maybe thirteen, fourteen years," Berthet said. "For years I made sketches, but only in my sketchbooks. Then, one day, touring this property, going around the sides, I looked and said: 'It's there!' "

"You mean: 'She's there.' "

"Exactly!"

"Who is she?"

"Nicole Jobert."

"Were you in love with her?"

"Yes, and I am still. Everything in life is a love affair, I think. I am a Frenchman."

Every curve, every ripple, every contour of the course is a replica of Nicole. One green is her left palm precisely. With the help of multidimensional cameras, the slightest creases and softest rolls were duplicated. Here, the rough is a Roman tunic tossed over her right shoulder. There, shrubs provide her a ruffled skirt. Tees turn into buttons to an open-backed dress.

The fifteenth hole isn't a dogleg; it's a womanleg. "If you knew Nicole, you'd know it's her leg," Robert said admiringly. "It's so obvious. The bump of the ankle bone, the foot, the print, are exactly hers."

Long and short patches of rough at fifteen delineate a stocking top and describe a garter. One is almost embarrassed to take a divot. "It's probably why I am playing so badly these days," Berthet sighed, "when everything reminds me of a woman."

Between the fifteenth and seventeenth holes, visible only from the sky, there's an indelicate, unplayable little marsh where the artist has decided to plant some lavender because, he thinks, an aroma may be called for. (Dave will vouch that my ball veered off single-mindedly in that direction before either of us suspected what was unfolding there.) "It's a little bit subtle," Berthet said. "The purpose of rough is to make the golfer hesitate. Then you have only a few minutes to find your ball. It's seldom enough time."

A few of the holes perform small pageants. Apple-shaped bushes with bites chomped out are nods to Adam and Eve. And a bunker tells a story of a mermaid. But always there is a mound of Nicole's shoulder or a dimple of her inner thigh. Even the practice putting green is her abdomen, her abdomen plus scores of breasts bouncing out of the grass, all emphatically Nicole's. In a few places, greenside orchards start to suggest a hairline, but the face is forever turned away.

"A detailed head wouldn't conform to the game of golf," Berthet said. "It all had to conform to the game of golf. Most of these things, you couldn't see until I showed you. But I think, I hope, you would have seen them over time, like a photograph revealing itself slowly in the developer's tray, month after month, year after year. My purpose wasn't to put aesthetics ahead of golf. That would be a mistake. Let them enjoy golf but also make them dream."

He has done this elsewhere. At Dunkirk, his Golf de Fort-Vallières is an explosion of sharp-edged bunkers and ramparts on the Channel coast. But it would be unfair to characterize his passion plays as gimmicks of the kind associated with Des Muirhead and others. As an architect, Berthet respects what naturally springs from the minerals.

"Sometimes it's the correct answer to move everything," Robert said, "but most of the time, no. The geology, the vegetation, has a lot to say, and maybe has more important ideas than the architect. Here we moved a ridiculous few meters of earth. Nicole posed at the drawing table, and she also came with me to the grounds. It's her skin, but it's God's anatomy."

Our hole would be the most difficult and most recognizable one on the course, the 430-yard, par-4 tenth. Its green is the bottom of a foot tucked up over an ankle with five sand traps for toes. We agreed to meet again the following morning to play it. In the meantime, Patrick had something he wished to show us—the twelfth century.

Stephanie was in America performing a play. They met on a blind date in London and courted in Kenya. "Do you share your wife's interest in wildlife?" I asked De La Chesnais in passing. His clipped answer—"I try to stay wild"—seemed to suggest he is not Mr. Stephanie Powers and we could leave her out of it for the moment. He drove us to Tournus and Cluny, "the most spiritual places in Europe," to visit the abbey and clamber down into the catacombs. "Isn't it a dream world?" he whispered in the icy crypt, where the devoted were walking the Stations of the Cross by torchlight. "Can you imagine? This is a thousand years old."

We had to hurry then to a hilltop for a river-valley view. "It's a beautiful light," he promised. "You'll see." We sped by herds of white Charolais cows, looking like snowdrifts on the lawns, and paused for just a minute to cheer the bowlers in a skittles game. From the hilltop, Patrick said, "If only you could see the red leaves of the wine harvest. It's incredible."

It wouldn't occur to us until the next morning that we'd had nothing to eat and drink all night but goat cheese and cognac. This is the nature of cognac. The man pouring the cognac was Jean Ducloux, the owner and chef de cuisine of Restaurant Greuze, where we never got around to dinner. He is seventy-five. Every night, his wife leaves the hostess's counter at eight-thirty. By a quarter to nine, his mistress has arrived to take over the watch.

"In Burgundy we have characters, strong characters," Patrick said. "I think this is the most important thing when everything else is through."

"Strong characters and strong cheese," Dave remarked, prompting De La Chesnais to tell the story of a man who won a goat in a lottery and began to milk the goat and now is the largest goat cheese producer in Europe. "If you are open for things to happen to you," Patrick said, "wonderful things will happen to you."

We resolved to make this our motto the rest of the way.

The Diabolical's Fourth Hole
430 Yards, Par 4

When we returned in the morning expecting to play only the first hole on the back side (a dangerous term to apply here), we were dragooned into a charity tournament. For a hundred francs apiece, Dave and I were pitted in a two-ball match against Robert and a comely brunette named Françoise. Pulling us aside conspiratorially, Berthet cautioned, "Don't mention Nicole to Françoise." He is a Frenchman.

Despite the fact that I lost two of Dave's balls (never mind what he said, he took it extremely well), we were just five over par alternating every shot and finished high up in the standings. Then we all returned to the tenth tee, where Patrick joined us. Shimmering poplars chimed off to one side. Rosebushes were blooming all around. "I'm planting 25,000 oaks too," De La Chesnais said happily. "It's not for myself, you know."

Dave locked eyes with me and cocked his head in the direction of Françoise's golf bag, which said "Hogan," of course. Robert yanked a yellow wildflower from some imperceptible pore of Mademoiselle Jobert and wove it tenderly into the brim of Françoise's straw hat. On Nicole's behalf, I thought: "Ouch." Jobert was an architect herself, an artist too. I wondered what she was like.

At Guadalupe in the French West Indies, a woman sat down to pen a letter. She was dark, half black, thirty-five years old, delicately drawn, astonishingly beautiful. Far from taking up a hundred acres, she was quite small. Her very long, very curly hair emphasized this. She fit her two homes, Paris and the Caribbean, equally.

She began to write: "I had two different glances about the conception of the La Salle Golf Club. The one of the beloved Lady, and the one of the architect, working with Robert Berthet.

"First of all, it has been a magnificent game, enlightening our love, but I were afraid it could break it. . . .

"I were proud sitting for an artist and being his Muse, the one who inspires the creation and gives its author the strength for accomplishing the work.

"This project was honoring me. I were truly feeling myself a Lady.

"They were, meanwhile, some moments of disappointment and anxiety for me:

"Thus, when I remarked that Robert's glance at my body was not a lover's one, but an architect's one. I became an object useful for his work, but I were not any more the beloved Lady!

"Or when I had to enter the photo studio: in the game we were sharing, Robert and I, we had to accept intruders—the photographers.

"Then, I had to undress in front of those guys! I could do it because Robert was present. I was doing it for him, for us. . . .

"I were dreading the glances of all those people busy around me with spots and cameras, but falsely: they were professionals. Thanks to that, the amateur model I, was never get in trouble.

"Being an architect helped me a lot not to give up before the end. I were not only sitting for the artist, I took part in the project, understanding the technical points and the process of conception, and I could follow the project until its end.

"Today, the golf course works, but, as for the photographic paper thrown into the developer, it will take some time to reveal fully the project. And I am impatient!

"In great love affairs, it is generally by the way of the words that we know what lovers made for each other.

"Here, at La Salle, a 64 hectares 'bas-relief' bears witness of our story and speaks for itself."

She signed it: "Nicole."

Leading off, Dave hit a fast-diving hook that left him dry but at the triangle point of a long water hazard widening almost all the way to the green. Obliged to lay up on one side or the other, he chose the left, hitting first a solid 5-iron to the wrong fairway and then what looked to be a wonderful wedge that tickled the front edge of the green and recoiled halfway to the water.

My drive flew over a line of dangerous trees to the right, but far enough to end up in the clear, if in the rough. Trying to lay up to the right, mindful of what Dave was doing, I accidentally hit a 2-iron on the green, admittedly about a hundred feet from the hole. "A hundred and twenty," whistled the architect. I was at the top of the small of Nicole's foot putting toward her uncallused heel with the five white toes to my back and the continuation of the water hazard churning in my face. The green seemed to be a bridge under which the brook could flow freely. It wasn't, but it seemed that way.

I thought I slammed the putt but, forgetting the dynamics of arches, I nearly rolled it off the left side of the green and came up a full ten yards short. I was still away. This one I rammed four feet past, making a four-putt probable. But I holed the next for a 5. Dave chipped to about six feet and missed it. The Irish were two up.

"Lot of holes to go," Dave said.

"I'm supposed to say that."

"Well, what are you waiting for?"

"Lot of holes to go."

"Thank you."

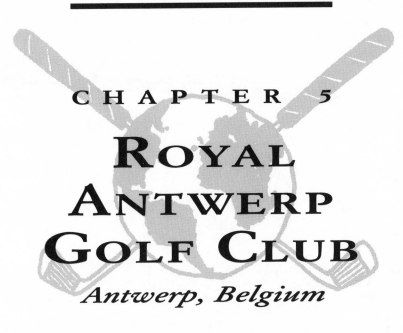

CHAPTER 5

ROYAL ANTWERP GOLF CLUB

Antwerp, Belgium

Where Dave Goes Looking for Mademoiselle Lily

FROM THE BURGUNDY country of France, Tom and I flew to Belgium, not for golf but for mystery.

It began in the summer of 1986 when I tried one more time to find the baseball cards. Maybe Mom had not thrown them away; maybe she had put them in a box inside a box and put those boxes into a bigger box. Then she might have put it all under a blanket inside a trunk shoved into a cubbyhole. So I pulled a trunk into the sunlight of Mom's upstairs storage room and lifted the corner of a blanket.

There was a little red book with a cracked leather cover on which was printed in fading gold: *Addresses*. A sleeve along the book's spine held a small wooden pencil. Two names were written in ink inside the cover, Mom's and Dad's:

A reporter, curious, wanted to know more. What would a World War II address book tell about Dad? The first page had English names such as L. C. Beachem, 29 Tyning Road, Bristol, England, as well as the Cookey Nook Cafe, 51 Church Street, Trowbridge. The entries were not in Dad's handwriting; they likely were made by the people themselves before his company, part of the U. S. First Army, left England for the D-Day invasion in the summer of 1944.

Dad never spoke of the war and would not watch movies about it. By nature reticent, he was silent about those years of his life. He brought home a German officer's cap and a German machine gun. Nothing else, not even memories he would share with us. He disliked the Red Cross; he said it existed to do favors for officers at the expense of enlisted men. Otherwise, nothing.

But here, in his address book, was a piece of that war. Here were names written at a time of his life which had been closed, or which his son growing up had never tried to open. Here in paper and ink and leather was a part of him I had never known. He was thirty-two years old and at war. The old address book put me in his time in that place. I could see him young and handsome handing the little red book to L. C. Beachem of 29 Tyning Road. "When this is over," I could hear him saying, "let's stay in touch."

I wondered what he said to the woman whose name appeared in bold handwriting on the address book's third page:

I wondered how the mademoiselle's life intersected Dad's. My mother's answer to that question was to say Lily had been a young girl, fifteen or sixteen, the daughter of a family in Belgium that provided Dad a room during his company's stay there from October 1944 to April 1945. "They raised rabbits in the backyard and Lily's mother made a fur coat for your sister that first Christmas," Mom said.

I took the address book home and for four years had no reason to open it. Then in 1990 Mom mailed a box of Dad's Army stuff: a military policeman's black MP armband, four battle ribbons, his separation papers and three old photographs. One picture was of a city street with row houses on one side and a six-foot-high wall on the other. What city? There was no way to know. The other photographs were contained in a paper frame advertising the C. Muller photo studio at 15 rue des Croisiers, Namur, Telephone 21543. Those pictures were of a young woman. One came signed:

En souvenir d'une petite amie
Lily

It was Lily Bemelmans. The portrait showed her about to become beautiful. She sat for C. Muller in a rabbit fur coat, mature and confident, her beginnings of a smile suggesting that she knew something you would like.

One of my failings growing up had been a blindness to anything except baseball, reading and writing. I knew nothing about Lily while my sister, Sandra, knew more than she cared to. When I called to tell her about the Lily pictures, Sandra said, "Do you want to see her letters, too?"

"Letters from Lily?"

"I'll mail them to you."

"What do they say?"

"You better read them for yourself."

They were letters mailed to Dad at his Army address. Mom gave them to Sandra because she had reached an age where she felt a comfort in passing things on. She wanted us to know the family history as well as she knew it. The letters from Lily represented a moment in that history. They were dated April 11, 1945, and June 6, 1945. Each was written neatly in both French and English, perhaps with Lily translating her own words.

In the first letter, shortly after my father's company had been transferred from Belgium to Germany, she wrote:

> **M**y love Johnny,
>
> I am despairing you no with me every day and every night. I am very much unhappy, Johnny. I believe you forget your little baby. Oh, darling, why you go, why? Johnny, if you please you be back, very fast. Every day I wait your return. I desire much to see you and your blue eyes.
>
> John, at present one Jeep stand before my house, I believe it is you, my heart beat very fast, but no you, it is one American soldier back from Germany with something for me from you. Thank you very much, Darling.
>
> John, 10 minutes pass, I foolish with despair. I believe you forget me. This hour I believe that I am foolish.
>
> Johnny, my little MP, you write much for me. You write when you believe you come back. I beg you, no forget me. I end this letter with my love you and with my kiss.
>
> Your Lily, for always, for ever. Lily.

The letter changed me. Until that moment, I had never thought of my father as a young man. He was Dad. It was an identity so complete I looked for nothing else. The people in this letter were strangers. A woman's voice I had never heard spoke about a man I had never known. She knew a young man who could make her "heart beat very fast." And that man was my father at thirty-two.

No moral judgments here. Just a sudden warmth. At war, with a wife and two small children at home, what would I have done? In a killing war, gone two years and only God knows if I'll get back home, would I have come to know a Lily? Yes. Would a Lily remember "for always"? I hope so.

Two months later, in June of '45, Lily apparently had heard nothing from Dad. She wrote:

> **M**y love Johnny, I hope that you have receive my letter that I have given to one MP of your company. I hope that you write for me in one little time and very much letter. Today my blue dress is finish and it is very nice. My little MP, can I hope you return? I want that you are always with me but this dream is too sweet and too nice for have existence. Johnny, you love me? Me, I love you and I never stop that! Believe me, please.
>
> Oh, if you please, Mister Kindred, John D., you not forget me in Germany.
>
> Here in the Belgium the weather is warm. I hope that it is the same thing for you. The photos are finished and when I see one MP of the 256 company I give him my photo for you. But I finish my letter with kiss and my great love. Your sweet friend, Lily.
>
> P.S. I hope that when you have one pass that you return to Namur very quick. My family give for you very good remembrance.

While planning the itinerary for our journey, I made a phone call for directory assistance in Namur, Belgium. I asked the operator if she had a number for the Bemelmans family at 9 rue de l'Industrie. She said she did and she gave it to me.

Leaving sweet Nicole's golf course, Tom and I were advised by Patrick De La Chesnais that the drive from Mâcon to the Geneva airport would be simple, no problem, just get on the motorway and you're there in an hour, no problem at all.

"You have no idea," I told Patrick, "how easy it is for us to get lost."

Not an hour later but three hours later, we arrived at Geneva after another high-speed escapade that produced more trembling-hand notes:

"Mad dash to Geneva at 100 mph after getting lost leaving Mâcon. Drove 80 miles north–south needing to go east. But we were trapped on a toll road with an exit every 40 miles. Kept missing the exit to Geneva.

"Went under a pedestrian bridge over the motorway. A nut in monk's robes waved a wooden dove at us. TC waved back and said, 'What if the poor fellow had by a miracle regained his sight at the moment we passed under him? What a wonderful thing if the first person he sees is a smiling, waving, good-looking American.'

"A death-lock on the wheel, careening along at 100 mph trying to get off a road with no exits, I grumbled, 'The monk's crazy. Find me a way off this road.'

"An hour later, we again passed under the monk with the wooden dove. TC said, 'Now who's crazy? The monk at least knows where he is.'

"We find the Geneva exit. Skid to a stop at the airport with five minutes to spare. Throw keys to rental people. Then can't find my passport. I open every bag and every zipper of every bag. Panic. I find the passport. Dash to the plane.

"Sit next to a guy who wants to know where we're going. I tell him. He says, 'You're going the wrong way around the world. You should be going west to east.' I resist an impulse to rearrange his eyebrows.

"Arrive in Brussels. Show my passport at customs. Go to baggage claim. Need to change money. Moneychanger asks to see my passport. It's gone. AGAIN! I don't find it this time.

"I fume and fuss, sweat and swear. I spin in ever tightening circles. Lost my passport twice in one day. What a hayseed. Loses his passport while waiting for his luggage.

"TC watches from a comfy seat near the rental car counter. He says, 'Dave, you've got the human shanks.'

"We leave the airport, me without a passport. We drive. We get lost. A car honks at us for dawdling. Car honks eleven or twelve times. As that car pulls alongside us, TC says, 'Hey, buster, we've lost our passport and we're not in a good mood. Don't mess with us.'

"At traffic light, TC runs our car into the guy's rear bumper. Guy jumps out, comes back to us and says, 'You no like my car?' TC has opened his door and unfolded himself out of the little car. TC comes out big. He has the red pirate's beard. He has the fighter's way of dropping his chin against his chest, daring you to find a way to it. TC is six foot three and he's got the Belgian guy by fifty pounds. TC says, 'Look, fella, I need to win my next three fights to get back to .500 lifetime. Let's get it on.'

"Belgian guy scurries back in car, drives away.

"Three days later, I get a new passport. Then I find my old one at the

airport's cop shop as we leave Belgium. So, with a bow to Jules Verne's heroes, Passepartout and Phileas Fogg, we become 'Passport Two' and 'Full of Fog.'

"What more could be perfecter?"

In Namur, a city of 50,000 people forty miles south of Brussels, we wandered most of a rainy morning until a policeman directed us to rue de l'Industrie: a short, narrow, curving street with three-story row houses on one side. Across the way was a six-foot-high brick wall. I looked at the street and looked at the photograph of an unknown place that my sister had given me. This was that place. In the summer of 1945, almost a half century ago, Lily had sent Dad a picture of the street where she lived.

No answer from the Bemelmanses' phone number in Namur. Now we had come four thousand miles to knock on the door at 9 rue de l'Industrie and ask for this Lily whose name appeared in my father's little red address book, who mailed pretty pictures of herself in fur coats and wrote memories of a war he wouldn't talk about.

When no one answered at the door marked with a 9, we went to number 7 and there a woman appeared, a Shelley Winters type, blowsy, blond and bountiful, her little black poodle yapping hello. The neighbor was friendly and helpful and, perhaps unknown to her, she wore a black open-weave shawl around her shoulders while leaving her considerable breasts bare to the rainy summer day. Tom and I took this exposure as a European

thing which, after a month in each other's bearded/mustachioed company, we found to be delightful, even doubly delightful.

Though our new friend's English was limited and our French nonexis-
tent, we came to understand that she didn't know a Lily Bemelmans, but,
yes, number 9 belonged to the Bemelmans family.

"Marcel live there," she said. "Not home now." She touched her knee
and mimed a limp, turning from the door to pull a cane from an umbrella
stand. "He in hospital."

I had never heard the name Marcel Bemelmans. "What about Mama
Bemelmans?" I said.

Again communicating by mime, the neighbor hunched over as if crum-
pled by old age. "Mama not here. Don't know."

"Where is Marcel? What hospital?"

She took our map and directed us to the hospital, a place called Domain
de Closière. She said, "House. White house. Great white house. Two kilometers."

We wandered around on a rainy morning in Namur until we bumped
into Domain de Closière. It was, in fact, an old white house two miles
from rue de l'Industrie. But for an hour there, the only time on our entire
trip, no one spoke English. I wrote down the name: Marcel Bemelmans.
But the hospital administrator shook her head no, no Bemelmans here.

About to leave, frustrated and not knowing where to turn, I noticed
three boards on the administrator's office wall listing the hospital's pa-
tients. There in Building 2, Room 46, was the patient THIRION-BEMEL-
MANS. "Here, here," I said, touching the name.

"*Ah, oui*," the administrator said. She made a series of calls and said
with a smile, "Marcel Bemelmans. Here, ten minutes. You wait."

No Marcel. An hour later, the administrator took me to a social worker,
Nathalie Bodart-Gavroy, whose English was good enough to let me know
Marcel was an outpatient who came in two days a week. "Do you come
with me?" Bodart-Gavroy said, going to her office where she asked, "Why
do you want to see Marcel?"

"It's not Marcel I want. I'm looking for Lily Bemelmans. A long time
ago, she lived at the same address Marcel uses now. Maybe they're brother
and sister."

The social worker looked at Marcel Bemelmans's hospital record. "He
is sixty-five years old. He has no sister. He has two brothers and his

mother, Mariette Thirion. She is ninety-seven years old. Nursing home, not able to speak."

Any reporter would doubt files created by civil servants. "How can it be," I said, "that Marcel has no sister? Lily Bemelmans, the same name, lived at Marcel's address in 1945. Are you sure? My father knew Lily Bemelmans of 9 rue de l'Industrie during World War II. Here, look at these."

I handed Lily's letters to the social worker, a young woman bright and pretty. Bodart-Gavroy read the letters with a smile, then a blush, and said, "Is a love, yes?"

"I don't know. Maybe. But it was a long time ago and I just want to find Lily now, to talk to her. Is there anything in the file that would tell me how to find Marcel? He's not at home now."

Bodart-Gavroy said, yes, the hospital records indicated Marcel should be home at five o'clock that afternoon.

Dad died in 1963 two weeks after a diagnosis of lung cancer. In the hospital he said, "I've got everything I ever wanted." My sister had been married that summer; I had become a father that spring. He was fifty-one, I was twenty-one. We had been given to doing, not talking. We played catch and he built a basketball court and a baseball diamond behind our house; he coached my junior baseball teams and with Mom drove thousands of miles carrying me to games. Because he had quit school after the eighth grade to support his widowed mother and sisters, he wanted more for me. The only thing he ever asked was that I graduate from college. Five months after my graduation, he died.

The older I got, the more I missed him. Not just his presence, but I missed not knowing him, not sharing his memories. He was Dad, always there. It would have been nice to know him as a friend.

So, to Namur. Lily knew the John Kindred of 1945. She shared a moment when he was young and at war. She could tell me about that man in ways no one else could. I wanted to know about a man who keeps a woman's letters. Such a man might want his son forty years later to find Lily. He might want her to know he had gone home to America and hadn't written and was sorry about it. He also might want her to know he hadn't forgotten.

At five o'clock that afternoon, with our breasty blond Shelley Winters helping us again, we stepped onto the sidewalk headed back to number 9 rue de l'Industrie—when she saw a slight figure in blue crossing the street. She called out, "Marcel, MARCEL!"

Marcel Bemelmans had no idea why two Americans were at his home; the blonde told him only that we wanted to talk. For that matter, we weren't sure he had any connection with Lily Bemelmans; the social worker insisted he had no sister. We were strangers standing in the rain on a little street unchanged since 1945.

Marcel, a kindly man, led us into a narrow hall at number 9. He pointed toward a cluttered living room. Even before I stepped through the door-way, I saw the photograph on the wall. My eyes went straight to it. In a group of Bemelmans family portraits, hers was placed in the center. The picture was nearly identical to the one I carried with me. It was Lily.

This was the place. I sat down, looking at the picture. Words floated around me, Tom and the blonde and Marcel making small talk, a murmur of noise distant and indistinct. I felt an odd sensation. I had been in that room before. I had been in that chair before, in that room with Marcel before. For those few seconds, I was in my father's body. I wanted to see Lily.

The small room looked like a medium's place, a séance due to begin. It was crowded with lush Spanish paintings of children crying. There were busts and statues of Napoleon. Scattered around were a dozen knives, including a Bowie knife with John Wayne's signature etched into the blade. Then I saw the rifles.

Marcel had two muzzle-loading rifles, each very old, each so familiar in this unfamiliar place that I stared at them as if by staring I could under-stand what was happening. Marcel Bemelmans, a man I had never heard of, collected muzzle-loading rifles and put them around his little room four thousand miles from my father's little room in Illinois, a room Dad built with his own hands for his collection of old muzzle-loading rifles.

Marcel asked the blond neighbor what we wanted.

"Do you know Lily Bemelmans?" I asked.

The neighbor translated and gave us Marcel's answer. "Marcel says, 'My sister is dead.' "

An emptiness. All this way and no Lily. I said, "When did she die?"

"In 1967, cancer."

Marcel didn't know why I was there. He didn't even know my name. I was just a stranger from America sitting in his odd little room. But now, with Lily gone, wanting to fill the emptiness, I needed to tell him more. So I began to unwrap a package carrying Lily's letters along with her photographs.

"Marcel, I want to give you some pictures and letters."

He walked over to my side while I fumbled with a string on the package.

And Marcel shouted, "John Kindred!"

I almost cried. In the package was a photograph of Dad in his Army dress uniform. Somehow, Marcel had seen it. And forty-eight years after my father left that room in Namur a last time, Marcel Bemelmans shouted his name with such certainty and such affection and such joy that the young John Kindred seemed to have walked back into that room at that moment.

I handed Marcel the picture and said, "He's my father."

"Your papa?" Marcel said. He held Dad's picture and turned so it would catch the light.

"Yes, my papa. Did you know him well?"

Marcel was thrilled. "Oh, yes. Yes, yes, yes. My brother, he has picture of Johnny in his other Army hat."

I knew then more than most sons ever know about their fathers. Few people leave memories that bring a flash of joy into an old friend's life a half century later. He must have been a good one, the John David Kindred who came to Namur in 1945.

For six months of 1944 and early '45, my father's company was stationed two blocks from the Bemelmanses' home. Marcel was a teenager who spent hours talking to my father about trucks and cowboys. I asked about the curious coincidence of muzzle-loading rifles; Marcel began collecting them only twenty years ago, and he didn't know Dad had collected them even before the war.

As for Lily and Dad, our blond translator/neighbor leaned over to whisper to Marcel and then translated with a laugh, touching a finger below her right eye, "Marcel says your father had eyes for his sister. He came to the house to see his sister. But she was just a young girl."

"Ask Marcel to read these." I gave the old man his sister's letters. He read them without saying a word. He put them down and said they were a young girl's daydreams, nothing more.

I had the feeling Marcel knew more than he said. Maybe Dad knew Lily only as the young daughter of a family kind enough to take in an

American soldier. Maybe the child's daydreams would become plaintive and passionate letters. But the name in a soldier's address book, "Mlle Lily," suggests a woman. A soldier at war for two years would share a laugh and a tear with a Mademoiselle Lily. And maybe this Lily, like a lot of European women in those dark years, would see in the American soldier the light of a hero.

The certainty is that Dad and Mom had each other for twenty-five years before, during and after Namur. On April 7, 1945, Dad left Namur headed for Germany. On June 24, 1945, the war ended for him and, happy to be going home, anxious to let her know, Dad wrote a letter to Mom. It was a letter she kept for almost half a century before giving it, too, to her children. Dad wrote:

Hi, Toots! Another week has passed and this is my first letter to you, but this is the one that I've been wanting to write for a long time.

Remember the last letter I wrote you? I told you that the 96-point men were leaving for home. They were a little short on their quota and there were 13 of us in Hq. that had 95 points. So they took us too. So, Honey, I'm on my way home.

Hank Pietschowski and I are still together. We are at a depot in France now being processed. I guess we will leave here about the 3–4 July and we should be home by the 25th. I'll call you as soon as I get in. It's hard to tell what will happen after I get to the States, but at least I'll get home to see you and the youngsters.

You will have to excuse the writing. I'm using the back of my mess kit for a table. And don't believe all you read in the papers about how nice they treat the guys on their way home, either.

Love, Johnny.

Shortly after the war, Lily Bemelmans was married. She had three children, a girl and two boys. The Bemelmanses never heard from Dad after he left Namur. Marcel said, "Lily never spoke of Johnny to me after 1945."

At every stop on his way from Germany to Illinois, stopping in Paris and London and Miami, Dad picked up a souvenir for Mom. He came home from the war and he loved us all and every Christmas he pulled us around the block on our sleds in his old Ford pickup truck with the oogah-oogah horn. He taught his parakeet to wolf-whistle every time Mom walked across the room, the bird's whistle followed by "Hi, Toots!" Yes, yes, it is true, Dad did take a while to make good on his promise to put up a backyard clothesline. He did it as a twenty-fifth wedding anniversary present, laughing with Mom at his side.

This story was important to me. But before writing it, I needed Mom's approval. She was reluctant. Like Marcel, she considered Lily's letters the result of a child's infatuation. But she also knew they were so compelling as to prompt other readings. In the end, Mom decided that her twenty-five years with Dad provided the only answer she needed for any questions raised. She told me to write it the way I saw it.

"I wouldn't have given you Lily's letters if there was anything to hide," Mom said. "If you write it, it's a good story and people will know your dad was a sweetheart. His very last words to me in the hospital were, 'I love you all.'

"The dates you have on him in Namur, I'm not sure those are right. It was only three or four months. He and his buddy Hank both lived with the Bemelmanses. They helped provide food so the family could survive the war.

"Johnny came home and got work as an apprentice carpenter on the railroad. It took him down to Alabama for a while and he didn't like it. He said he'd been away from home long enough. So he quit the railroad and joined the carpenters' union.

"No, he never talked about the war. The Red Cross some. There was one thing he said. As an MP, he had to help hang an American soldier for rape. He never got over that. No war movies, no war talk. He didn't want anything to remind him of any part of it.

"The funny part of the clothesline thing was that a doctor had told me I couldn't have a clothesline. I had a heart problem and the doctor said I couldn't raise my arms over my head to hang clothes. Your dad used that as an excuse for the longest time. He said he was following doctor's orders not to put up that clothesline—until I reminded him, 'Oh, yes, you do have to put it up. You promised me a clothesline for our twenty-fifth wedding anniversary.'

"So he put it up, there in the backyard, right behind the garage. It was the best clothesline any wife ever got."

The Diabolical's Fifth Hole
426 Yards, Par 4

Herbert Warren Wind once wrote that Royal Antwerp Golf Club "comes close to being a masterpiece of its kind . . . the type of course that wends its way through woods of pine and silver birch, heather and shrubs."

As I sat on the bathroom sink using the Brussels Hilton hair dryer to blow-dry my socks—travel is educational—I knew that a masterpiece of any ratzenfratzing kind was the last thing my golf game needed.

Things would be going along. Sun shining. Spring in my step. Tom the finest Irishman in the hemisphere. And then, for reasons unknown, I would hit a ground ball to shortstop. From Portrush to Mâcon, I topped a drive a day. Some rounds, two or three of those soul-destroying little dribblers would take eighteen hippity-hops and vanish into a volcanic fissure, quicksand goop or stinkweed.

My game in these days cried out for the remedy so often suggested by witnesses to its imperfections: Take two weeks off and then quit for good.

Fat chance of that. Were golfers capable of such rational thought, we would never have begun our devil's dance with the crooked sticks that change shapes.

One day a 9-iron is a precision instrument, part of our being, a physical manifestation of our thoughts—until the Stephen King thing happens and the divine tool becomes a spitting cobra and we're holding it by the tail. Now, try hitting a pitch shot with *that*.

Early in our travels, my driver and fairway woods stared up at me with disdain. They whispered darkly, my 5-wood hissing, "We are ill-designed implements, remember that and never forget it. There is no way to hit that itty-bitty ball with these misshapen chunks of metal. And if you try, this cobra will bite your ankle. Take two weeks off, Dave, and then quit for good."

So my greatest ambition at the masterpiece Royal Antwerp was to make it through a day hitting all fly balls.

For an hour or so, I managed civil conversation with our host, the club captain Robert Van Blerk. I told him I'd come to Belgium because my father had been stationed in Namur in 1945. Van Blerk said, "Ah, one of the American soldiers who gave us the life we have today by pushing the Germans out. Welcome, welcome."

As for golf in his country, the captain said, "Belgium had nine courses when I began to play forty years ago. Only fifteen years ago, we had fifteen. Now, it's sixty. The same with France. Golf in Europe is going boomingly because of television. People see it on TV and want to play."

Robert's son Philip, a lawyer, delighted us with a brief about course conditions which he promptly delivered to the club captain: "Bare spots everywhere, Father. High rough so near the fairway. Such *punishment* for so small a mistake."

We came to the sixth, our diabolical hole, a par 4 of 426 yards. "Several holes," Mr. Wind had written, "are compelling in their design and beauty. The 6th curves around an elbow of woods and narrows like an hour-glass where a long drive finishes, and a mound before the green stirs memories of St. Andrews."

Though my drive finished well short of the hourglass, it did have the virtue of flight. My 5-wood second shot, however, was a ground ball to short. It left me with a 5-iron shot that bumped against Mr. Wind's precious St. Andrews mound. From there a miserable chip caught a ridge and rolled twenty-five feet left. Such punishment for so small a mistake.

Tom's long drive bounced into knee-high rough. He wedged it back to the fairway, put a 3-wood right of the hole's only bunker, chipped on to forty-five feet and made that cross-country putt for a bogey 5.

Making twenty-five-footers for a half is a doubtful proposition at the best of times, let alone during a stretch when you believe you hear your 5-wood whispering darkly.

Naturally, I made the putt. Golf is temporary insanity practiced in a cow pasture.

CHAPTER 6

VISBY
GOLFKLUBB
Gotland Island, Sweden

Over the Baltic by Barking Boat
and Bubbly Balloon

A LETTER CAUGHT up to us, postmarked Belfast, stamped H.M. Belfast Prison, handwritten in a smooth script on looseleaf:

Dear Tom and Dave,

Sorry I was unable to play with you this year but as you can see from the above address, and as you now know, I was well and truly indisposed.

Some time when you are over again, I will tell you the whole story. Suffice to say at the moment I am being held on remand on holding charges accusing me of burning my own hotel and contributing to para-militaries.

To put it very briefly, my hotel was burned and the persons who were responsible then contacted me and informed me they had burned the hotel, they knew that I had a claim pending for insurance and, as they put it, they wanted £60,000 as I stood to gain from a fire which they had caused.

The demand was put to me as one I couldn't refuse, as a refusal would mean that my wife and four children would not live long enough to enjoy our new house. I started to pay and now I'm here because of the circumstances explained above.

My legal representatives say that I have no case to answer and at the end of the day I'll be free. But in the meantime, while the wheels of justice grind slowly onward, I'm held on remand.

That's a brief summary of the situation and I was not involved in any of the allegations. I'm quite confident that I will soon be released. I got your message. It was extremely thoughtful of you to try to visit me. Perhaps next time you're over we will enjoy a game. Mind you I'll be very rusty.

I hope you enjoyed your golf in Ireland. The Royal would have been in good shape as it's not long since the Amateur Open was played there. I believe the weather during the Open was very rough, not what you Americans are used to. I think only one American out of thirty entrants qualified as one of the 64 players going into the match play stage.

I'd like you both to know how much I appreciate your good wishes. Hope to see you sometime in the future.

Regards,
Roy

People said Phileas Fogg resembled Byron—at least that his head was Byronic; but that he was a bearded, tranquil Byron who might live on a thousand years without growing old. His companion was nicknamed Passepartout because of a natural aptness for going out of one business and into another. In his time, Passepartout had been an itinerant singer, a circus rider, a rope walker, a professor of gymnastics and a fireman.

Full of Fog was bearded but far from Byronic and very far from tranquil. As for never growing old, he had been the oldest young man almost anyone had ever met and only recently outgrew his unofficial title (bestowed on him many years ago by Edwin Pope of the *Miami Herald*) as "the world's youngest curmudgeon." Hardly a flibbertigibbet, let alone an itinerant singer (as we will certainly hear in Thailand), Passport Two was a confirmed old newspaperman and likely to remain so.

Landing in Scandinavia, they made for Gamla Stan, Old Town, the original Stockholm of seven centuries ago, and quickly became addicted to goulash soup and tiring, interesting walks along the brick Stortorget, the Great Square. They were in direct sight of the Grand Hotel just across the Strömmen canal and in spiritual contact with Alfred Nobel. But they couldn't see the city, which was described to them as unseeable from either too high or too low, clearly discernible only from a balloon.

Now this was perfect. Every spin around the world in eighty days or less is a homage to Jules Verne, but here was a paean to Mike Todd, as there was no balloon in Verne's book, only in Todd's movie. Full of Fog and Passport Two had toasted Verne already, on the Orient Express, when the stationmaster called the village of Amiens, France, where Verne died in 1905. So they looked up "balloonists" in the directory and set out to commune with David Niven.

Ballooning, they came to find out, is servile work. The riders pay for their passage in more than kronor. They are expected to wrestle the basket off the truck bed into a field and stretch the canvas skin of the prehistoric monster like circus roustabouts. Then they lurk for an hour in the fly-infested weeds while the pilot sits cross-legged in the middle of the pasture launching little trial balloons and worrying at how swiftly they reach the setting sun.

Eventually he shrugs, as if to say, "You only die once," and calls for the passengers to man the lines like the *Hindenburg*'s ground crew while he heats the air with a blowtorch until the dome is taut and they jump in the basket and are away.

Stockholm isn't a city at all. It is a bewilderment of islands connected by a latticework of bridges. Lights were blinking on in the half-darkness. It rather resembled a stadium. To an Icelandic "hiss of heat," they climbed from 1,000 feet to 2,000, mainly to reassure the palace guard in the King's residence straight below, but then impulsively kept soaring in defiance of an approved flight plan until they were just a speck in the sky. "The rain goes away," the pilot said. "Perfect."

Passport Two, who thinks in metaphors, said it was as though they were in a little press box floating farther and farther away from the game. He knew Full of Fog had been thinking of this.

What had made Fog an old-young codger was his affection for the battered fedoras still holding forth when he arrived in the sportswriting business a quarter century before. He gravitated toward the old crocks and away from the dormitory rats because he preferred the crocks' conversations and didn't care all that much about rock and roll.

The way Pete Rose bootlegged memories from the elderly pitcher Waite Hoyt—to the point where Rose could recall the exact position of the embroidered "BR" on Babe Ruth's terrycloth bathrobe—Fog became a contemporary of dinosaurs. Through no credit of his own, he was the last best friend to Red Smith. Most of us have the touch of a blacksmith. Only Red had the touch of a Red Smith.

Old sportswriters operated under a buddy system. Grantland Rice took young Walter Wellesley Smith under his archangel wing. Later, Frank Graham and Smith were 1 and 1A. Eventually the firm came down to Red and Jack Murphy of San Diego. They took in a junior partner.

After Jack died way too soon, Fog walked alone with Red and talked him columns in hotel rooms if he couldn't make it to practice. When Smith finished bringing himself to the subjects, it shamed Fog to read how much better they were in the translation, and made him extraordinarily happy. Even when it came to Murphy's funeral, Red had whispered, "Be my legs. Take notes."

With Red's death and the death of a sweet old giant from Dayton, Ohio—Si Burick—Fog's false age caught up with him at last. He still loved the words. He liked the games well enough. And the new rock and rollers were nice men and women, terrific writers too, many of them. It just wasn't as much fun.

Although the athletes of the day also seemed less compelling, Fog knew this was a function of his own diminishing enthusiasm. Johnny Bench wrote in a book how he once dreamed of punching Fog and going to jail for it. On the golf course subsequently, Fog turned to the great catcher and said, "You know, you ought to try dreaming of Ingrid Bergman at the top of her game." Johnny had to laugh. Isn't that an odd brand of vinegar to miss?

The basket hit the ground with a thump, and if Passport Two had been daydreaming too, they might have been dragged all the way to the Strombron bridge. Laughing and rolling around like children, they squashed the wind out of the bag, and the pilot rubbed champagne in their scalps and named two new islands mysteriously in their honor:

King's Hat Island (was that because Passport Two had such a shiny crown?) and Bird Island. While they drank the rest of the champagne in the dark, the pilot told a story about convicts in Paris and balloon rides and champagne. Full of Fog, half listening, looked back up at the stars winking in the night. He missed them.

Gotland Island sits in the middle of the Baltic 120 kilometers off the Swedish mainland. Starting altogether below the surface, it slowly rose out of the sea, submerged and reappeared again in stages of thousands of years. The 57,000 people who inhabit Gotland — good-natured people with chapped faces and strips of rug sampling for eyebrows — contend alternately that the island came up to stay when somebody named Tjelvar patented fire or that it still sinks below the waves every evening when the sun burns low. Because Dave and I were assured a 586-yard, par-5 hole was worth the bother of possibly drowning, we pulled the car onto the *Nord Gotlandia* at Oskarshamn and set rudder for Visby Golfklubb aboard a boat that barked.

The miscalculation was our own. Both of us had seen the decal of a proud profile of a German shepherd over the ticket window where the seats were purchased. Neither of us understood we were buying our way onto the poop deck. Evidently, Swedish dogs are well traveled enough to warrant their own sections of the ships, and the timing of the biggest dog show of the year in Visby somewhat worked against us.

As we sat petless in the mammoth and jammed pet section, looking as pixilated as Jimmy Stewart in *Harvey,* feeling like stowaways on the Ark, an undercard of light preliminaries broke out around us. Champions of every breed snapped and lunged at each other while their humans held the leashes with one hand and munched shrimp sandwiches with the other. In the eye of this bedlam, a quartet of Brits, each tethered to a little Winston Churchill, was playing English Monopoly, where Mayfair and Park Lane replaced Boardwalk and Park Place.

"It couldn't have been the Miss Sweden pageant, right?" Dave said.

Just then, two wolfhounds or Afghans — anyway, they looked like Vanessa Redgrave and Meryl Streep — decided to divvy up the Churchills, and the main event was on. We docked in Gotland littered with hair and laughter.

The island's centerpiece is Visby, a walled-in city of roses and ruins, where Vikings and pirates stashed things of imprecise value and dreamers are still searching for them; including Jack Trask.

We encountered Trask in what should have been the simple process of asking directions. (Only when you're already lost is asking directions unmanly.) He immediately threw over his sandwich board, advertising a coming production of *Two Gentlemen of Verona,* and took us on as full-time charges.

A cotton-haired grandfather with a radiant pink face, maybe seventy, Trask was prosperously dressed in a blue Oxford shirt buttoned to the neck and a striped seersucker sport coat. Stashing his sandwich board in a private crevice of the tallest of the Ringmuren's guard towers, he cavalierly dropped the information that he intended to portray one of the Two Gentlemen personally, though he hadn't made up his mind yet which one it would be. He didn't seem to know very much about the play.

Never mind. He hurried on to say he was a professor emeritus at "C. W. Post University in America," although he didn't appear to know where C. W. Post was in America. "How did you happen to pick C. W. Post?" I asked him, probably not very kindly. Ignoring the skepticism, he went on.

So we were golfers, eh? Well, not being a golfer himself, he couldn't tell us very much—that is, nothing about "swinging the cabers" or such as that. But he was intimately familiar with the grounds of Visby Golfklubb in that all six of his children were conceived on the property, one on each of the first six greens.

Dave and I looked at each other.

Yes, he would gladly show us the golf course, but first he wished us to stand him a drink and he would repay us in advance by showing us two wonders of the world. The first was a road he called "the Dutchmen's Road," where he delivered us excitedly. That is, he was excited. It looked like any other road to habitués of the road. But Trask insisted it was haunted. "If I had a horse, I could prove it to you," he grimaced. "A horse won't go up this road. A little child neither."

"We'll take your word for it," Dave said. "Good one."

The second sight was an ordinary-looking stone inlaid in a humble cottage that, according to Trask, glowed like a star, but only for the pure of heart. "Can you see it?" he asked earnestly, shading his own eyes from a searing glare.

"Let's get that drink," I said darkly.

At the arboretum-bar of the handsome Visby Hotel, under a leaning and glistening skylight, a young man in a tuxedo was playing the piano for the brunch crowd. "Ah, *Pagliacci,*" Trask sighed, sipping his Bloody Mary, "one of my favorites. I used to be a concert pianist, you know."

"Play something," said the hostess, who overheard. "Won't you, please?"

"No, I haven't got my music."

"Oh, please?"

"He hasn't got his music," I said.

The customers began applauding, first hesitantly, then avidly, then insanely.

"He's overdue at the golf course," Dave mumbled, panicking. "He has to show us where they keep the cabers and, you know, uh . . ."

But the swells had collected Trask by the elbows and swept him to the piano bench, where he sat motionless for a long, terrible moment while Dave and I looked at each other miserably. Finally, he began to play.

He played like an angel. For ten minutes, nobody moved. He stopped only for an instant, to smile at Dave and me, to shrug his apologies and nod farewell. The Gentleman of Verona had his music after all. We could still hear him playing almost all the way to the course.

The Diabolical's Sixth Hole
586 Yards, Par 5

Not wanting to be too forward, we teed off backward. For some reason, we just had to hit a ball into the Baltic. This was pressing our luck but we were feeling pretty lucky.

Visby is a self-service Golfklubb. One fills out an elaborate three-carboned chit, drops his kronor into a slitted strongbox and takes a pop-up paper number to the first tee. So many foursomes were stacked up at the tee, there wasn't even waggling room. On-deck hitters had to fan out into an adjacent woods, where the hatchet sounds of their anvil chorus could have drowned out a Boy Scout Jamboree.

What Dave and I didn't know was that reserved tee times kicked in at certain intervals, and after waiting patiently (relatively speaking) for over an hour, we stepped on the tee only to be black-flagged by a severe female authority figure interceding on behalf of four sizable Swedes. One of them had a head as big as a nineteen-inch color television set. Behind them waited four others, four others and four others.

We presented our serving numbers. She waved them off, saying the number system had expired thirty seconds earlier. I told her we had come a long way to play the thirteenth hole. She wasn't visibly moved. Then I thought of something incredibly stupid. I flashed my *Golf Digest* Course Ranking Panel Gold Card, the absolute last refuge of a scoundrel. Whereupon Dave pulled out his own irrelevant credential, heretofore unused. Maybe they were dazzled by the gall, but the natives reacted as if we had predicted a solar eclipse. They bowed and we hit, the wrong way off the tee far into the ocean. Mischievously then, we walked backward all the way up the fairway.

Golf in Sweden is exploding. The country has fallen completely in love with a sun-speckled and uninhibited redhead named Helen Alfredsson, who screeches at her golf ball in profane Swedish and makes it listen in polite English. She is the third or fourth best player on the LPGA Tour. Anders Forsbrand, the standard Swede at the Masters, has been thrown over in the hearts of his countrymen for a long-hitting young matinee idol, Joakim Haeggman. Tennis is out, golf is in. Every course is teeming with national enthusiasm.

At the Emmaboda Golfklubb on the mainland, we had whiled away most of a morning gobbling chocolate pastries and waiting for a Hogan 3 to curl down to the front of the starter's rack. Our eventual playing partners, two Swedish schoolboys (one a Haeggman worshiper), explained that Emmaboda was prized for its glimpses of water and rare is the golf course in Scandinavia that ever won a fight with an environmentalist.

Visby is practically *in* the water. A few of the tee boxes are literally boxes, small wooden platforms or crates backed up against the sea, carpeted with a wiry brown textile that will take a peg but doesn't really require one. Off the back of the third tee, twenty-five swans congregated in the shape of a gallery. "You're the cob!" none of them hollered. It was a shiny afternoon, but reminders of what must be an astounding winter wind were all around. Even in peaceful weather, the trees lean in permanent, ghostly distress.

Our hole was a par-5, straight over a lake, then hard to the left. You could bite off a bit of ground to the left but, in any case, the minimum carry was probably two hundred yards. I hit my maximum drive in the optimum direction and barely flew the water, bouncing on a curb of rough just onto the fairway.

"Did you get all of that?" Dave asked.

"I caught it up on the neck a little bit," I said, which, decoded, means I crushed it.

"I thought so," he murmured.

Setting up significantly right of my ball, Dave hit a splendid, rising drive well onto the fairway but miles from the green. And now the wind was dead against us. He struck a perfectly acceptable 5-wood, followed by a more than passable 3-wood, and wasn't home yet.

Meanwhile, after hitting a 3-wood that stood up in the wind just a touch, I pulled a 5-iron that missed both the green and the greenside bunker to the left. Pitching over the bunker to twelve feet, I botched the putt. Dave chipped to eighteen feet and two-putted for his own 6. No change in the match.

One third along, we could say we had been playing okay for us—good and bad—but also a little scared on the big hole.

"I think we're choking," Dave stated flatly. "It's in the books, a pair of bogeys. The pressure's off. Let's play it over just for fun."

I hit the same drive a little to the right. He hit the same drive a little to the right. He hit two good fairway woods again. I hit a slightly lesser 3-wood and a slightly better 6-iron. We both chipped from the edge and two-putted for 6s.

"So, what do you think?" I asked.

"I think we're a couple of 14s," he said.

"I think we're a couple of 14s who are choking dogs," I grumbled, "and I think we came over on the right boat after all."

"Arf," he arfed.

CHAPTER 7

MOSCOW
COUNTRY
CLUB
Moscow, Russia

Cruising in a KGB Limo With the California 6

MAYBE ONCE A month the boys and girls in Alice Pryor's seventh-grade class hid under our desks as protection against the moment the Russians dropped an atom bomb on the rich black dirt of central Illinois. How a pine-top school desk would deflect radioactive waves, no one thought to ask. Good Midwestern children of the 1950s did what we were told. Even Miss Pryor, a white-haired lady who loved everyone, taught us during bomb drills to be afraid of the big bad Commies trying to take over our country.

In the summer of 1993 the Adult recognized that Moscow had become a bum huddled under rags and a threat only to himself. Still, the Seventh Grader was nervous about flying into Moscow, even a toothless Moscow.

It was further unsettling to be seated on Swissair's flight 492 and hear a Germanic voice demand: "Passenger Kindred. Please present yourself to a flight attendant. David Kindred."

My good buddy Mr. Callahan said, "I know what it is. The X ray has picked up that collapsible golf club you're carrying in your luggage. They think it's a rifle. They've ID'd you as the Jackal. But don't worry. I'll get you a good lawyer the minute we get to Moscow."

On my first trip to Moscow, for the 1986 Goodwill Games, passengers on a British Airways flight were ordered not to take photographs once we crossed into Soviet Union airspace. I later was detained at customs when a guard saw an odd instrument in my briefcase. He apparently thought I might overthrow the USSR with an antique buttonhook. Only after a lengthy discussion did the guard understand the sweet nature of buttonhooks.

No such Cold War chill this time, nor had Interpol spied an international assassin. As it happened, the Swissair attendant needed to tell me the baggage handlers had found my golf clubs and loaded them. The attendant did ask a question we had heard before and would hear again: "Why do you take golf clubs to Moscow?"

The cheeriest folks on the Moscow flight were three dozen Jehovah's Witnesses going to an international convention. They were up and down the aisles in conversation, each witness wearing a name tag with printing visible from a distance. The printing promised/threatened DIVINE TEACHINGS. Well, what more could be perfecter for two broken-down sportswriters entering the Evil Empire than to enter with divine teachers?

Outside passport control, we said hello to the cheery Witness Helen Farrell of Bandon, Oregon, who bore up cheerily under a black hat the circumference of a Goodyear racing tire. When Tom noticed Hasidic Jews in their traditional black hats moving through a passport stall, he said to Mrs. Farrell, "That must be the funny-hat line. You should try it."

Mrs. Farrell took a look at the Callahan lid, a flat cap with a look suggesting burlap scraps yanked from a bear trap. She said, "You should talk."

Then with a smile: "What are you gentlemen doing in Moscow?"

"I can't really talk about it," Tom said. "It's a secret plan that involves the dark of night, a moving van and Lenin's tomb. But until it's a 'go,' we'll play some golf."

"Golf in Russia?" she said, choosing to deal with the less preposterous half of Callahan's blather.

"Jehovah's Witnesses in Moscow?" Tom said. "Anything's possible in these times."

It is Callahan's theory that all stories fit eventually. As proof, he said, "Helen, no offense to Jehovah's Witnesses. But we're newspapermen and we have a religious poem you might be interested in. It was told to me by a great man, Si Burick of the *Dayton Daily News*. It goes like this:

"Someday I'll pass by the great gates of gold,
And a man will walk through unquestioned and bold.
'A saint?' I'll ask, and St. Peter will reply:
'No, he carries a pass, he's a newspaper guy.'"

Mrs. Farrell laughed. "You really believe *that?* You better read *this.*" They don't get past the Kindred porch in Georgia. But at the Evil Empire's doorstep 6,000 miles from home, a Witness handed me a pamphlet entitled: "What Do Jehovah's Witnesses Believe?"

Moscow's airport is the first circle of hell. It is dirty, dusty and dimly lit. A mid-July afternoon becomes so hot that perspiration boils aromatically on the foreheads of unsmiling soldiers in the customs lanes. One such soldier said, "Fifty dollars?"

"Fifty dollars to pass through?"

"Fifty dollars?" he said. A disembarkation form reported that I entered Russia with more than $50. He motioned me away from his lane, in which I stood alone, toward a lane of three dozen people.

"No one travels with less than $50," I said. "Why do we all have to stand over there while nobody goes through here?"

"Fifty dollars?" Only his bottom lip moved. He might have been a wax figure with a motor behind his eyes. In the other lane a Hasidic Jew returning home said, "If you'd lied and said you didn't have $50, they would have let you pass through. They wouldn't have checked."

"Why not?"

"This country," he said. And he moved a finger in little circles next to his temple.

After bargaining for a taxi ride to Moscow Country Club, we settled on 50,000 rubles: $50 for an hour's ride on dusty crumbling roads past crumbling dusty buildings in a tiny dusty dirty rattling groaning sweltering jalopy with grease-smeared windows.

I said to Callahan, "These buildings are so bad you can't tell if they're being built or being demolished. Russia needs a new recipe for concrete."

Tom looked out the taxi window at the debris which passed for Russian construction. "You know, Dave . . ." And right away I knew. Any time he begins a sentence, "You know, Dave . . ." he is liable to commit a pun. Callahan had applied such punishment for years. He said Si Burick taught him the punning trade and asked him to carry on in his memory. And there in the taxi, he did it: "You know, Dave, as bad as the Russians are with the abstract, they're worse with the concrete."

"Oh, puh-leeze."

"A groan, thank you very much," Tom said. "I consider groans testimonials. You are very kind."

Our taxi turned off a busy road and passed through a gate into a birch forest. There the driver wound his way down a narrow, dark road toward the Moscow Country Club. The only light came from the moon full and high. Another mile or so into the woods, the moonlight fell on an open space. And not just an open space. More than that. In there we could see a high tee and a fairway bending left to right. Amazink. Golf in Moscow.

Once upon a time, golf and Moscow were mutually exclusive terms. Marxists believed the game smelled of a bourgeois decadence practiced only by enemies of the people. But with the USSR now on the bone pile of history, what the old Moscow would have outlawed as bourgeois decadence is encouraged by the new Moscow as capitalistic enterprise.

With a Chicago-during-Prohibition air to it, the new Moscow embraces gambling casinos, strip-tease clubs, hooker bars and discos in sports stadiums with 35,000 people at $15 a head. "Russia has shot from puritanical austerity to self-indulgence [wrote *The European* newspaper] as fast as it slid from zero inflation to hyper-inflation."

In the summer of 1993, Russia was a shambles. The ruble was in free fall. Where an authoritarian government had created order, a ripped-from-the-womb democracy created chaos. City officials expected bribes from businessmen; traffic police shook down motorists; baggage handlers at Moscow's airport stole what they wanted. Car thieves took orders by make, year and color.

All in all, criminals figured it was a good time to be alive in Moscow, provided you could stay alive. From the *Moscow Times* of July 21, 1993:

Four Dead in Moscow Gangster Shootout

Next door to a police station, seven men with machine guns and pistols entered an automobile showroom and exchanged gunfire with employees. The newspaper called it a "Chicago-style shootout which bore all the signs of a gang war." Alfa-Romeos and Jeep trucks were riddled by bullets. Police said the assailants wanted overdue "protection" money. The shooters left behind a Mercedes with a hand grenade on the front seat.

Russia's dance with capitalism brought Rolls-Royce to Moscow along with McDonald's quarter-pounders. At a downtown traffic light, we stopped alongside a Lincoln Continental, a Mercedes-Benz and a Jaguar. The Red Square department store GUM sold fashions and cosmetics from Estee Lauder, Christian Dior, Galeries Lafayette and Benetton. Fortune 500 companies rushed into the economic vacuum.

Golf, the capitalist's tool, could not be far behind. Though there is no record he advised his friend Vladimir Ilyich Lenin to take up golf, the late American industrialist Armand Hammer tried for years to build a course near Moscow. In 1988 a Swedish outfit built a nine-hole, par-3 course downtown. By 1993, though, Golf Club Tumba Moscow existed as little more than scruffy wasteland, and even that existence was too much for a nearby church, which claimed its centuries-old cemetery had been lost under the golf course. "They play and ride their carts on the bones of my ancestors," an old woman told the *Moscow Tribune*. "This is unbearable."

A California developer with a gambler's high-stakes moxie moved in where Hammer and Tumba failed. Jim Anderson sold the Russian government on a $120 million idea. He would bring Las Vegas to Moscow. With the Russian government of Boris Yeltsin as his partner, Anderson planned to create a luxury resort. It would include a hotel, casino, lake, sports complex, business center, restaurants and theater.

Before any of that, it would have golf. The Russians gave Anderson three hundred acres and buildings once used as a private retreat for visiting heads of state. The California entrepreneur hired the architect Robert Trent Jones, Jr. Half the land became the Jones-designed golf course.

By July 1993, the Moscow Country Club had nine championship-caliber holes in grass. Imagination being kinder than Moscow's winters and spring rains, I could see a big-league layout under the mud, standing water, washouts and weedy fairways. The other nine holes, cut through the silvery birch forest, waited to be planted.

It would be Russia's first eighteen-hole golf course, the first on a land mass which is one sixth of the earth's surface. At its latitude it would be the only course between Japan and Poland, some 5,000 miles.

The "California 6," as the Moscow Country Club salesmen called themselves, were fortyish bachelors who in the spring of 1993 dropped everything on the beach and caught the next plane to Moscow. They would sell club memberships for $17,500 to individuals and $85,000 to corporations. They would sell $500,000 dachas. The sales pitch would go this way:

> **"Y**ou're in Moscow. But you wouldn't know it. With these trees and terrain, you could be in North Carolina or Northern California. You know Robert Trent Jones, Jr., one of the world's best golf architects. Bobby has built two hundred courses everywhere in the world and he puts Moscow Country Club in his top five.
>
> "Have you been to Moscow lately? The air is unbreathable. But out here—we're forty miles from Red Square—it's 300 acres of clean and pure air. You want quiet? We got quiet. From the first tee late in the afternoon, you can hear the cooing of a Eurasian cuckoo. We have twenty-four-hour security to protect our clients' privacy. Elvis might be here and nobody'd know it. I can tell you this: George Washington didn't sleep here, but Chairman Mao did."

"What we're building here," said the beach boy Bob Trietler, "is a clone of Warner Springs Ranch in San Diego. It'll be just fabulous and our first market will be American corporations doing business here. Moscow is a difficult location to live and this will be a great escape. Germans, Italians, the multinationals, the Fortune 500 people. Our last marketplace will be rich Russians."

Most Russians are poor beyond an American's imagination. The Brussels Hilton did six pieces of laundry and charged $42; Moscow C.C. did thirty-one pieces for $16.95. The most expensive entree on the club's dinner menu was roasted chicken at $3.30. You could order bubble gum for a dime.

Amenities and services weren't much. The hotel furnishings came in seven browns, each a darker shade of depression. Trying to call Atlanta, I could not make a collect call, could not use a phone credit card or pay in rubles. Dollars only and in advance. When I argued the point, the phone clerk said, "You must speak to Bondarenko."

A sign behind the clerk's desk advertised "COMBELLGA. The World's Most Sophisticated Digital Telephone Network. Always at Your Service." But I chose not to press a complaint. Another rule of life: when in Russia, never argue with anyone named Bondarenko.

Finally, to escape our Moscow C.C. escape, Tom and I hustled up a golf game with another of the California 6, the breezy John Oehrlein, a mustachioed wisecracker with a loops-inside-loops swing and a bachelor's wanderlust. Soon enough he asked, "What are you guys doing tonight?"

"We're open to suggestions," someone said.

"The most beautiful girls you've ever seen are at a place called Night Flight," John said. "They start at $300, but you can negotiate."

"We've talked to Jehovah's Witnesses," Tom said. "Might as well give the other side equal time."

Headed for Night Flight, the California 6 rode in a black limousine which they said had belonged to the KGB. There was an ominous darkness to it and the doors slammed shut with an armor-y thud. The beach boys sat deep in the limo's darkness and imagined themselves as adventurers going into the night. This cool, clear, starry night in July 1993, they took us to Moscow's highest-priced hookers' bar where I, for one, loved Svetlana.

Let me rephrase that.

I met Svetlana and found her very interesting.

She wore a rumor of a red dress. Her black hair glistened in Night Flight's smoky light. She leaned a shoulder against mine. She looked like Michael Jackson would look if Michael Jackson wore a red dress. Quite the hooker conversationalist, I said to Svetlana, "You look like Michael Jackson."

Svetlana didn't understand. She looked to her buddy, Natasha, who exhaled cigarette smoke, admired herself in a mirror while rubbing her black teddy's lace and spoke in Russian to Svetlana.

Svetlana laughed and said, "Meekel Jahkson!" She pushed the tip of her nose upward. "Meekel, *nyet!* Me like Janet, *da!*"

Beefy security guards in black leather boots, camouflage uniforms and bulletproof vests stood hand on pistol by Night Flight's door at 17 Tverskaja Prospect. Their job: keep the riffraff out. The oldest profession had gone upscale in downtown Moscow. Inside the jam-packed, two-level, $15-cover-charge, $20-a-drink joint, maybe fifty microskirted professionals trolled the bars and dance floors. Night Flight's chrome, mirrors and glitterballs suggested a New York disco of the seventies.

"It's Studio 54, circa 1978, or Berlin, 1936," Tom said. He took a drag on his first cigarette of our journey, narrowing his eyes against the smoke. Bogart-in-Casablanca style. "Tell me, Dave. Am I looking exceptionally good tonight? Lucia seems to think so." He introduced me to Lucia, a blonde in white.

Lucia told Tom she was twenty-seven and had been married to a man who beat her. ("They all hit you.") Not to be too foolish about this, but in another time and another place, Lucia might be a stockbroker or lawyer. No such choices existed in Russia for a bright woman needing to feed her parents, brothers and sisters. Tom told Lucia she should move to New York and study art. Why, he asked, do women do this? With perfect English and perfect sense, Lucia swept her gaze around the meat market and said to Tom, "Why do men do this? Let's talk about something else."

The talk in Night Flight was easily monitored because most customers shouted their sweet nothings above the music's roar. Pieces of conversations moved on the smoky air:

"Me not married. I was been married. Now I marry you. I go with you to hotel, okay?"

"Come to the flat and help me with my rent. [He then asks how much help she needs.] Two hundred dollar. [He says he doesn't want to buy the flat. He suggests $80.] I go now. Bye."

"I'm from California, too. Small world. Do me a favor when you get home. Call my mother and tell her you met me in a hooker bar."

"Prostitutes in Moscow? With AIDS, isn't that literally Russian roulette?"

"Stay all night. Cheaper than hotel room in Moscow."

"Ludmilla is exquisite, gorgeous, stylish, the kind of woman you'd see in New York on Fourth Avenue getting into a Rolls-Royce. But cold, man. I sat with her here in a corner with three or four other people. I asked if I bought her a drink—meaning $20—could we talk a little bit? She turned her head away and said, 'What for?' Cold bitch."

Anyway, Svetlana in the red dress said to me, "Where you stay?" She could speak English, after all.

"I'm staying at the golf course." Thinking how odd that must have sounded, I began to elaborate when Svetlana interrupted to say, "Where you from?"

"The United States."

"Want to have dance?"

"I won't dance, don't ask me." Odder by the moment, now I stammered in Ginger Rogers lyrics.

Poor Svetlana, confused and finished with her night's supply of English sentences, then spoke in Russian to Natasha, who said, "Svetlana wants to know why you don't dance."

The temptation was to tell the truth, that this night out was a sociological dig for our book and nothing more. But that explanation had nothing to do with the whole truth. The truth is, I never dance with women who look like Michael Jackson in a red dress. So, in keeping with the male tradition of never telling any part of the truth in a hookers' bar, I said, "A war injury. Bad leg. No dance. Ever."

An attempt at translation ensued, followed by quizzical looks, after which Svetlana and Natasha moved away to set up shop at another corner.

Near midnight, the California 6 left Night Flight in their KGB limo. They hadn't gone one block before two women demanded the car stop so they could get out. (Financial negotiations had broken down.) But sad-faced Luisa rode out of Moscow into the night. A beach boy did his impression of Elvis singing "Hunka, hunka, burnin' love." Luisa almost smiled.

At midnight, Tom and I walked into Red Square. The vast public place was paved with dark cobblestones over which rockets, tanks and soldiers had passed on May Days. We stood outside the walls surrounding the Kremlin. These were siege walls thirty feet high with gun towers at regular intervals. Mongol khans came to Russia once upon a time. The Turks came. Swedish lords ruled Russia. The Japanese, Poles, Lithuanians. The

British and French. The Germans came last. They all wanted Moscow. This place, for a thousand years, had known siege. You might have built a wall yourself.

We stood near Lenin's tomb, its door slightly ajar. The 1917 revolutionary was preserved for display in a glass coffin, refrigerated, his fluids flushed and replaced regularly. Technicians making $50 a month change his blue suit and red tie every year or so. You never know. He might rise one day and walk through the door into the square to ask how the revolution is going.

"Here we are," Tom said, "at the Kremlin Kooler. It'd be a night like this when we'd take Lenin's body. We'd have a little plane land in the square to get us outta here."

At a corner of the Kremlin wall, a turreted gun tower rose high into the night, its spire topped by a lighted red star visible for miles. Below it stood St. Basil's Cathedral, the centuries-old church with its fabulous onion domes of happy spiraling colors, the work of artists who couldn't know the darkness soon to smother the Russian people.

Beauty had faded in Russia. We walked around a downtown train station, a grand building gone to grime, now a bazaar of human desperation. Unwashed and unshaven, toothless and raggedy, Russians with no place to go slept in dank darkness on bags of potatoes. Some riffled through pornographic magazines. Outside, they sold sorry vegetables and sad fruits, knockoff boom boxes and shoes with paper soles.

They sold bread and onions, peaches, plastic shopping bags, eggs, carrots and tomatoes (two traffic cops took a pound without paying), broiled chickens, sneakers, salami, candles and beer, fish and coffee—all for sale, a week's work for a family hoping to earn a dollar or two.

A little girl's eyes were dark with circles of sleeplessness. Her pregnant mother begged me for a dollar. I had none. The woman made the sign of the cross and asked again for a dollar. I had only traveler's checks.

Then the little girl with haunted, hungry eyes came by herself and tugged at my hand. She put one finger against her nose and said likely the only English she will ever know. "One dollar, please. One dollar, please."

All I had was a Swedish 10-kronor coin worth maybe $1.25. I gave it to the little girl, who gave it to her mother, who looked at it with no recognition. She moved away then, the little girl at her side.

In Red Square, a voice came from the night. "Are you German or Norwegian?" It came from a stocky man, craggy and without some of his teeth, looking older than his fifty-nine years. He had Solzhenitsyn's cut of beard.

"American," I said.

"U.S.!"

Adolph Ivanov was a high school geography teacher in Moscow. He often came to Red Square with a friend selling photographs to tourists. Because Ivanov seemed eager to talk, Tom asked him, "So are things better in Russia today?"

"We have more freedom, yes. Is good. But economics is bad. We buy at tall prices and are low sellers. The people have very little money. The ruble is going down. For old people like me, is hard because things worked better before. But young people, they have time for this to be good.

"Right now you go down in the subway, you see sign on the wall. 'It is necessary to clean the subway.' They must have people to clean the subway. They pay only 250,000 rubles a month, which is what? Two hundred and fifty American dollars. For teachers at the university level, pay is 350,000 rubles. Not good."

Ivanov pointed to a building at the end of the square. "See that? Amazing building with amazing artifacts. The Lenin Museum. It has been closed ten years now because no money to operate it."

Even during my Goodwill Games trip in 1986 the suggestions of the Soviet Union's decline were obvious. No way the U.S. would lose World War III to a country that figured your restaurant bill on an abacus. Now I asked Ivanov about Russia's future.

"They say twenty years everything will be fine. Not so. Two, three generations at the least. We are not like East Germany. They had Communism, yes. But they had a real economy before Communism. They know about real economy. We have not had real economy for almost one hundred years. We do not know and we must learn.

"Our problem now is workers. We have none. They are alcoholics. Engineers, crazy alcoholics. In building, in construction, ninety percent are crazy alcoholics. Ahggh!"

Each time he mentioned alcoholics, Ivanov rubbed the back of his fingers against his throat and spat onto the Red Square cobblestones. Suddenly he swept his right hand toward Lenin's tomb.

"That son of a bitch! Communism gone two and one half years now and that bloody cadaver is there. No more Communism. Never again! But that son of a bitch is still there. They still march sentinels to his door."

Even that ceremony would change shortly. Boris Yeltsin put down the parliamentarians who became itchy in the fall of 1993. He then ordered an end to the goose-stepping sentinels. For more than a half century, every hour, they had come. In 1986, at three fifty-eight in the morning, I watched them. From the gun tower two hundred yards away, four soldiers goose-stepped on a concrete walkway. Against their right shoulders, they carried rifles with bayonets glinting in the dim light. Their left hands, in white gloves, swung in precise, measured, strong rhythms. Their footfalls echoed across the cobblestones, heavy with threat.

And then the guards were in front of Lenin's tomb. They were young men, barely more than boys. They were men who were small boys when they first saw this glorious thing done. They were a thousand years of Russia under siege.

That was 1986. On our night in July 1993, the footfalls were lost under the hubbub of tourists' conversations. No longer an ominous march but a performance—and a performance honoring a man whose life's work led his country to the edge of the abyss.

"Look at the door," Ivanov said. "At the second sounding of the clock-tower bells, the sentinels will change places. The new ones march up in front of the old ones. Then they do it. So quickly. Like cuckoo clock. You might miss it. They whirl like puppets on strings."

Then Ivanov became a capitalist entrepreneur: "You want a sentinel's army cap? I can arrange to buy one for you. It would be $15, American. Uniform jacket, $65. Winter overcoat, $100. You want? I talk to sentinels for you. American tourists like caps."

"No, but we're thinking about taking Lenin's body," I said. "Has anyone ever tried to steal the cadaver?"

Ivanov laughed out loud. "Oh, yes."

"And how'd they do?"

"He's still here."

"And what happened to the body snatchers?"

"Hah, ask me another," Ivanov said, and the way he raised an eyebrow made me think of firing squads.

"Maybe we'll just stick with golf," I said.

"Golf! I remember golf." It was 1959, he said, when he held a golf club in his hands. "Good balance," he said. "Perfect wooden head." He closed his hands gently around an imagined golf club. "But golf too expensive for Russians. One club cost $100, yes?" We told him it might run to $250. "A month's salary in Moscow."

We started to leave Red Square. The geography teacher first asked if we could give him $2.00.

"Sure," Tom said. "Now, Adolph, you come to New York sometime. And then I expect to get this back."

"Travel now legal," Ivanov said. "But Russians, we cannot afford a ticket. To New York? I could save all the money from all the rest of my years' work and not have enough for airplane to New York."

We walked toward our taxi. Ivanov waved good-bye and called out one more sentence, his voice echoing around Red Square. "Give my regards to your clever country."

The Diabolical's Seventh Hole
430 Yards, Par 4

"No cow-pasture pool today, it's billiards," Tom said. "A Twilight Zone hole — a hole with no hole at all."

Through the kindnesses of the California 6, we were allowed to play Moscow Country Club two months before the official opening. So the club had not yet cut holes into the greens. We dropped a head cover on the green and said five-footers were gimmes.

The ninth hole, the one we had seen while driving in the moonlight, was a par 4 of 430 yards which turned right through a silvery birch forest and climbed to a green with deep, angry bunkers at its slopes. Off the front of the ninth tee there was a small pond which would come into play only if some poor soul topped his tee shot weakly to the left. Now, who would be such a foozler as to hit a ground-ball tee shot into a frog pond?

The frogs began a raucous impression of Pavarotti gargling. Perhaps they were to blame for what happened next, not that it will be described here. The sports editor of the *Bloomington* (Ill.) *Daily Pantagraph* once covered an amateur-league baseball game that wound up with a silly score like 23–6. Jim Barnhart's entire story that night: "The Bloomington Cubs last night defeated the Mattoon Cardinals, 23–6. If you can't say something good, don't say anything. Here's the box score."

Saying nothing about my performance on this diabolical, I offer only a bare note from my journal: "Topped drive past frog pond, topped 5-

wood, fat with 5-iron, 9-iron on, two putts. If I ever, ever, EVER IN MY LIFE again express a desire to play golf, I want Doc Kevorkian to come to my place right away."

Tom put a nice drive just off the right side of the fairway. His 6-iron second fell in a grassy bunker at green's edge. He made par with a chip shot four feet from the head cover. He was three up after seven holes.

At the Moscow airport, Tom said, "Glad to have been here. More glad to leave."

Our next port of call would be Johannesburg, a two-continent, two-hemisphere, fourteen-hour flight away. During our layover in Zurich, with daylight dying, we rented a car and drove across the border into a German village named Nack. We teed it up on a nice course cut through cornfields and hills. From a high tee, we heard a tiny sound that grew more distinct until we recognized it as hoofbeats. In Ireland we had almost driven into a horse and sulky; in France we saw trotters training near Patrick De La Chasnais's estate. We had come to think of horses and sulkies as happy omens. And now, at twilight, escaped from Moscow, standing on a high tee in Germany, looking over cornfields to a small road, we saw a painted pony pulling a sulky with a small blond girl in the seat.

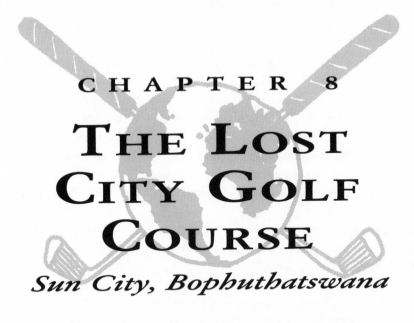

CHAPTER 8

THE LOST
CITY GOLF
COURSE

Sun City, Bophuthatswana

While Moses Leads His People out of Soweto

BERNARD KGANTSI'S mother, who did not know how to play golf, taught him. "She thought it was like tennis," he said, smiling at the memory. Somehow or other, they had come into possession of two worn irons and a nearly round ball. One boy would hit it; another would hit it back. "When I eventually saw whites playing golf, I couldn't believe it," Kgantsi said. "They all had their own ball! Nobody hit it back!" He became a scratch player, then a pro. Now he is the chairman of the entire South African PGA, white and black. Mostly white, of course.

In 1992, in the process of profiling a young comer named Ernie Els, I met Kgantsi. He introduced me to Moses Hadebe. He introduced me to South Africa.

"Here we are now," Hadebe said. "This is the start of Soweto." It's called a township, but really it's a reservation, a handy labor pool far enough from the whites (a half hour outside Johannesburg) but near enough to the work. The matchbox houses on the cramped lots weren't so awful, just a little sad. The corrugated tin squatters' camps on the medians of the roadways were horrible: rows and rows of waterless, sewageless crates overflowing with families. We drove by a cinder-block wall sprigged with barbed wire and spray-painted with the slogan "One settler, one bullet."

"That's a play on 'One man, one vote,' " explained Hadebe, a Zulu. "By settler," he added with a lilt of mischief, "they mean you. Here we are, Soweto Country Club."

As Kgantsi had foretold, "Soweto Country Club" was an exaggerated title for the only black golf course in South Africa. ("A bloody goat track," he actually said.) It was a municipal course of wild grass and dust, home field to 5,000 golfers counted among the 4 million citizens of Soweto.

"Sports, especially golf, might seem to hold a low priority in our troubled country," Hadebe said. "But sports develop heroes, and heroes develop hope. I think it's important." He is the head of the PGA's junior development program, a 7-handicapper.

"When I was a small boy, I used to climb the fences of real courses wherever the most remote corner of the property might be and play fourteen, fifteen and sixteen; fourteen, fifteen and sixteen; fourteen, fifteen and sixteen, until the sun came up, before the members arrived. Then I'd hide in the bushes and watch them. I didn't think of it as being surreptitious. I was just having fun and loving golf. Then I caddied. Caddying got me to school, the University of Zululand, Natal."

"Why golf?" I asked Hadebe, a scholarly-looking middleweight, thirty-six years old then, with a trim mustache and tortoiseshell glasses. "What was it about golf?"

"Because it was the hardest," he answered simply. "You only need a pair of sneakers to pound the road. You don't even need the sneakers. But running wouldn't prove anything. I heard golf was a white man's sport. That drove me. You know, you had to be very inventive to survive the apartheid system. You had to work out some kind of coping mechanism. Mine was golf. I taught myself to imagine there's no bunker there. I taught myself to imagine there's no apartheid here. I proved to myself, and hoped to prove to others, that myths are incorrect."

A worker pulled up on a tractor, unleashing a typhoon of dust. Hadebe introduced him as Mike Nompula, president of the club. "In the States," I told him, "the presidents don't do that much of the tractor work." He smiled fabulously. "Is that so?" he said. Nompula poured drinks out of a mammoth Coca-Cola bottle. "I drink Coke to keep my dark complexion," he remarked, "and my sense of humor."

The star of the round was a caddy named Walter, who recommended I hit a 7-iron at the only water hole on the dire property. When I hesitated, Walter observed solemnly, "If you've got the nerve to play here, you've got the nerve to hit the 7." He was thirteen. "Walter," I exclaimed, "you're the greatest caddy who ever lived!" "Yes," he said, "I think so."

Near the end, the flags ran out. The poles ran out. The half poles ran out. Until, finally, sticking poetically in the eighteenth cup was a stripped tree branch with a small leaf left on top for a pennant. It whipped about in the swirling South African winds, but stayed.

"You and Dave must play the thirteenth hole at Lost City," Gary Player pronounced with finality. "That's your hole. That's it. I'm going to call right now and have them feed the crocodiles." Pressing his hands to his thighs, he bent over at the waist with delight.

Four hundred black children go to school every day at Player's ranch, Blair Atholl, in Lanseria. Their song permeates the premises, lingers with the squeak of gumboot dancing and the smoke of learning. "Education is the light," he said. "South Africa is at the crossroads and the children are the key. They'll lead, as usual."

Player is the son of a gold miner who had only four years of schooling but could speak three black languages. "Never in my father's life did he make more than $200 a month. We lived in a crummy little house. One day in 1952, Dad rolled up with a set of Turfrider Wilson clubs. He told me just: 'I had a bit of money.' Eight years later, the bank manager explained how an overdraft had to be taken to buy those clubs. When I began to win golf tournaments, my dad would put his arm around me and just cry."

As Player became one of the most famous golfers in the world, he inevitably turned into an international symbol of apartheid. To American blacks in particular, his signature black clothing had the insulting effect of a minstrel's makeup. "I know there are many people who think we're all racists here," he began to say slowly something he wanted to say clearly, "and they certainly won't believe me when I say this. But there's definitely greater love between whites and blacks in South Africa than there is in America. No question."

Staying at the Sandton Sun Hotel in Johannesburg reminded Dave of staying at the Renaissance Center in Detroit. I thought back to a Tigers World Series, and he was right. Both are self-contained Emerald Cities that pretty much eliminate the necessity of being where you are. "You weren't in South Africa," a travel lady would sarcastically chide us down the road. "You were at the Sandton Sun."

But you could hear the weeping there, and the newspapers shook with hand-grenade explosions and AK-47 ambushes that killed twenty and thirty people a night for just the hope of slowing down democracy. In a matter of months, free elections were scheduled for the Transvaal. President Frederik W. de Klerk and the former prisoner Nelson Mandela, the Nobel twins, would be changing places. ("De Klerk has the courage," Player had said, "of a bloody lion in the bush.") A coalition of many black political parties, led by Mandela's African National Congress and Zulu Chief Mangosuthu Buthelezi's Inkatha Freedom Party, figured to cogovern for a period of reconciliation preceding normal majority rule. South Africa is eighty-five percent black.

Meanwhile, black marauders were tossing Molotov cocktails into churches and pulling over the distinctive little white vans that township domestics take from station to station to station to station on their endless relays between work and home. The passengers were separated into ANC or Inkatha supporters, and one or the other side was executed. The murderers may not be on any side, except the side against change.

On our third morning, we turned right out of the Sandton Sun and veered left down the hill into a firefight. Like the earthquake at Candlestick Park, it was over before we realized what was happening. Some escaped prisoners were being reapprehended, that was all. One of them was curled up in a blood pool on the street. Passersby acted only faintly interested.

We were on our way to the Wanderers Golf Club, Harold and Graham Henning's course. The name was irresistible. Dave wanted a cap. It was a short, narrow, heavily wooded course. Tom Weiskopf, Hale Irwin and Corey Pavin have won tournaments there. But it was hard for either of us to concentrate on the game. The fact of golf going on as though nothing were happening seemed so odd.

That night, Moses Hadebe came to dinner at the Sandton Sun. I was anxious for Dave to know Moses and to see Soweto.

My Zulu friend was resonating with good news. His transfer was complete. He had moved his family out of Soweto. "Those who can move, should," he said, continuing with a twinkle: "I would have moved much earlier if not for the fact that it was against the law for me to do so." His mother, a seamstress, and his father, a truck driver, remained.

Hadebe and his wife have a daughter, four, and a son, eight, who shares a birthday with Tom Watson, Moses's particular hero. "My son doesn't see color," he said proudly. "One day, when he was four, he came to me and said, 'Daddy, we're brown people, aren't we?' I replied, 'Do you remember that accident we saw on TV? The blood that comes out of everyone is the same kind.'

"I want him to see things in his own time and go through life in his own way. He doesn't need a complete undercoating in the dark old days of apartheid. But I try to answer his questions.

" 'Do white people hate black people so much?'

"No, everyone isn't that way."

" 'But why was Dr. Mandela in jail for so long? What did he do?'

" 'Who would kill Chris Hani?' "

Moses shifted uncomfortably. Explaining these things isn't easy.

"When we were growing up," he began, "there was what we called The Struggle. It had a life of its own. All of us, when we were young, wanted to be identified with The Struggle. Some of us wrote poetry. On Sunday afternoons, we'd meet and read our poetry. This was a history of what it was like to grow up in the townships, the positive sides too, such as the women who raised twelve kids.

"A lot of us got ourselves arrested. Detention without trial was one of the ways to prove we were part of The Struggle. Until we realized, the fewer arrested, the fewer marked men, the better for all.

"But I went on causing small trouble. I had to make a noise. I forced my way into movie houses that didn't allow blacks. 'What color is the movie the other people are seeing?' I'd ask. My wife—my girlfriend then—would go shopping with me for shoes. We demanded to be treated like customers. 'Go ahead,' my wife would say, 'arrest us for shopping.' They knew we were right. We got the shoes."

For leading a food revolt, Hadebe was tossed out of the University of Zululand. He finished college via correspondence courses, studying by candlelight. Then he got a little successful and became quieter.

It was a colleague at Johnson & Johnson who spurred him back to golf. Hadebe had risen to the position of products manager. Before a company outing, the man motioned pointedly from his neck to his head and said, "Golf is played from here up." After that, Moses practiced in a fever. "I didn't have to win the tournament," he said, "but that man had to finish behind me." And he did.

On the outskirts of Soweto and the other townships, able-bodied men wait every morning on corners. In Mexico, they're called *braceros,* "shoulders." They stand ready to perform a day of work at menial tasks for 25 rand.

"I was intrigued," said Hadebe, the successful man who had stopped making noises but was still listening. "I parked my car one weekend morning, put away my spectacles and took my place on the corner. I was picked up by this guy. I spoke to him in pigeon English. In a way, it was a disappointment. The family treated me very well. They brought me food while I worked in their garden and washed their car.

"At the end of the day, when we got back to the corner, I said that was fine. But he insisted on taking me wherever I was going. So I had him drop me at my BMW. I got out and unlocked the door. He was just amazed. As I put on my glasses and drove away, I'll never forget his expression. I wonder if this is a funny story for him today as well."

Dave asked: "Do your neighbors resent you for moving?"

"Oh, no," he said. "There has been a party for each and every one of the families that has left. It's sad, in a way. But you're creating a hope. 'Who knows?' everyone in the neighborhood association tells you in turn. 'We may be following you.' Now we live in a place called Douglas Dale forty-five kilometers away. Doesn't it sound safer? But even now I think Soweto will always be home. I ran into another escapee in Douglas Dale. 'We should revive that Soweto thing,' he said. I laughed. That Soweto thing. He meant the association, the families, the love, The Struggle, everything."

The next day, our last in Johannesburg, Dave and I were ready to leave for Soweto, to which Moses had agreed to conduct us, when he telephoned. "I'm in Soweto now," he said. "I came ahead to scout around, and it doesn't feel right. I think it's a bad idea." Fliply, I asserted first how tough and then how expendable we were. "I would not forgive myself," he said. Hadebe's voice, not his nerve, was cracking. His heart was breaking. Soweto will always be home.

"Go to Bophuthatswana," he said. "Play the crocodile hole. Take a slow backswing. Make a good turn." Referring to golf but much more than golf, he added: "Be frustrated, that's OK. But don't be pessimistic. And come back."

He paused a moment. "The first time I traveled abroad, my mother was distraught. 'Come back,' she whispered. When I did, she learned to trust me. I already trust you, but come back anyway."

We promised.

Bophuthatswana is another pseudo-independent state, another apartheid creation, 187 kilometers north. We made it to the frontier all right. But, from there, eight different direction givers (all of them questioned by Dave over my manly objections) led us back to the same wooden zebra outside the same desolate gas station. In what might qualify as the smartest dumbest move so far, we decided to follow the first Mercedes-Benz that whizzed past, and it led us straight to Sun City.

Next to the Palace of the Lost City at Sun City, Caesars Palace in Las Vegas is a model of restraint, good taste and understated elegance. Sol Kerzner, the entrepreneur, has created a myth of a lost tribe ("Centuries before tall ships were ever dreamed about, long before the dawn of a Western civilization, a nomadic tribe from northern Africa set out to seek a new world, a land of peace and plenty . . .") and furnished it awesomely with towers and domes and mosaics and tapestries.

The driveway passes through a dry forest of coral and camel's-foot trees, crosses an ornamented bridge over a tumbling stream and arrives at a monstrosity of elephant-footed columns, a fountain of bronze cheetahs and 8-meter-high doors to paradise.

"The tribe wandered for many years in search of such a magical place, and at last their quest was rewarded. The land they discovered to the south became the legendary valley of the sun, known today as the Valley of Waves. Not only did they bring with them a rich culture, but also architectural skills which were exceptional even by today's standards. Something special was created: from the jungle rose an amazing city with a magnificent Palace, a world richer and more splendid than any they had ever known.

"Then a violent earthquake struck this idyllic valley. The survivors fled, never to return, and left it to be found and restored by archeologists centuries later. We have today restored it to its former glory. . . .

"Discover the most extraordinary hotel in the world!"

Before I could take in the full effect of my ridiculous room with the leopard motif and four-poster bed, Dave telephoned from the water buffalo wing to say: "Check out the lamp beside your bed. Do you see what I see?" "Yes," I laughed. "You're right."

It was Louise's chocolate monkey.

The Diabolical's Eighth Hole
178 Yards, Par 3

Just as Dave prepared to hit over a tree, a community of monkeys screeching something like "Hold your fire" threw out their weapons, low-

ered themselves from branch to branch, scampered down the trunk and generally abandoned ship.

Unoffended, Dave turned to his caddy and inquired academically: "What kind of monkeys are those?" The teenaged boy answered with a perspicacity that surpasses understanding.

"Regular monkeys," he said.

Regular monkeys, giraffes and rhinos give an air to the Lost City course, which abuts the Pilanesberg national preserve. "An elephant rolled a car of tourists and killed a German a while back," Mike Leemhuis said, making it sound like the elephant held a particular grudge against Germans. "Lions are on the way," he added cheerfully.

Leemhuis, the general manager of Lost City, and Phil Jacobs, the golf course designer, were our playing partners on a dry, brilliant day over desert ground reminiscent of Arizona, notable for its brown panoramas framed by mesquite-like trees whose surreal antlers couldn't have been embellished much by Salvador Dali.

The course was young and fast. Not just the greens, although they were glassy and thrilling. A few seeds had blown off the new greens to make scatterings of tiny greens all around. The whole course was lightning. Balls that smacked the middles of the fairways bounded and ran until they found their way off one side or the other. We were hitting a lot of decent shots and making a lot of sixes.

The mountains were studded with baobabs, but the king of those obelisk monuments stood over a shoulder from the thirteenth tee, our hole. It resembled a giant knobby ginseng root. "Mixed with water," Jacobs lectured, "the milk of the baobab tree makes a potion that supposedly renders one invisible to crocodiles." So, we had come to the crocodiles at last. "Do you want to test it?" No.

From a tee constructed on a side of a mountain, we looked down on a green shaped like Africa. It was flanked by bunkers of white, yellow and red sand. The white was as bright as sugar. The yellow was dull, mustard-colored slimestone from the gold mines. The red was natural African sand as sticky as Augusta clay. In a stone pit in front of the green lurked forty crocodiles, up to 14 feet long, yawning, sunning and swimming. BEWARE OF CROCODILES, the sign didn't have to say. The ground under the crocs was peppered with abandoned golf balls and the relics of unfortunate chickens. Two large baboons took seats in the rear of the amphitheater to view the performance.

By the grace of a par at twelve, Dave had the misfortune to go first: 178 yards, but straight downhill. He took a 6-iron and hit it gorgeously, right at the hole. But, by inches, it wasn't enough club. The ball chipped a back tooth of the moat and bounced backward into the crocodiles. Only one of them even looked up, languorously hoping it was Frank Perdue.

Lucky to have gone second, I put back a 7-iron and hit a 6 onto the high left side of the green, approximately at Kinshasa on the map. The pin was all the way down in Durban. Dave hit his third from the drop area, which wasn't any bargain. He had to chip along a narrow path to a minuscule opening in the green. If he pulled it even slightly left, he was back with the beasts. Deftly, he almost holed it for a par.

Naturally, I three-putted. Another halve. Later, Dave would be presented a trophy: a rubber crocodile with a golf ball clamped in its jaws. To show how touched Dave was, he discarded the toy and was playing that ball by the time we got to Mauritius.

As we swung on, I chatted with Jacobs about his golf-course-designing business. He was a graceful, likable man, soft-spoken, unassuming. One got the impression the multicolored traps weren't entirely his idea, perhaps Player's. "The economy is so poor," he said. "There's so much political uncertainty." But, on the brink of historic change, wasn't he excited, hopeful? "I'm not particularly optimistic."

It was South Africa's apartheid system, Jacobs insisted, that had kept the tribes from slaughtering each other, just as the Communist system in Eastern Europe had served to keep the ethnics in line. We didn't say too much after that.

If only there were a corner for all of us to wait on, like "shoulders," so we could spend a day in the opposite world. "We know their world," Moses had said. "We work there. Our mothers grew up in their homes. But they don't know us. They'll have to come out of their cocoons to meet us. A cocoon is no place to grow."

Dave and I pulled out of the gaudiest cocoon in South Africa, looking and longing for a lonely island.

"What kind of monkeys are we?" Dave asked softly as we drove.

"Regular monkeys," I said.

CHAPTER 9

LE PARADIS
GOLF CLUB

LeMorne, Mauritius

Where Shots Ring Out on the
Old Man's Mountain

WE FIND THE lonely island and we're driving lickety-split. It's raining and it's night and there is no light, not even moonlight, and we're
driving lickety-split on a black road with a jungle crowding in on both
sides of the car.

Tom and I are in a rattling rental car with fogged-over windows. We're
leaving the Mauritius airport after the Budget Rental kid pointed out
seven dings in the car, pointing out the dings he wouldn't charge us for
on our return. The kid circles the car and says, "Here. Here. Here. And
here. Here. See this one? Here." We think: "We roll this tin can into a
ditch and it won't look any worse."

We want to get from the island's southeast edge to its southwest edge,
a matter of thirty miles on the map. We're fog-blind in the rain-black
night headed through a jungle tunnel and we have a map with no road

numbers. (Not that it matters. There are no road signs.) All we know is we're on an island speck in the Indian Ocean a thousand miles east of South Africa. This is the last place anyone saw a dodo. We're specks on this dodo's speck and after driving two hours we decide: we are lost, really lost, so extravagantly lost this time that no one in the world even knows we are lost. We have become a future episode of "Unsolved Mysteries."

We're in Mauritius mostly because the plane stopped here on the way to Kathmandu. Then, too, we've never hit a ball into the Indian Ocean and where better to do that?

So here we are, rattling through a black jungle, lost in the eerie night, both of us wiping mist off the window. Then we drive onto A Road With No Number into A Town With No Name. We stop. I get out of the car and put our map down in front of the car headlights. A citizen comes up and says, "Can I help you?"

As a matter of fact, I say, we might have made a wrong turn. "We want to get over here." I point to the map's southwest corner.

"This is Quatre Bornes," the good samaritan says. "You should drive to Flic-en-Flac. You must go back and turn to the right."

It was to have been an hour's drive. Our dark dash through the wilds of Mauritius takes three hours during which time our rattling tin can of dings bounces into and out of four million potholes on goat-track roads. We pass the hulking shadow of a rhinoceros that, on closer inspection, turns out to be a steamroller. We pass road graders, tractors, backhoes, cement trucks, bulldozers and a sign: EXCAVATION IN PROGRESS. Really.

We make six U-turns, three O-turns (circles of indecision) and one slam-on-the-brakes-back-up-and-go-right-at-the-rhino turn.

"So we're lost looking for Frick-and-Frack," Tom says. "In the movie, this escapade is nothing but a car's headlights making circles on a black screen."

What we hadn't seen in the night we saw in morning's soft light.

Just outside Le Meridien Paradis Hotel, a mountain rose straight up from the beaches along the Indian Ocean. The Dutch settled Mauritius in 1598. Then came pirates arguing with the French and British, not because they wanted the island's sugar cane and bananas but because they coveted its strategic location on shipping routes. All this came in a package with white powdery beaches, emerald lagoons and mountains soft in the morning light. Few baubles of such beauty ever hung from an imperialist's charm bracelet. Joseph Conrad, sailing to Mauritius in 1888, wrote of "this blue, pinnacled apparition, the astral body of the island risen to greet me from afar."

A coral reef a half mile off our beach caught waves and turned them into silent white spray. The lagoon behind the reef was crystalline and more than one lagoon swimmer wore less than all her bikini. On the sunny beach, oils were rubbed onto tanned bodies and lovebirds shared champagne.

I said to Tom, "Interesting, that all these girls wave to me."

"To you?"

"To me."

"What, do they think you're Albert Schweitzer?"

At the hotel office, a public relations person told us that most guests are Europeans and South Africans who visit Mauritius for two reasons: "Because it's a honeymoon, or because they're hoping it leads to a honeymoon."

"Does anyone," I asked, "come to Le Paradis for the golf?"

"Oh, yes."

"Like who?"

"You and Mr. Callahan."

We had driven three hours through jungly tunnels of darkness—there was sugar cane alongside the road—because Le Meridien Paradis had the island's only eighteen-hole course. And a pretty, tough, memorable course at that. Even a man with no intention of hitting a shot into the Indian Ocean would soon find himself on the sixteenth tee knowing full well he was about to hit a shot into the Indian Ocean. The sixteenth is a par 5 bending right to a peninsula green with water all the way up the right side.

The prevailing wind at the sixteenth comes from the right with such force that trees have grown bending to the left. That wind may be strong. It was not, however, strong enough to push my wild-right tee shot onto dry land. O diary. First the Atlantic off the Northern Ireland coast. Now the Indian. The Pacific awaits.

Because we needed visas for entry to India, we were told to drive to the capital, Port Louis. There we should ask for the India High Commissioner, a Mr. Kumer. He might or might not have five minutes to help us if we arrived in his office before twelve-thirty that afternoon. It was nine-thirty. It was an hour's drive. No problem.

"We'll get lost, but that's okay, because we have plenty of time," Tom said in our dingmobile. "Have you noticed, by the way, that when we get lost you're always driving?"

"Say what?"

"I've noticed that."

"And you, the 'manly' inventor of the U-turn, you're Marco Polo finding China on horseback? I now understand that 'manly' is a synonym for stupid."

"Just an observation, partner. When I'm driving, we don't get lost."

"We're too busy playing demolition derby with Belgians."

"If we get lost again, fine with me," Tom said. "We'll just stay in Mauritius a few years. Miss a few Super Bowls."

Three hours into our one-hour trip, we bumped into Port Louis. A human anthill, it was a filthy, foul, falling-down place choking on the palpable stink of internal-combustion exhaust fumes spewed by coughing traffic stalled on alleyways pretending to be streets. The honeymoon trade cannot be brisk in Port Louis.

Because the place offered two parking spaces for every thousand cars, we squeezed the dingmobile into a space beneath a sign that said: RESERVED FOR HIGH COMMISSIONER.

It was 12:35 P.M. when a fellow in a turban advised us that Mr. Kumer would be out of the office all day and could we come back next week? The turbaned assistant to Mr. Kumer not only seemed insensitive to our predicament, he made the mistake of saying to Mr. Callahan, "You should have taken care of this visa before leaving America. It is your fault, not the High Commissioner's. There is nothing we can do to get you a visa here."

Those increasingly familiar tendrils of smoke began to rise from the Irishman's red beard. "Look," Tom said, "one swipe of your pen is all we need. Just change the date of our visa two weeks, okay? And we'll get out of here."

"Only Washington can do that, sir," the turban said.

I had played the good cop, Tom the bad cop. Now negotiations moved beyond such parameters. And what an entertainment it was for a meek Midwestern boy to see Mr. Callahan's display of Irish Republican Army instincts. Rhetorical bombs were thrown. Metaphorical damage was widespread. All of India soon came under siege by Mr. Callahan, who told the turban on our way out, "You haven't heard the last from Passport Two and Full of Fog."

Sunset's gold caressed the mountain by our hotel by the time we found the place again. I was fascinated by the rock rising a thousand feet from the beach. It was covered halfway to the top by small trees, tall grasses and yellow flowers scattered in the winds that moved off the Indian Ocean and around the rock's big-shouldered bulk. The mountain's high face, scarred by time's erosions, changed character with the dying light: now soft and sweet in twilight's gold and in the dusk as foreboding as King Kong's place.

For the sake of an after-dinner drink, we sat at the hotel's open-air bar in the moonlight and watched a stupendously amateur cabaret show called *Formidable*. It featured lip-synching to Josephine Baker records by a French chanteuse of an indeterminate age. The show's dancers we recognized as the hotel's maids, waiters and clerks, who hoped enthusiasm covered their sins of footwork. Tom said, "Reminds me of the guy who wouldn't let anyone else clean up behind the circus elephants. 'What? And quit show business?'"

Headed to bed, I looked at the mountain one more time. Pitch-black then, it had disappeared into the night. I asked the hotel bellboy how high up the mountain a climber could go.

"You can't go on mountain at all, sir," he said. "It's private property."

"A mountain is somebody's property? Whose?"

"He lives in the house on the side of the mountain. His name is Allan Gambier."

At seventy-two, the mountain man Allan Gambier was a tree stump: wide, thick and likely unmovable. Bald, bullet-headed, bull-shouldered and bellicose, he had a bad eye and a bad ear, on opposite sides, so his head was always turning. Most days he appeared to be the Great White Hunter wearing leather boots with white knee socks, khaki shorts and a safari shirt with epaulets. There was a rifle on the front seat of his four-wheel-drive truck when we rode with him one summer day in 1993.

We rode in circles up and around the mountain on a bumpy, rutted, spiral path he had chewed out with a bulldozer years earlier. Gambier shouted French into a radio mike while using his free hand to keep the

bucking-bronco truck on a skinny little dirt ledge over which a truck and its passengers could fall a thousand feet into the Indian Ocean and make a really big splash. TWO AMERICANS MISSING IN MAURITIAN MOUNTAIN PLUNGE: WHY WERE THEY THERE?

The mountain man had said, "Get in," that's why.

Gambier's great-grandfather took possession of the LeMorne land in 1872. By 1919 the estate covered 4,400 acres. Gambier himself took over in 1942 and sold, as unprofitable, all but 1,200 acres around LeMorne Mountain. In exchange for a one-seventh interest in Le Meridien Paradis Hotel, he had given the developers 500 acres. Since 1979 Gambier and his son, Patrick, had bred deer to be killed by paying customers. Some customers sat in wooden stands on the mountainside and waited for beaters, usually Mauritian women, to drive the deer before their gunsights.

Deer not good enough for the hunt were butchered in sheds built on the mountainside by Gambier's thirty workers. Clambering up and down the wooden stalls and runways, Gambier told us with enthusiasm of his deer and their destinies: "We take them in here. Then we use a pistol with a silencer. We knock them down in the head."

Even as Gambier spoke, the sound of gunshots came from a distance. A hunt was on.

"Then we slit the throats and hoist them up by the hind legs and the blood drips into the drains in the floor. When the blood is gone, the carcass is butchered, skinned and gutted and sent to different spots to be sold. We say a little prayer over the meat for Jews and Muslims."

A man at home on his mountain, Gambier once climbed to the mountain's summit, 1,860 feet above the ocean, 500 feet higher than the Rock of Gibraltar. "Today it is not possible to climb it the way I did," he said, "and there is a history behind that."

Gambier said fugitive slaves hid atop the mountain in 1838. The British governors of the island had abolished slavery three years earlier. But French landowners refused to free their slaves. So runaways went to the mountain. When British soldiers climbed to the slaves with promises of freedom, many would not believe the promises. They threw themselves off the mountain.

The British soldiers reached the remaining slaves only when they found a way to cross a chasm in the brittle volcanic rock. They laid a twelve-foot oak door across the gap. They brought the door from a prison.

In 1945, more than a century later, that prison door still bridged the gap. Gambier was twenty-four years old, freshly returned from schooling in South Africa. On the notion that anyone climbing this mountain should take God's helping hand, Gambier persuaded a priest to join him.

"The door is still up there," Gambier said. "But no more is it across the gap. The cyclone of 1975 knocked it down and now it is in the chasm below. In 1892, my great-grandfather put up a cross on the mountaintop for the slaves who died there. Lightning hit it and burned the top of it. But the upright is still there."

In one voice, Tom and I said, "Can you show us?"

He waved the back of a hand toward his truck. "Get in."

For an hour, we bounced along the mountain's bumpy dirt ledge of a road, moving higher and higher. Had the passenger-side door fallen open at thirty-five miles per hour, a sportswriter or two would have been pitched into the sky without a parachute. The sportswriter nearest the door put his left arm up on the back of the truck seat. He held on.

A boulder must have rolled down the mountain into our path. Gambier said, "They're a nuisance. They break fences. They live forever." It was no boulder; it was a tortoise maybe a hundred and fifty years old. We drove around it rather than wait for the thing to move.

We saw wire pens filled with screaming monkeys. "For research," Gambier said. (Tom whispered in my ear, "Make a note. This guy is Stephanie Powers's worst nightmare.") To our left, skittering under trees, we saw wild boars.

Gambier again: "Very savage, the boars. The mountain, it has all the birds, you know. It has Mauritian kestrels, very rare in the world, like small hawks. Also the pink pigeon, just as rare. We kill boars, but never the birds."

On the ledge road, we drove past a dozen hunters in camouflage, some with their small sons in tow. Gambier maneuvered his truck around deer killed and dragged down the mountainside to the road to be taken home.

Tom asked, "The deer, being raised in paddocks, do they lose their instincts of being in the wild?" Unspoken was the further question about the equity of such a hunt, the game simply paraded before the crosshairs of hunters waiting in easy chairs. Just as well the second question was unspoken because the first went unanswered by Gambier, who may or may not have had his bad ear turned Tom's way.

We saw on this drive, from halfway up, the remnants of the slaves' memorial cross. And from the edges of the mountain we saw the ocean far below, the water shimmering, changing with the light, the water turned white by the island's reef catching the waves a half mile out. We saw the lagoon pure and still with white sails moving slowly toward the mountain. We saw mountains in shadows marching toward Port Louis where, I must confess, we hoped India's High Commissioner breathed deeply of the city's charms.

The Diabolical's Ninth Hole
474 Yards, Par 4

The seventh hole at Le Paradis Golf Club was a 474-yard dogleg right par 4 curling tightly around the foot of the old man's mountain. By the time you reached the green, you felt you had climbed halfway to the prison door.

The seventh demanded a drive dead straight 260 yards past a stand of towering gum trees. The second shot was more than 200 yards to an elevated green. Miss either shot to the right and you were in trees, jungly trash and volcanic rocks fallen off the mountain. Miss left and the hole became six miles long.

Or you could make the hole a real challenge. You could miss left with shots six inches off the cut grass and that height only because they bounced off the occasional earthworm that hadn't heard the air raid siren, three longs and a short, warning everyone to go underground. Kindred had a wood in his hands.

And I had thought the miseries were done. A new grip. A new swing thought. I even tried to share the wonder of my improvement with my good buddy Mr. Callahan. I was about to demonstrate my changes when he said, "Don't bring that typhoid near me."

Yes, I hit another grounder, another 18-bouncer and why? This was not the U. S. Open. This was not Michael Jordan a million bucks down to a sharpie. This trip was the cheery mother of all boondoggles. Have fun. Relax. Sure, right after I throw my fool self off Gambier's mountain.

At our Diabolical hole, after cold-topping my drive, I slash-topped a 3-wood before my white-knuckle-skulled wedge bumped against a hillside and stopped thirty feet from the cup. Two putts completed a disgraceful bogey.

Meanwhile, Tom took the jungle route. His drive, maybe 260 yards, landed in boulders along a road in the right rough. A 5-iron second put him over the gum trees into the weedy trash. From there he pitched onto the green twenty feet from the hole. Two putts for a hero's bogey.

So, at the turn on the Royal & Diabolical Global Golf Club's course, Mr. Callahan was three up and Mr. Kindred wrote a postcard home to his swing guru, the *Atlanta Constitution* golf writer Tom McCollister:

Old Tom,

Halfway around the world and I have forgotten how to play. Helppppppp!

Yours for better golfing,

Choking Dog Kindred.

Blessedly, we then hit the road again, on to India where we would catch a plane to Kathmandu. We were blown toward New Delhi by 125-mile-per-hour monsoon winds that shook the airplane for hours. At one point during the nervous turbulence, the Mauritian Air pilot came on the public address system to ask, "Is there a doctor on board? If so, please present yourself to a flight attendant."

Tom said, "At least he didn't ask for a pilot."

CHAPTER 10

ROYAL NEPAL

Kathmandu, Nepal

Where a Himalayan Monsoon Drops
Us Among Windswept People

CONSIDERING THE QUALITY of the ride from Bombay, we weren't inconsolable to be stuck on the ground in New Delhi. In fact, we absorbed our first canceled connection of the entire trip with a grace and equanimity that awed the Indians. (It would have flabbergasted the turbaned gentleman at the Mauritian Embassy.) For five hours, starting at five in the morning, we camped serenely on our luggage in the dormant terminal. Actually, it could have been four forty-five or it might have been five fifteen. Time changes had begun to befall us at half-hour and even fifteen-minute intervals. When that happens, the clock loses much of its moment.

Just before the airport awoke, I pulled out my putter and a black Akureyri ball (more visible against the Arctic snow) and began testing the grain in the marble floor. Dave joined in and we took to putting at each other's splayed feet, first ten feet away, then twenty, thirty, fifty, a hundred. Eventually we were the length of the concourse apart, dots in the distance, barely touching the ball and slowly, slowly rolling it over three hundred feet.

Clump by clump, a gallery gathered, customs agents and baggage handlers at first, almost everyone ultimately. They formed a chute. Whipping out fistfuls of rupees, they started betting and cheering. "Yes, no, yes, no, yes, yes, yes . . . no-o-o-o!" Occasionally, an exuberant winner broke ranks and danced around the spinning ball like a dervish. The business of the airport that hadn't come to a halt was obliged to conduct itself around us. Nobody complained. The great hall echoed with the festivities.

It took the ball almost a minute to traverse one lap over the slick stone. The spectators picked up the quiet rumble and rolled it into a roar. This is the only fun I've ever had with a putter in my hand.

When our flight was finally called, to the despair of the parimutuels, we were swept through customs like VIPs and forgiven the overweight duties on our clubs. "I do one good deed per day," said the immigration man, "and you've already done me a good one at that. Be happy."

In the jitney to the plane, a downy college girl who smelled like butterscotch wondered if we were celebrities. Her name was Virginia Olente and she was en route from a Paris school to a Kathmandu hospital in the service of Mother Teresa. Neglecting to notice our stomachs, she asked: "Are you trekking in Nepal?"

When we told her what we were about, she reacted with a start, followed by a waterfall laugh not meant to be insulting. There *was* a certain disparity in the nobility of our causes. "And you have been out how long? And you have how long to go? And it's for golf, truly? Just for golf? Ooo-la-la."

Twenty-five hours and nine minutes after leaving the hotel, we set down hard in the signature stop of all merciful missions and nutty pilgrimages: Kathmandu.

The most pagan of the godless Super Bowls was held in Houston in 1973. The game itself was relegated to Rice Stadium. The more crucial business, the party, took up the entire floor of the Astrodome. Updating the fatted-calf sequence of Cecil B. DeMille, cows and pigs were roasted on spits while their live progeny milled sad-eyed amidst the revelers.

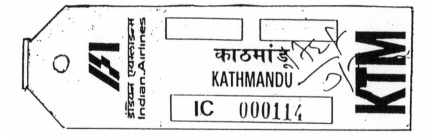

The expressions of the Kathmandu cattle brought back those damp faces—as they were categorically opposite. Blatantly aware of their sacred status, the Nepalese cows were sitting down in the middle of the busiest thoroughfares, across the sidewalks, on the steps of public buildings—or wherever the hell they wanted to sit—looking more contented than either Pete Rozelle or Harry Vonzell could ever imagine.

Tooling its way around the livestock, in a cloud of blue smoke, was a panzer division of makeshift Mad Max vehicles that ranged from haphazard three-wheeled contraptions (constructed fundamentally of two-by-fours, lawnmower motors and umbrellas) to chopped-down rototillers that looked like praying mantises but lurched like Tennessee walking horses from one side of the road to the other, the perfect transportation for the bovine slalom. In Kathmandu, plowing with a machine is a sacrilege. Turning the air into a kerosene haze isn't even a venial sin.

Adding marginally to the pollution but significantly to the racket were flocks of gravel-gargling motorbikes carrying self-satisfied young men sporting colorful fezzes and, hanging off the back, demure young women sitting sidesaddle. All of these motorists queued up in marathon lines at the petrol stations, repairing their own tire punctures while they waited for the pump.

We went directly to the course, the lavishly identified Royal Nepal Golf Club, which turned out to be a nine-hole amazement squeezed up and down and sideways into a holy gulch between the Pashupati temple and the airport. A gnomelike caddy master invited us into a dilapidated clubhouse, where the evidence of the club's royal designation was there to behold. In a priceless photograph, His Majesty King Mahendra Bir Bickram Saha Dev was signing the inaugural proclamation, September 5, 1965, by the glow of a Zippo lighter held cautiously to the parchment. Just as the King lifted his pen, the electricity had blown out, a nightly occurrence, we would find out later, at the Everest Hotel.

As we took our practice swings, a body floated by on the shoulders of three little men, bundled in a bright orange wrapper, on its way to eternity.

The secretary of the Royal Nepal Golf Club, Major Sam Hamilton, sized us up the next morning like recruits to the Gurkha Rifles and ordered us henceforth to wear shirts with collars. He was a retired British Army officer, a Scot, and looked the part in every way, silver and slender,

balding and bespectacled, conveying no impression of frailty, rather of strength, like a cable. He had come to Nepal originally with a regiment from Hong Kong to play soccer. As the Major told it, he had been everywhere in the world at least twice in the service of king and country.

"Everywhere," he repeated. "You name it, I've swept it up. In 1969, I was with the first battalion that went into Northern Ireland."

For twenty-seven years he was married to Patricia, an Army nurse with a stupendous spirit, born on St. Patrick's Day. She had been dead now eighteen months from cancer. In a way, she bequeathed him Kathmandu, their happiest former post.

"Diagnosed in February, dead in November," he said in his clipped style. "But, in two ways, she got me ready for her going. First, unbeknownst to me, she pledged I would run a certain number of miles in a sponsored marathon for the purchase of a new dialysis machine. Hell, just

when I was ready to go into mourning, I had to go into training. Then she requested that half her ashes stay in the UK and half be delivered here to the temple river. That's what brought me back. You see, she planned the whole thing." Along with being the club secretary, he was the coach of the national Nepalese golf team.

In an Army mess some few weeks after Patricia died, the Major saw six aging officers at the bar, three widowed, three divorced, "all slowly getting pissed," and instantly resigned his commission. With the half-filled urn under his arm, he raced like an imagination for the Himalayas. And, like Conway, he refound his Shangri-la.

"I made a little boat, a real nice one with flowers," said the Major, "and sent her off down the river toward the Ganges. Of course, she knew as well as I did that most of the ashes dispensed from that spot wash up in one of my bunkers. You've heard of people who spend a lot of time in sand traps? Most of the people here, whether they know it or not, spend forever in mine.

"So, a short ways down the stream, I took back the sand and built it into a house. I don't say that to the Nepalese. They get frightened. They think: to the Ganges, then up to heaven. I think of my house, and of the spirit of Patricia, and of an interesting life in Nepal. It's not a way of life; it *is* a life. You have to live it. Day to day. No reserve. People who live in places like this are interesting people. Patricia knew all this, and also that the partner left behind can lose his incentive and might easily call it a day. That's the real religion of it. Go on to the temple. It's just a few steps down the road. Have a look."

Monkeys, mendicants and madmen. It was like a scene out of *The Arabian Nights*. Terraces and temples. Staircases to nowhere. On several landscaped tiers beside a canal, white-bearded holy men sat according to rank, one of them wearing a steel colander on his head like Don Quixote's shaving dish. Across the canal, on two of four platforms jutting out into the water, bodies were burning. Smoking feet stuck out of the wood chips. Yet, just upstream from the curling toes, skinny-dipping boys splashed and carried on like Huck and Tom at the ol' swimmin' hole.

Eleven phallic gods preside in the grandest of the small shrines, the ones infidels are permitted to see. The great church that rises in the trees behind the pyres is off limits to non-Hindus. As an advertisement to the

procreative power of jade and gold, all of the monkeys (regular monkeys) seemed to have a baby in tow—and a dog in pursuit. Eight mother monkeys and eight mongrel canines finally squared off in a relatively fair fight that made the *Nord Gotlandia* look like the Westminster Kennel Club. The holy men scattered. Even Cleveland Amory would have run for his life, and we did so hilariously, laughing like monkeys, mendicants and madmen.

Once we were in the clear, children tried to sell us things, like little silver perfume bottles with intricate blue designs. Or black fossil rocks indented with fish vertebrae. For around $50, Dave bought a Gurkha knife with a delicately carved handle and the distinctive dogleg blade. The young vendor glowed like crêpes Suzette, as though he had just sold the suit that gets the salesman to Hawaii.

Looking up, we found ourselves at Mother Teresa's infirmary and went searching for Virginia Olente. A tiny brown woman in a tired sari said Virginia had just gone off shift, but the woman invited us in anyway. Standing in the dark, low-ceilinged ward, we would have felt like unconscionable intruders if the shrinking people in the beds hadn't pressed their palms together, bowed and smiled so generously.

We tiptoed through the ward back out into the light of a courtyard, where the ambulatory followed carrying unusual horns, drums and stringed instruments. Sitting cross-legged under an eave, they played us a concert as slow and sweet as honey sifting through a comb. Fortunately, sportswriters don't cry.

As we departed, Dave crammed all of the money we had on us into the slit of a collection box. "It's either $8,000 or sixteen cents," he said. "I'm not sure."

Shimmering from the last dark wall, like a shadow shape in a puppet show, a winter scene flashed across the senses, a fading but still glorious projection of a clean, fresh, pine-scented dream world. It was a calendar, obviously out of date. It said: "The Eudora Bank, Eudora, Arkansas, 'The Oldest Bank in Chicot County.' "

"Come on in, you two," the Major called from the back room of the clubhouse. "Say hello to George and Ruth Hunter. They're windswept and interesting too."

Having completed their game, the Hunters were mixing beer and Sprite into Scottish shandies. "You can get canned shandy now in Scotland," said Ruth, who is actually from England. "No doubt, soon, *diet* canned shandy," grumbled her husband, who is as Scottish as Carnoustie.

A military couple, they would shortly be changing stations. But two Nepalese artworks will be going home with them: a doe-eyed boy named William Krishna (after the Hindu god of love) and a baby girl they call Esme. "Everyone says these children are so lucky," George said, "but they're wrong. We're so lucky."

Still blinking from a blizzard of an adoption process, he said, "The Nepalese are wonderful, open, hospitable people, but they have this— what's the word for it?—'in the hand of God' mentality. It's like, after the massive landslides, when the crops have been washed away and the people killed, they recultivate and rebuild in the same denuded place. It's quaint and charming and heartbreaking. They go back in the hand of God. The trick, dealing with the adoption bureaucracy, was to suggest, just suggest, that maybe He had sent us."

And maybe He had, because the godliest sight we saw in Kathmandu was the Scotsman with his Camcorder racing around everywhere making a memory for his children. "William's a Tamang," he said. "They're hill people. I want him to know it." Mount Everest couldn't have been much more inspiring, even if we had seen it.

The race to Everest with our regular cab driver was a spine-tingling dash, probably not unlike the Pikes Peak Hill Climb. We weren't actually going to Everest, only to the high ground of Nepal where, on a clear day, you could see just the tip of the giant mountain. The regular hops to

Everest via a period piece of a prop-engine airplane had been canceled in deference to the most recent crash. "When you're there," Major Hamilton said, "it's a living thing. Even at the base camp, you feel like you're halfway up. You bounce around with the aura, the sheer awe of it."

Thinking of Muhammad Ali, we wanted to get as close as we could to Tibet. In his favorite fantasy, the big fight was always going to be in Tibet. Shadow-boxing with Budd Schulberg on a bank of the Zaire, Ali said he couldn't make out the ultimate opponent but he was sure of the ultimate place. Now and then he'd bring it up again with a lovely laugh.

On the morning after Leon Spinks beat him up in Las Vegas (Ali would outmaneuver Spinks later in New Orleans, but he knew the die was essentially cast), Muhammad sat uneasily in an easy chair in his hotel room surrounded by a handful of the passengers who had so enjoyed his dizzying ride. "I'm sorry, men," he said somberly. "We never made it to Tibet."

"Champ," spoke up Ed Schuyler, a gravelly imp from the Associated Press, "with this guy, we'll be lucky to get to Scranton, Pennsylvania."

Ali roared. It was the greatest laugh he ever had, maybe the greatest one anyone ever had. Luckily, sportswriters don't cry.

We never saw Everest. The day was too cloudy. We went on to the Indian embassy, where the clouds had parted. Overtrained for Round Two of our visa fight, I was humbled by a gentle-spoken, snow-haired man who, before I could say anything impolite, took it upon himself to add extra days to our passports. "You may want to see more beauty," he whispered. Then we had to get back to pick up the Major, who was officiating our match.

Actually, the view from his roof beat the one on the hill. "You can see," he pointed out, "where God took his Gurkha knife and cut the Chobber Gorge, leaving this beautiful, fertile valley. Look, there's an island that still floats where a lake was and, over there, a Buddhist shrine guarded by a troop of monkeys."

On the ride to the course, Dave was furiously scribbling another of his relentless postcards. This one was to Muhammad Ali, Berrien Springs, Michigan. It read: "Here's as close as we ever got to Tibet."

The Diabolical's Tenth Hole
456 Yards, Par 4

We drove off the elevated first tee into an outfield of forecaddies. The Major's entire work force of seventeen-year-old boys, who all sadly looked twelve, appeared to have been activated in an all-out alert. Some of them wound in their kites before joining us. The sky was unusually clear of those candy-colored delights that dance all over Kathmandu.

At Royal Nepal, even balls hit in the "fairways" plunge and disappear. The boys find them, dig them out, clean them up and stand them fetchingly on tufts in conformity with the local rules. "A ball lying in play anywhere outside a hazard may be nudged with the clubhead up to six inches. In the event the lie of the ball or the player's stance is affected by animal droppings, the ball may be lifted and dropped clear without penalty."

The second hole didn't have a green. It had what was called "a brown," which was really a black. "If on the brown a player's putting stance or backswing are affected by the surrounding bank, the ball may be taken off the brown and played without penalty." Dave and I both had only wedge second shots to the brown, but the Major warned it wouldn't hold

even a sand wedge. "You have to bounce it on," he said, "and it's better if it bounces twice."

Before we putted on the oiled sand, my caddy smoothed it out by dragging a burlap sack. When he was finished, I somehow could visualize a straight track to the hole and putted along that rail right into the cup. However, before I could feel too good about it, he discreetly showed me the thumbtack he had hidden in the burlap.

Dave's caddy was an undersized local legend named Harry Bendari, who once was such a promising player that the club sponsored him, dressed him and made him a caddy-member. But he never got any bigger. Bendari's star blew out. His membership was rescinded. Now he was back caddying exclusively. "They eat at the house of whoever worked that day," the Major said. "No reserves in Kathmandu. Life on a day-to-day basis."

The third was our hole, a 456-yard par 4 from a platform tee leaning hard left against a wire fence (to keep the holy cows out) and the airport road under a billboard ad for Mount Everest and the late little airplane. A steep, shaggy hill had to be carried to a blind landing area with bunkers right and left. I hit an anemic drive down the middle that at least carried the hill. Dave hit a much sounder one a shade left.

Overestimating the caddies' tuftability, I tried to hit a driver off the ground and mashed it fat, fifty yards short. Dave's 3-wood over a "nullah" (a drainage ditch for the monsoon season, which was in full flower) landed hole-high to the right side. He hit a handy pitch to within about eighteen feet.

Unhappily, I had shot first, dropping an inspired sand wedge like a bomb down a stovepipe right on top of the green flag. Of course, we were playing the blue flags. I bounce-putted a thirty-five-footer to within four feet and made that for a 5. With aplomb, Dave slammed in his par for a win. The margin was back down to two. Considering one of those holes didn't even have a hole, only a head cover, the difference seemed negligible.

"Yeah, yeah, yeah," he said graciously.

Four of the last five Royal Nepal holes were par-3s, although one of them plumped to a 4 on the "back nine" when different tees came into play. On the jungle side of the course, where every tee shot appeared to be *from* a slant *to* a slant, the players and caddies did a lot of splitting up. The boys would hand us a 5 and a 6 and head en masse to the green. The trouble was, we always needed a 3 or a 4. "Is this supposed to be a compliment?" Dave wondered.

At the seventh hole, a 134-yarder down an alley of vegetation, we hit through a purple silk screen of dragonflies, setting off a grasshopper alarm. It felt as though we were back in the cathedral at Burgundy. "That's a holy river," the Major said, pointing to the left. "I'd like to change it, but its course is determined by God. Priests come here sometimes and do amazing, sometimes pornographic, things. Having to do with fertility. Well, don't tell anyone, but I have diverted it slightly."

He casually warned us to look out for leeches, conjuring Bogart's back and Hepburn's salt box in *The African Queen.* "On second thought, don't worry about leeches," he said. "They'll crawl into your socks, take a little swig and climb back out again before you know it. In fact, it's better you don't realize what's going on. If you tried to pull them out, you'd probably leave the heads in and end up with a lot of septic infections."

Yeah, yeah, yeah.

Afterward, over shandies, he rolled out his dream of a new Royal Nepal Golf Club, a crinkly gossamer drawing from the architect Ronald Fream of Santa Rosa, California. In the Major's heart, you could see the perfect greens already, and the orchards in bloom, and the sand traps that would make no washed-up passerby long for the Ganges. It was a windswept and interesting course for windswept and interesting people.

And, when I took off my shoes that night, the left sock was full of blood.

CHAPTER 11
ROYAL CALCUTTA GOLF CLUB
Calcutta, India

Where the Mistress of Tollygunge Serves
Us Eggs Rumble-Jumble

THE EAST INDIA RAILWAY revolutionized travel so completely in the 1880s that many a passenger became anxious speeding from place to place at ninety miles per hour. "Train fright was a matter for jokes," a history of the period reported. "There was the Brahmin scholar who duly consulted the stars with the help of the Almanac, and fixed upon Thursday for the journey as a 'lucky' day.

"He fortified himself for the expedition by bathing three times in the river, and repeating the name of his titular god 937 times. He went as far as Hooghly but declined to undertake the return journey, because, said he, 'Too much traveling in the car of fire is calculated to shorten life, for seeing that it annihilates time and space and curtails the length of every other journey, shall it not also shorten the journey of human life?' "

A bird of fire, the India Airlines Airbus 320, delivered us six hundred miles from Kathmandu to Calcutta, the only shortening of life being that produced by the anxiety of buying an India Airlines ticket. In the first four months of 1993, the airline had four hijackings and two major accidents that killed seventy-five people. Hearing these numbers, Callahan said, "A crash might put a damper on the trip, but a hijacking could be interesting."

(I made a note about a fellow in the row ahead of us: "Nepalese man, fidgety, talking across aisle to a friend [accomplice?]." On arrival without incident, we cleared customs together and the fellow even smiled our way. Maybe he had made a note: "American behind me. Fidgety. Talks to big man with red beard [accomplice?].")

We had come to the Tollygunge Club, a historic Calcutta haven named for the Major Tolly who operated a gunge, or market, on the grounds. The London newspaperman Ian Wooldridge had written of the club as the last outpost of the British Empire: "When the British Raj lowered the Union Jack in 1946, it left behind 100 acres of England which are more English than England has become in recent years. . . . You turn off a teeming filthy street into a high walled world of order, strict convention, impeccable manners and sport: riding, golf, croquet, tennis, billiards. Most of its members are Indians whose accents hint at Oxford or Cambridge, in some exaggerated instances both."

Waiting for us on Tollygunge's first tee was our new best friend, R. S. Sabharwal. He had chosen not Oxford but the University of California at Berkeley. His degree came in nuclear engineering. We knew we had wandered into good fortune once again. Dressed for golf, R.S. seemed to have bought one of everything from the pro shop. He even wore a golf visor tugged down and around his turban. The visor's elastic band was stretched like carnival taffy to accommodate the turban's girth, both headgears a daffy shade of purple.

Halfway around the world, in the black hole of Calcutta of all places, we teed it up with a nuclear engineer in a visored turban who knew more about *Golf Digest* than we did. One year Sabharwal organized the club's handicapping system after reading in the magazine how to do it. His knowledge of PGA Tour esoterica (from John Daly's swing weight to Paul Azinger's workingman's grip) came from the dog-eared magazine.

"Before Star TV," he said, naming the Rupert Murdoch satellite television network created to cover Asia, "*Golf Digest* provided everything we knew about golf. For the first week, the magazine is mine. Then I give it to a friend. In exchange, he gives me his *Golf World*. This way, we know what is happening on the golf scene."

Calcutta or California, R.S. spoke a language understood by anyone who ever took up the crooked sticks and beat upon the good earth. Each leg of our journey gave us a greater appreciation of golf as an international language based on shared feelings, discoveries and joyful miseries. In places as different as Akureyri and Calcutta, people as different as fire-making old widows and turbaned nuclear engineers suffered the game's confusions and came back for more. Golf became our passport to good will at every stop for 37,000 miles.

"I love golf courses," R.S. said. "At Tollygunge, sometimes you cannot drive straight because of the leaves. So many trees, so many colors. It is so beautiful. I always make it a point, when I'm traveling, to visit golf courses even if I'm not able to play. You get so attached to this sport."

In 1989 he went to St. Andrews. "When I walked out there, I almost started crying. It was like a dream coming true.

"And there I met Sean Connery. What a big man. So tall, the clubs looked like toothpicks in his hand. He saw me in my turban by the first tee. He walked right up and said, 'Hello, Mr. Singh.' He was so nice."

People with no hope have always seen Calcutta as a city of hope. Millions of refugees have run from their homeland's despairs to reach Calcutta. The mystery is why. No place can be more desperate than the streets of the city we saw in the summer of 1993.

We saw naked skeletal little boys five years old blotched with graying mud. Their eyes were unblinking in hollow spaces of malnourishment. We saw babies on garbage heaps pushing at pigs to find food among the stinking wet black muddy garbage.

Barefoot men pulled ox carts stacked with rusting sheets of tin picked up who knows where. With the tin and stalks of bamboo, these men go near Mother Teresa's hospice. There they use rope to tie the tin and bamboo to a bridge. They make a roof. They make three walls.

The leave open the front so they can crawl in. These people looking for hope live there.

Hundreds of these shanties are filled with human beings tied to bridge railings by hope. They are tied by rope and bamboo and tin, their skeletal desperate big-eyed children competing with pigs for garbage. This is hope? Hopelessness has a smell in Calcutta: the smell of human urine and feces, animal excrement and exhaust fumes and food so rancid it burns your nostrils, food dumped onto babies' garbage piles on Calcutta's sidewalks, left there for weeks, buzzing with flies, picked over by vultures who dare little babies to put a hand toward their discovery.

A Calcutta newspaper argued during our visit for more tax money to get rid of garbage: "Over the years, Calcutta has learnt to live with a thousand sordid images of urban vice. And among the most vile of them are the mounds of solid wastes on the streets of the city. . . . To avoid the stink rising from the rotting garbage, it is quite common to see passersby covering their noses and quickly go through."

To know the darkness of Calcutta is to know nothing. In 1780 a fire destroyed 15,000 thatched huts housing Calcutta's desperate poor. In the fifteen years after World War II nearly 10 million immigrants came to Calcutta. Knowledge of despair is not preparation for the sensual assault of Calcutta.

You smell human decay on sidewalks where people live. Buzzards caw at babies. You see black pigs in mud under burned-out cars overturned on sidewalks. A woman frail as famine bathed in water dipped from a gutter with her hands. Garbage slapped slick against my ankles.

Unreasoning senses best measure Calcutta's wretchedness. It is inevitable, irresistible and irreversible. And not just in one neighborhood. It is everywhere. A cityscape painted in revulsion.

We saw a man with no legs push himself on a roller board. He had no legs and yet, somehow, he had feet. They grew upside down from the back of his thighs. He pushed his board through traffic on the street.

We drove on. We passed a huge stadium built for soccer, a monument to entertainment in a city of wretchedness. We drove on to our hotel, the Taj Bengal, where a movie star, said to be "India's Rambo," leaped from his limousine as if to hurry from the squalor into the luxury. In the lobby of the hotel, an Indian boy wore a Michael Jordan/Scottie Pippen T-shirt.

Now and again, Tom and I asked variations of his question first raised at the Maze in Northern Ireland. Moscow, could you live there? How about Kathmandu? What would it take, now that we're in Calcutta, for you to stay here a few years?

Nothing short of a jail sentence would have kept me in Calcutta, and I say that mindful of the gracious welcome by everyone we met in that desperate city. Samuel Coleridge asked readers for a suspension of disbelief. To live in Calcutta would demand a suspension of the senses.

Beyond the real threat of nuclear war with Pakistan, India is a snakepit of political turmoil. A television news-magazine show promised its correspondent would ask a political figure "inconvenient questions." Then the screen went black for ten minutes behind these words: "The story which was to follow here has been deleted on the orders of the censors board."

A headline out of the *Calcutta Telegraph* said, 35 MALDA "WITCHES" KILLED IN 2 YRS. The story began: "Forty-year-old Fulia Aheri insists that a month ago Kondan Aheri unleashed a ghoul into her hut. Last Wednesday, Kondan and five others were brutally murdered in a 'witch-hunt.' In the last two years more than 35 tribal women have been killed as witches. Almost all were murdered after village sorcerers, locally known as *mahan* or *gyanguru,* branded them as " 'practitioners of witchcraft.' "

And this: "Twenty persons severed three right hand fingers and slashed the neck of a reporter of a Tamil weekly for writing against a Tamil Nadu minister."

Live in Calcutta? We were reminded of our question the first night at dinner when a handsome young man at the next table said, "Are you Americans?"

Mohammed Amir had lived in Houston for a year, and after a year back in Calcutta was delighted to speak English again. "I heard you talking," Amir said, "and it reminded me of how much I missed America. Please excuse me. I loved America."

He had returned to India at his parents' call. "I am an only son. It was emotional blackmail. One day, I hope to go back to the States."

Twenty-five years ago, the celebrated writer Khushwant Singh did an essay that began, "Why am I an Indian? I did not have any choice: I was born one. If the good Lord had consulted me on the subject I might have chosen a country more affluent, less crowded, less censorious in matters of food and drink, unconcerned with personal equations and free of religious bigotry.

"My head tells me it's better to live abroad," he wrote, "but my heart tells me 'get back to India.'"

No such ambivalence for our turbaned friend R. S. Sabharwal, who left Calcutta at eighteen to attend Cal-Berkeley. He spent seven years in Houston, Detroit and Chicago (where Americans introduced him to golf). Though he liked and admired the United States, he always wanted to return to Calcutta.

"My business is here, my friends are here, I grew up here," he said. "Going to the United States, going back to visit and yet living here—it's like having the best of both worlds."

Tom said, "But isn't Calcutta a hard place to live?"

"It's true we need to get out of the city to a place like Tollygunge. But Calcutta is not a hard place to live if you're above a certain standard. You feel sorry for people on the streets because we have seen the other side of the world. But you have to balance it. On balance, Calcutta is a good place to live. Bombay and Delhi are materialistic, but Calcutta is warm. In Delhi, it's how big your house is. Bombay is 'Bollywood,' where India's movie industry works. Bombay asks, Do you drive a BMW? In Calcutta everybody is equal. Anybody can be friends."

With all due respect to R.S., it made no sense to say the people of Calcutta were equal when a taxi ride down any city street was proof of inequality. To suggest equality was to confirm a blind eye. What the affluent people of Calcutta didn't want to see, they didn't see. These were parallel universes, existing without intersecting.

"Come tonight to a party and you will see the warmth," R.S. said. "Every Saturday night, our group gets together at a different friend's home. Come tonight to Buljeet's and Puppy's. There will be thirty people there. The chief of India's IRS. The police commissioner. The director of a steel company. And all are golfers."

From the other side of Anne Wright's door, we heard a dog greet us. "YAP YAP YIP."

Another agreed, only faster. "YIP, YIP, YAP!"

Louder from a third, "YAP, YIP, YAPPITY-YIPYAPITTY!"

We had been forewarned that five cocker spaniels and a Labrador retriever would run to the door yippety-yapping. A small, handsome woman of authority, the mistress of Tollygunge quieted the kennel with a word. "We are," Anne Wright allowed, showing us in, "overdogged."

When we mentioned in Kathmandu our intention to visit the Tollygunge Club in Calcutta, the retired Major Sam Hamilton all but came to attention and said, "You must see Bob Wright. He is the heart and soul of Tollygunge."

Wright had been a Tollygunge member forty-five years and the club's general manager for twenty. Before our arrival, he had left town on holiday. Even as we spoke by telephone with his wife, Anne, she was packing to go off to England herself. Still, she said, "Come to breakfast tomorrow at eight-thirty. Do, please."

Tom and I arrived on a Tollygunge morning of the sort Ian Wooldridge had described: ". . . a morning of ethereal beauty. The early sun electrifies the plumage of the blue jays and golden orioles circling above. White egrets, no longer required to sacrifice their feathers to the headwear of viceroys from afar, stroll confidently about."

Breakfast waited in a room the size of Idaho. Eight ceiling fans fifteen feet above the floor marched the length of the vast space. Silver trophies took the shapes of thoroughbreds. From the Wrights' second-floor balcony we saw traces of the club's old steeplechase course. The start-finish pole stood by the golf course's first tee, reason enough for Mrs. Wright to speak of her passion for horses.

"On the club grounds, in our fine stables, we have thirty horses, and so I do get in my share of riding," she said. "And in Delhi, where we do some breeding, I have a full sister to Little Current." Even the mention of that great old American runner brought a happy light to Mrs. Wright's face. It was reason enough, in turn, for Tom to tell his Snow-and-Secretariat story.

"His legit name," Tom began, with Mrs. Wright eager to hear any mention of Secretariat," was Frank Snowfields. But they called him Snow. A little, gray-haired black man who worked the stables for Claiborne Farm as far back as Bold Ruler. Every Derby Week, Snow took out-of-town guests around to visit the farm's stallions.

"He'd pull out Buckpasser, Riva Ridge and Tom Rolfe, Mr. Prospector and Nijinsky. But the prize of the tour was Secretariat. Snow'd make a little whistle and Secretariat would gallop across his paddock, always the one closest to the barn. He'd come running, thinking Snow had a carrot or some such for him. One of the elegantly dressed out-of-towners asked Snow if it would be all right to pet Secretariat's nose. Snow said, 'Oh, yes, ma'am, that's okay. He'd like a finger.'"

Tom had more, bringing Mrs. Wright to a full laugh. "One Derby week I was there for Snow's show and a lady asked, 'Have any of these horses ever won the Kentucky Derby?' Snow had Secretariat by the bridle and he said, 'Oh, yes, ma'am. This one here has won it twice.'"

On with breakfast now, Mrs. Wright asked how we would like our eggs. "Scrambled," I said, and she answered, "Here we call scrambled 'rumble-jumble.'"

"Better yet. Eggs rumble-jumble."

Our toast, with its edges trimmed, stood in silver holders.

Born in England and brought to India at the age of one by her father, a career British civil servant, Mrs. Wright had been both horsewoman and participant in tiger hunts. She shot "anything that moved."

She came to regret the hunting. "I suppose I just got disgusted with the slaughter. Pigsticking still goes on in some areas, but tiger shooting for sport is now totally banned. Since 1972 you can get fifteen years in prison for shooting a tiger that's only minding its business."

On tables and desks around the room, we saw a family history in photographs, many of them showing Anne or her daughter Linda, a *National Geographic* documentary maker, in the company of a big cat: a lion, a tiger, a leopard. Mrs. Wright knew the life story of each cat.

"Now they're killing tigers for the bones," she said.

"The bones?" I asked.

"They grind up the bones and sell the powders as cures. Dreadful stuff in a bottle."

A glimpse of the Calcutta police commissioner at Buljeet's and Puppy's party was enough to remind us of a John McPhee line. Kowaljit Singh's dark and bearded face conspired with his dark and mean profession to suggest the darkness McPhee once saw in the Romanian tennis star Ion Tiriac, of whom he wrote: "Tiriac looks like he makes deals in the room behind the back room." No one, I thought, would be in a hurry to enter a back room with this Mr. Singh, whose thick body compounded his air of menace.

"Here in Calcutta, we believe in law and order," the commissioner said. "There is respect for the law that there is not in other cities."

The Calcutta police had been involved in a controversial exchange just the day before. Thousands of demonstrators led by a woman, Mamata Banerjee, had gathered downtown to protest what they saw as governmental oppression. Those demonstrators had come under rifle fire from the city police. The public outcry was harsh.

So, making party small talk, I asked the police commissioner, Mr.

Singh, "The demonstration yesterday, what did you think of Mamata Banerjee?"

Here's what Mr. Singh did then: he allowed his dark eyelids to move slowly over his dark eyes. He said nothing. He said nothing for a long time and then said, "Where do you go next from Calcutta?"

Maybe thirty friends gathered in two rooms of Buljeet's and Puppy's apartment, the small living room and smaller bedroom on the fifteenth floor of a luxury high-rise looking over the odious Calcutta of a parallel universe. On the bedroom bookshelves, Michael Crichton thrillers stood beside Danielle Steel romances. Recurring brownouts, a fact of life in Calcutta as in Kathmandu, periodically shut down the apartment's air conditioning. Only Tom and I seemed to notice the 90-degrees-at-11 P.M. heat.

Barefoot servants glided through the rooms serving drinks. A buffet table held shrimp, curried chicken, rice, yams, beans, mangoes, cheesecakes and another six dishes that could be categorized as unidentifiable-by-Yanks-who-ate-it-all.

Women in the world's most beautiful dresses—silk saris in peacock colors, the diaphanous cloth alive with magical prints—gathered in the larger room to speak of families and children. Along with the police commissioner, a dozen men gathered in the bedroom to speak of golf in laughter and lies and at least one happy truth born of pain.

S. R. (Sam) Dastridar was a little white-haired man who had played India's "fast games" of soccer, squash and tennis. An auto accident drove his left femur through the hip socket. Doctors said Sam would not walk again. Even when he proved them wrong, ten years later he was barely able to stand for five minutes. An orthopedist suggested he take up golf. He was fifty years old. The doctor said the fresh air couldn't hurt.

"Four holes, six holes, eleven holes, then fifteen, finally eighteen holes after a year and they had to carry me off the golf course," Sam said.

Now sixty-five and a 13-handicapper, he loves his friends' eight- and twelve-ball matches. (They toss balls to decide partners, then spend happy hours at the nineteenth hole calculating the damages.) Sam said, "I carry the pain with me. The golf is worth it."

Golf is twenty percent mechanics, Grantland Rice said. "The other eighty percent is philosophy, humor, tragedy, romance, melodrama, companionship, camaraderie, cussedness, and conversation." Even in Calcutta, Granny was right. We might have been in Orlando, the talk sounded so familiar: a father reporting on his son's college team; a manufacturing rep lamenting the poor quality of golf instruction at his club; a videotape playing on the bedroom television of the group's last golf trip.

In one of the curious ways we learn how small our world is, we heard Ben Hogan's name at this party. We had seen Hogan's image on the Iceland pro shop's door and heard the Scottish caddy Tip Anderson wish he had made the trip to Carnoustie in 1953. In the Burgundy country of France, the fair Françoise, the architect's girl of the day, carried a golf bag with Hogan's signature. And 5,000 miles later, R. S. Sabharwal, an Indian with a Cal-Berkeley degree, invoked Hogan's name after saying, "It's too bad Mallik isn't here."

Hashok Mallik was a national amateur champion who played for India in World Cups from 1958 to 1968. His father, Sardar Mallik, was the first Indian allowed to play in the Indian Amateur.

"Hashok is a living legend of Indian golf," R.S. said. "His father was a great player, too. He played with Hogan and knew him well."

Near midnight, the evening soft and kind, the police commissioner said no, no, no. But his friends persisted. Please, they said, please sing for us. And as he sat on a sofa with the night sky at his back, the dark and menacing Mr. Singh of the Calcutta police began to sing in a voice so sweet it seemed impossible to be his.

R.S. told us, "These are Punjab folk songs," and with each song there came murmurs of satisfaction and approval. The songs took the friends home again, to the Punjab region of northwest India, where their families owned the country's richest farmlands. They liked the warmth of that journey and urged the singing police commissioner to go on. He usually did.

Too soon it was midnight and time to go. R.S. and his chauffeur drove us to our hotel on Calcutta's nighttime streets. When Tom mentioned the beautiful saris at the party, our host said, "I paid $25,000 to buy my daughter a silk and gold sari, a work of art. It will be her wedding present one day." We saw people sleeping naked on the sidewalk. They slept in orderly rows, heads to the buildings, feet to the gutters. Even on the sidewalks, there isn't enough room in Calcutta for all of them.

We drove on.

———

Again, Hogan's name. Again, the great man's ghost.

"We've got to go to Texas and see Hogan," I said.

Tom said, "You're right. Let's go. He doesn't talk to newspapermen, but what the hell, Texas is only 18,000 miles from here. Let's do it."

So, before we finished this trip, we would go to Fort Worth. Maybe we would see Hogan, maybe not. We had to try.

The Diabolical's Eleventh Hole
457 Yards, Par 4

Anyone stronger than John Daly, straighter than Tom Kite, a better putter than Ben Crenshaw—I have won every hole in Asia, a total of one, during which streak I am even par and have yet to ground out to shortstop—such a mighty hero is eager to take on a hole so fearsome it has been called the terror of Indian golf.

So I stood heroically on the seventh tee at Royal Calcutta, the oldest golf club in the world outside the British Isles. Founded in 1829 by Britons and Scots serving in the Queen of England's imperial forces, Royal Calcutta showed that golf could be played on grass in tropical climates (even grasses with silly names, such as "dhoob" and "creeping dog's-tooth").

At St. Andrews early in our journey, George Wilson, a high muckety-muck of the Royal & Ancient, showed us a tall silver cup, first known as the Cashmere Cup and now the Calcutta Cup.

"Members of Royal Calcutta," Wilson said, pausing to sip at his afternoon glass of port, "visited St. Andrews in 1884 and were bowled over by the hospitality. When they returned home, they said, 'We must do something for the Royal & Ancient. What can we give them in return for their hospitality?'

"Of course, the Calcutta was as poor as a church mouse. So they instituted a swear box. For every transgression of the rules of golf, and for every oath uttered on the golf course, the perpetrator had to drop one Indian rupee into the swear box.

"Within three months, the box was filled. The club then melted the rupees and made this cup you see here today, a hundred and nine years later."

On a summer day in 1993, we admired Royal Calcutta's wide and flat fairways decorated with mighty trees. The course could play 7,331 yards but with its pleasant parkland feel it seemed benevolent enough. Besides, playing on a hot streak of one entire hole, even the prospect of crossing Royal Calcutta's notorious tanks didn't bother me.

Tanks are ponds. The Indians call them tanks because water is stored in them. On the seventh, a par 4 bending left 457 yards, a tank waited in the dogleg's corner. Once past that tank, a second tank yawned wide and deep. A hero would take one look at the abyss and say: "Hot-diggity, the Grand CANYON! Piece of CAKE!"

It is one of the sad facts of a 14-handicapper's golfing life that he can hit lots of bad shots and persuade himself that each one was a mistake unlikely to be repeated in his lifetime. But let him hit two good shots in a row and he is certain he has figured the game out. He becomes a new man whose name is Norman Severiano Faldo. Tanks, what tanks?

We hit two good drives, Tom's better than mine. We were maybe 230 yards from the green.

Considering a second shot, needing 200 yards to clear the tank, I first said, "Fore." After that: "Fore, please." Then I threw a ball at the goats.

Because a refugee village crowded against the club's boundaries, villagers and their goat herds often walked across Royal Calcutta's fairways. It was an ambience enjoyed at few golfing venues anywhere. On the second fairway, we met an eight-year-old villager named Junda. He was, as they say in Iceland, amazink, yes.

No taller than a driver, barefoot and skinny in raggedy shorts, Junda had a beautiful golf swing. He threw down a golf ball and hit it with the bare nub of a curved tree branch stripped of its bark. The prodigy Seve Ballesteros hitting balls off a Spanish beach with a rusty 5-iron may not have done it much better.

So there I was, shooing the goats away. Mr. Hero of the Ages had a chance to fly the tank with a whistling 3-wood shot. Instead, Mr. Hero wimped out. I chose to lay up short of the hazard and be happy with a bogey.

"Nine-iron," my caddy said. To be safer than safe, I used a pitching wedge. Unfortunately, I hit it very good, very smoothly and solidly. So good it had to be bad. The ball went into the tank, putting a small fright into a mother and her child doing the wash down there.

Tom's second, a 3-wood, cleared the tank easily and left him a short pitch to the green.

My fourth shot, an angry 5-wood, somehow flew 190 yards to within twenty feet of the cup.

Tom pitched on to twenty-five feet; we both used two putts, and he again went three up in our titanic struggle.

CHAPTER 12

GREEN VALLEY COUNTRY CLUB

Chiang Mai, Thailand

Where the Rooster Crows at Midnight
(and two . . . and four . . . and . . .)

ONE YEAR AT the British Open, when the tournament was in Sandwich, England, I bed-and-breakfasted with a family in Canterbury. The man of the house was a silent brickmaker who didn't seem to own any shirts. He was constructed of his own hard clay. His wife and mother, who talked more than enough for the three of them, prepared the breakfasts.

Every evening, after the long drive home from Royal St. George's, I would dictate my column over a telephone in the foyer. As soon as I got the operator, the brickmaker would come out of his room, take a seat in the shadowy hallway and quietly listen. When I finished, he would go back to bed without comment.

"Do you like golf?" I asked one morning.

"On television," he said.

"You've never been to the tournaments?"

"That's for millionaires."

"No, it's not," I told him. "Find yourself a shirt. We're going Sunday."

At an athlete's pace, and with young eyes, the broad-backed strongman followed Jack Nicklaus every stride of the final round. Afterward, I introduced him to Nicklaus, who wasn't just gracious but kind. It hadn't been Jack's happiest week. Back in Columbus, one of his teenage sons, the special one who always resisted golf, had rolled the company station wagon—on the Jack Nicklaus Freeway!—and been tagged with a DWI. Nobody was hurt, to Jack's immense relief. But he was a father that week, not a golfer. And the few minutes he gave the brickmaker were part of the clearing gentleness that follows the emergency.

The next morning, as I packed to leave, my host came to say good-bye. He was shirtless again. "I know what you do," he said gruffly. "Here's what I do." He handed me an ordinary—that is to say, unextraordinary— but sharply cornered and perfectly rectangular red brick. "I make bricks," he said. So, sportswriters don't cry?

Oh, to be able to make something as substantial and essential as a brick.

Of course we rode elephants then. We were in Thailand.

Coming from Calcutta to Chiang Mai was like going from the darkness into the light, but the sensation was surprisingly disagreeable. The reappearance of Kentucky Fried Chicken stores and Pizza Huts—even three-storied malls with food courts and banana slush and yogurt stands— somehow rubbed us both the wrong way. Dave drew his adjustable golf club like a terrible swift sword and instructed the driver (admittedly of a swanky black Chiang Mai Orchid Hotel limousine) to head for the hills.

From the moment we left Atlanta, Dave had been champing to improvise an implausible shot. Arnold Palmer once drove a golf ball off the Eiffel Tower that, by the restrained account of his ineffable Boswell, Doc Giffin, bounded along the rue a good 500 yards before rolling into a sidewalk café and ordering itself a cup of hot chocolate. Astronaut Alan

Shepard swatted a one-armed 6-iron on the moon that, he says, flew weightlessly over two hundred yards—with just the nicest fade on it. Chipmunk reporters ached to ask him: "If you could have the shot over, would you still hit the soft 6 or would you go with a hard 7?"

Mac O'Grady, the pro from outer space, recommended Dave cut a little 5-iron over the tomb at the Taj Mahal, as he once did. O'Grady went so far as to share with us the Zen master's secret of where a particular Titleist happens to be hidden on the property. Mac's the one who hid it there, just in case he might find himself in Agra sometime without a golf ball.

Still, standing on the edge of an upcountry jungle, smashing dialed-up 5-irons at arbitrary landmarks, I couldn't help but think of Carroll Rosenbloom. That scoundrel, the late owner of the late Baltimore Colts, used to hit brand-new balls by the gross into the ocean waves behind his Florida beach house. Mysteriously, he drowned in those waters. I was kind of glad to move on.

As we went, the driver cum tour guide said hesitantly: "I'm confused. Isn't the object of the sport to get the ball into a little hole, a specific little hole marked off someplace?"

"No," Dave explained patiently. "The idea is to lose the ball as quickly as possible in as spectacular a way as possible."

"Oh-h-h. Now I see. Very good. Good shots."

For dessert, he offered us orchids, butterflies or snakes; we chose snakes. At a roadside snake farm of the ramshackle sort associated with Okefenokee alligators, acrobatic little men in black pajamas and red head-bands swam with giant pythons and stared down spitting cobras to the accompaniment of Billy Joel warbling "You May Be Right, I May Be Crazy."

When, late in the production, the bamboo shelter began to quiver above us and the ground proceeded to quake beneath us, Dave murmured ominously, "Ted Turner." I looked around and whispered in a spooky drawl, "And what about the elephants?"

On the occasion of the first Goodwill Games in Moscow, Turner spent an afternoon trying to convince us a U.S.-Soviet track meet could save the world. At the bottom of a memorable tirade involving Hitler, Jiminy

Cricket, François Mitterand, Helmut Kohl, General George S. Patton, Verdun, the National League, Robert E. Lee, Marshal Zhukov, Caspar Weinberger, Jacques Cousteau, Carl Sagan, pigeons, mountain goats ("I killed one here last winter and they just delivered the stuffed head to my hotel room"), Perez de Cuellar, Horatio Nelson, Mikhail Gorbachev, Howard Baker, John F. Kennedy and Lester Maddox, Turner concluded: "All the things we've done—our books, our art, our literature—and what have we done with our opportunity? Get ready to blow ourselves up. And not just ourselves. What about the elephants?"

Dave's elephant was more amenable to climbing the steep jungle hills. Their elephant boy didn't have much to do but walk alongside and marvel at the viewfinder of Dave's camera. My elephant didn't like the draw. He refused to ignite until he was jump-started from behind with an unloaded slingshot snapped by a tiny terror of a dark-eyed child who answered

every question put to him with the same rapid-fire litany: "Bye-please-thank-you-and-I-am-pissed." When he tired of stinging the reluctant elephant, he vaulted onto its bumpy head and pulled its dappled ears and thunked it mercilessly on the noggin with the butt of the slingshot. "Bye-please-thank-you-and-I-am-pissed," he said.

To spare the elephant these beatings, I slid off the padded chair and straddled his neck, probably not much of a trade-off, from the elephant's point of view. Dave did the same. We looked like reinforcements coming to drive Hannibal to suicide. At the top of the hill, we came into a clearing. Far below, we could see farmers working in rice paddies and teenagers sudsing down water buffaloes like jalopies. Clouds of butterflies dived in formation and soared in a tropical breeze.

Going downhill, the elephants were incredibly surefooted and as reinvigorated as rental horses headed back to the stable. "Well, another conveyance," Dave said, updating his statistical lists. That night, the tuk-tuks made still another.

Bangkok, to the south, is the R & R capital of the Vietnam generation, where fat American men of the Vietnam age, who have never been to Vietnam, come to be with overyoung girls certain to ignore their girths and credit their stories. We elected Chiang Mai, thinking it might be different. But it wasn't really. It was pretty much one, big, dead-eyed massage parlor. Even the tuk-tuks, the dune buggy taxicabs, were strung with lurid ice-blue lights.

Sportswriters are reputed to be fervent drinkers, a newspaper-wide anachronism left over from the fedora days. All but gone are the reeling rummies who, five minutes from deadline, call for a *Herald Tribune,* patiently tear out Bill Corum's column, painstakingly paste it to a sheet of copy paper, carefully roll it up into the typewriter, thoughtfully type "What does Bill Corum mean by this?" and send it.

All the same, it is fair to say, Full of Fog and Passport Two drank beyond their usual requirements on a bleary, blustery, highly musical but otherwise unredeemable evening in Chiang Mai. Lest he join me on the waiver wire, I should hasten to mention Dave was the soul of both good manners and monogamy, a fact that can be corroborated by the talcum teacake in the green satin dress loosely labeled his date at the karaoke club. (Honest, Cheryl. All we did was sing.)

My companion for inexpensive drinks was a less glamorous, terribly petite, heartbreakingly young hill girl named Patra. If her tale was the rehearsed and standard one detailing the slavers in her own family and the inevitable baby back home with Grandmother, Patra's delivery at least sounded fresh to one who was on his fifth gin and tonic without the tonic. She was looking for a man, she said (what else?), who would "touch" her, for once, "in a real place." She said, "I only want someone who think of me as loved, not lover. He need to love. I need to be loved. Share life, not time. Not only talk, listen. Laugh together. Cry together. Sing duet."

With a voice as light as a scarf, she sang the Thai lyrics crawling across TV monitors scattered all about the dark bar in which we seemed to be the only foreigners. Where a corresponding video wasn't available, neutral scenes of spring and romance were substituted. Patra sang into one of two silver ball microphones that floated from table to table.

Without microphones, Dave and I attempted to sing along by the syllables. I once knew a Jesuit priest who, noticing declensions weren't being memorized at the rate of Top 10 lyrics, took the unconventional step of setting his high school Latin classes to music. "Sum . . . es . . . est, sumus . . . estis . . . sunt, eram . . . eras . . . era-a-a-t, eramus . . . eratis . . . era-a-a-nt." He was known as "the Mitch Miller of the Punic Wars." The more we drank, the clearer it all came back.

Dave's date, girl, pal, acquaintance, stranger (nothing, she meant nothing) vanished for a minute and returned with a catalogue of English-language requests. Just like us, the selections were irretrievably dated. They ran from Frankie Laine's "Mule Train" and "That Lucky Old Sun" to Frank Sinatra's "Theme from *The Cardinal*" and "Strangers in the Night."

"I think I know that one," Dave said. "How does it go?"

"Dooby-dooby-doo," I demonstrated.

"Doughby-doughby-dough," he repeated.

Gack.

"Wait a minute, here's an easier one," I said. " 'True Love.' Bing Crosby and Grace Kelly. You can be Grace Kelly."

"How does that go?"

"So I give to you . . . and you give to me . . . true love . . . true love . . . and on and on it will always be . . . true love . . . true love . . ."

"Jesus."

A few moments (or was it drinks?) later, our number came up on the screen. We tapped microphones with trembling hands, cleared our well-oiled throats and waited for the first note. I felt like I was back at the Peabody Conservatory in Baltimore.

When I was a boy, I played the violin. At least I tried to play the violin. That is, I pretended to try to play the violin. In the early Chicago days, my father liked to joke that mine was the only violin case in Chicago that actually had a violin in it. But I was one of those kids who, on the way to the weekly lesson, customarily hid the violin in the brambles and played baseball. The teacher screamed but never squealed. He probably needed the $3.00.

Eventually, like the fathers of River City, my father wanted to hear some music. My sisters played piano, and all of them performed recitals at Peabody. When was the boy's recital? In a loamy panic dwarfing my own, the teacher tried to install like software the simplest program he thought I could get away with in a recital. The title of the piece was: "Pony Boy."

It was going along okay—a woman I had never seen before was accompanying me on the piano—when I came close to the end and couldn't remember how to finish. So I went around again. This time, I could make out the exit ramp through a cloud of resin dust in the atmosphere. But, screeching and hydroplaning, I couldn't veer off in time. So I went around again. The pianist started to perspire.

Five times around, we raced at the hellish pace of Charlie Daniels, until somebody in the audience finally laughed and ultimately everyone joined in. Miraculously, the sixth time around, I stumbled out of the labyrinth and finished totally out of breath to a standing ovation. Isaac Stern never heard such cheering at Carnegie Hall.

When I broke through the stage door, the Irishman was waiting. He was leaning against the wall with his hands in his pockets and a Lucky Strike in his mouth. All he said was, "You don't have to play anymore," and I never did.

"... Country road ... take me home ... to a place ... I belong ... West Virginia ..."

God, it was John Denver. Trooper that he is, Dave kept singing, faking the words, half a beat behind Denver, holding the microphone like Liza Minnelli. "... Take me home ... country road ..."

Desperately, I rifled through the pages for other numbers. No. 81—Sam Cooke's "You Send Me," No. 74—Rosemary Clooney's "Hey There," even No. 31—Conway Twitty's "It's Only Make Believe." They all came out John Denver.

"... Radio reminds me of my home far away ..."

It was a nightmare, "Pony Boy" all over again.

A smartly dressed and pencil-mustachioed local, about the size of Bill Shoemaker, leaned over the back of our booth to say something to Patra. "What is it?" I asked. She replied: "He say, you play that song one more time, he gonna kill you." I laughed. "Tell him not to worry," I said. "If they play it one more time, we'll kill ourselves."

Nobody got killed that night, but a rooster almost did. Drunk or sober, Dave resents roosters that crow in the dark, especially outside his window. He roused me in the middle of the night to help him locate it and, in his queer phrase, "execute it." My memory's a little hazy, but I'm pretty sure we circled the building two or three times with his adjustable club dialed to a 1-iron. And I'm positive, when the night clerk couldn't grasp the situation, Dave cock-a-doodle-dooed in the lobby. "All I can say," I said, "is bye-please-thank-you-and-I-am-pissed." Four hours later, we were on the golf course.

The Diabolical's Twelfth Hole
235 Yards, Par 3

After Royal Nepal and Royal Calcutta, the Chiang Mai Green Valley Country Club was a real golf course, beautifully appointed, impeccably manicured and, once again, a bit offputting. There was virtually no rough. The only trees were tall palms topheavy with green coconuts. An intricate system of lakes came into play at least once on all but a couple of holes. Typically, you had to overfly one lake to the fairway and another to the green, including floating greens connected by cedar footbridges. Pink flower arrangements bobbed in the water. Fountains and waterfalls conspired with the morning sun to splash misty rainbows across mountain shadows framing the horizon. As George S. Kaufman would say to Moss Hart, "It just shows you what God could have done if He had the money."

In the morning paper, a senior golf tournament, somewhere else in

Thailand, was trumpeted at length. It seemed half of the field had the surname Thabpavibul and none of the Thabpavibuls broke 80. When the pro shop cashier asked a second time who we were, I said, "Tom and Dave Thabpavibul," and he smiled with recognition and assigned us two girl caddies. The immediate order of business was to find out exactly how much English they had.

The first time I encountered female caddies, some years ago in Japan, I was playing with a Japanese assistant pro at an airport course on my way out of Tokyo. Other than from interpreters, I hadn't heard any English for ten days until I met this friendly young pro who had studied at UCLA. That kind of language deprivation can lull you into the dangerous supposition that nobody understands a word you're saying. It can also increase your propensity for saying stupid things, even if that's already quite high.

Although I was enjoying the round, I mentioned to the pro that I thought the $300 greens fee a trifle rich. "Yes, but for that," he said, "you get nine holes, a nice lunch, nine more holes and a bath." Beholding the beautiful, mute young woman who was pushing our clubs, I asked: "Does she give the bath?" She looked at me and smiled. I smiled too.

"I give the yardages," she said.

Thank Buddha, neither of our caddies had a word of English. In fact, the wrote the yardages on their hands with ballpoint pens. In a charming

improvement over the familiar peasant dresses and beekeepers' helmets, they wore uniforms reminiscent of sulky drivers' silks, cream-colored with green piping and jaunty jockey caps. (Sulkies again, our old good luck charms!) Printed across the back of Dave's caddy were the numerals 007. Of course, he immediately dubbed her "Odd Job."

Scurrying around like assistant managing editors, the caddies did everything except swing the club. They marked the ball. They cleaned the ball. They replaced the ball. They repaired the ball marks. They fished the ball out of the cup. We would have felt even more sluglike if ours hadn't been the only group on the course without parasol holders, insect fanners and ice-water bearers. If you think the dollar is weak, you ought to see the baht. Just in front of us was a "foursome" of twenty-one people. It looked like a press conference.

Hoping to be waved through, we got right on their bumper and tailgated them for eleven holes. At the twelfth, a 181-yard par 3, they at least invited us to hit up after all four of their balls and most of their cocktail shakers had reached the green. Dave striped a killer 3-iron just off the back. My own 3-iron is a little harder to describe. Swinging out wide to the right, the ball turned straight left somewhere over the green and started clanging and diving like a submarine ducking depth charges until it struck the base of a palm (I'm going to say twenty yards left of the green) so flush that it shot straight back almost into the hole.

"I never see such thing before!" exclaimed one of the Thabpavibuls on the green.

"You don't say?" I said pleasantly. "Play faster." (A little less hung over, I'm a lot more cordial.) Anyway, they took the subtle hint and let us bypass their safari.

The last par 3 was our hole, the 235-yard sixteenth, a scenic drive—out of a garden, more than off a tee—across a stream and bridge to a distant green with the water, the bunkers, the flag—everything—tucked to the left. As a par 3, it was fitting company for Calamity and the Crocodiles.

I hit a driver that got a piece of the green but ran into the highest bunker on the left. Dave also hit a driver, straight but short of the green, leaving an uphill pitch of sixty feet that bounced once and sucked right next to the pin for a tap-in par. Expecting to take two shots in most bunkers, I was surprised when I blasted out to six feet. I was not surprised when I missed the putt. A 4 and a 3. Again, the margin was back to two.

As was his habit after the match holes, Dave lingered to take a few snapshots around the green and back toward the tee. Sitting down in the grass, running her fingers through a patch of clover, Odd Job nodded approvingly. She concurred with our choice.

CHAPTER 13
SINGAPORE ISLAND COUNTRY CLUB

Singapore, Singapore

Where Chewing Gum Is a Crime and Johnny Two-Thumbs Is Still Dead

AFTER THE MONKEYS and madmen of Kathmandu, after the co-bras and B-girls of Chiang Mai, we were headed back to the real world. Our route was determined one night when we studied a globe and discovered Singapore four inches above Australia. The city sat in the corner of a dogleg left from Chiang Mai to Singapore to Beijing. Otherwise, we had no good reason to go to Singapore, save, perhaps, that suggested by our London adviser Ian Wooldridge. "In Singapore," he had said, "you'll stay at Raffles, of course. And you'll go to the Writers' Bar for a Singapore Sling."

The travel writer Paul Theroux prefers trains because airplanes are too much like submarines for his taste. But the birds of fire have their moments. One moment came above Singapore. We descended through clouds so thick and white they might have been snowdrifts. They were suspended in a turquoise sky. For that moment, we floated inside a watercolorist's imagination.

Even Mr. Callahan roused in his seat to take a look. Then the summer stock trouper and aide-de-camp to aging songstresses said, "Singapore! Sing-ah-poor? No, no. I sing-ah-good. Take me, please, to Raffles."

Raffles is a five-star hotel left over from British colonial days. It was named for Sir Stamford Raffles, the East India Company administrator who in 1819 stepped ashore on the banks of the Singapore River and decided that, local pirates be damned, Singapore should be Great Britain's trading base. Raffles then finagled the purchase of land that in 1824 led to the British buying the entire island. Michael Jackson, on his "Dangerous" world tour in 1993, commandeered an entire floor at Raffles a month after our visit and waved to the masses from his penthouse window.

Because we didn't want to pay the Raffles single-room rate of $480—we had run away from home, not away from bill collectors—we limited our visit to a round of Singapore Slings. We did the drinking at the Writers' Bar where Rudyard Kipling, Somerset Maugham and Joseph Conrad earlier had pursued inspiration. Their photographs sat behind the mahogany and brass bar, each scribbler looking solemn even without the burden of carrying golf clubs.

Until we landed at Singapore's Changi Airport, we had no idea what the city might be. We learned quickly. If Moscow's airport was the first circle of hell, Changi was a paradise. It was at once efficient, beautiful and suggestive of all we would see in Singapore. From the balcony of a forty-seventh-floor room at the Westin Stamford Hotel, we saw a pastel city sparkling in the night, a tiny jewel set between the Indian Ocean and the South China Sea.

Skyscrapers carried neon signs: the Pan Pacific, the Marina Mandarin and the Hong Kong Bank on the edges of the city's deep-water harbor. From our aerie, the world's busiest port looked like a bathtub full of toy boats. There were hundreds of ships, yachts, ocean liners and freighters.

As I made notes of the Singapore revelations, Callahan had another thought working. He thought: tattoos. Having worked in San Diego, another sailor-y place, Callahan stood on the forty-seventh-floor balcony and said, "Sing-ah-poor, port to the Far Eastern world. You know, Dave, this would be a great place to get a tattoo. Let's do it. Ask yourself: 'What tattoo in what position can I live with the rest of my life?' "

I pretended deafness. Tom went to the phone book to look up tattoo parlors.

The last tiger in Singapore was captured on the hilly grounds of a jungle that now is the Bukit course at Singapore Island Golf Club. These days only an occasional iguana or monkey threatens the player who climbs through eighteen holes of Bukit's "verdant paradise." To quote Herb Wind: "The greenery suggests a pleasant coolness. . . . To play golf there in the early morning, right after sunrise, when the fairways are still wet with dew, is a delight. To tee off late in the day, coming in as the sun disappears, is another unforgettable golfing experience."

Uninvited but trusting in our golf-as-passport theory, Tom and I arrived at Singapore Island G.C. with crooked sticks hanging off our shoulders. There are no public courses in Singapore. In the summer of 1993, a Singapore Island membership cost $170,000. The club, with four golf courses, swimming, tennis and even bowling, was 6,627 members with another 6,759 spouses and children.

The club secretary, Gurmit Charl, sent us to the first tee where we met the gracious John Cheng and a skinny Singapore pro who talked with a hustler's patter, who wanted to play the PGA Senior Tour, whose hair looks that way because he lost a beery midnight bet and who handed us a business card identifying himself as:

Dan the Pro

Golf & Tennis Consultant, Golf Course Designer, 1985 Singapore Open Golf Champion, Represented Singapore in Putra Cup, Nomura Cup and Eisenhower Trophy, 1968 and 1975 Singapore Open Tennis Champion, Winner of many Golf & Tennis tournaments, Singapore's Davis Cup Coach, Singapore's Best ever Tennis professional.

"The later it became, sitting here on the patio"—we join Dan the Pro
in mid-narrative—"the more beer we drank. The more beer we drank, the
better player I became until about midnight I was damned good.

"The bet was I would cut off my hair. I had very long hair, long all
over, and I wore it in a pony tail. I bet I could make a par on the first
hole—in the dark. It was midnight, partner. We couldn't see at all. And
I'm going to shave my head if I can't make a par.

"Almost did it. Had it fifteen feet, but three-putted. I think the beer
had more to do with that than the dark. I wouldn't cut my hair all the way
off, though. I cut the front and kept the rest."

In his round with us, Dan the Pro hit the ball great distances off the tee
but, curiously, he never took a putt. He said he saved his putts for real
rounds. A guy, he said, has only so many good putts in him. We'll drink a
Sling to that.

Under "Tattoo Parlors" in the yellow pages, the Irishman on the forty-
seventh floor of a Singapore hotel found one establishment of particular
interest.

I heard him say into the phone, "Is Johnny Two-Thumbs in? . . . Dead?
I didn't know he was sick. . . . But you still do tattoos? . . . If I wanted
one, when would be a good time to come over? . . . Will a taxi know how
to get there? . . . Thanks, bye."

By Singapore, we had been on the road too long. Callahan wanted a
tattoo—of what, Marilyn Maxwell's profile? He also had broken into song
again. In France, he heard the architect Robert Berthet speak of Adam
and Eve; in Belgium we passed a bronze statue of the Garden's mademoiselle; in Mauritius we walked by tanning bodies unburdened by bikini
tops. These occasions moved Tom to his youth and he became Lancelot
singing from *Camelot* . . .

> *"I never stray from what I believe,*
> *I'm blessed with an iron will.*
> *If I had been made the partner of Eve,*
> *We'd be in Eden still."*

No songs for me. A beautiful blonde led me through a maze to a dentist's office. The dentist was a black-haired doctor rehearsing for a soap

opera. He sat in an easy chair wearing a robe. I told him, "I know your real name. It's Johnny Berardino and in the 1940s you were an infielder for the St. Louis Browns. Good field, no hit."

Here a door opened and four women entered, each a circus fat lady. I sat on the doctor's staircase. One woman kept coming toward me, nearer and nearer until I couldn't breathe.

Then I woke up and moved a pillow off my face.

It is illegal in Singapore to chew gum. It is illegal to not flush a toilet after use. It is a crime to drop a cigarette package on the street. (A three-time loser at this cigarette thing sweeps city streets three days.) Singapore cuts criminals no slack, as noted in red print on a traveler's disembarkation card: "DEATH for drug traffickers under Singapore law."

Anyone waiting in the visa section of the United States Embassy can copy down these reminders from a sign on the wall:

> Under Singapore law, it is presumed until proven otherwise that a person possessing more than 2 grams of heroin or 15 grams of marijuana is a trafficker. (28 grams = 1 ounce) Conviction for trafficking in heroin is punishable by a minimum sentence of five years and five strokes of the cane.
>
> Traffickers possessing more than 15 grams of heroin are punishable by a mandatory death sentence.

Strokes of the cane are whippings done with a four-foot-long piece of rattan cane, a finger's thickness and splintered so it will slash and scar the skin of a prisoner's back. At dinner one night, a Singapore doctor told us the cane has a name: "It's called son of a bitch." Dr. Un Hong Hin also told a cane joke: "A doctor was brought in to oversee a caning. On the first stroke, okay. On the second stroke, okay. On the third stroke, the *doctor* fainted."

We met a young American businessman who had lived in Singapore eight years. He said the city is an authoritarian society pretending it's a democracy. Yet, when it comes down to it, he likes the trade-off: freedom for safety.

"The ACLU back in the States would be wigged out," the American said. "Screw them and the white horse they ride in on. You can walk the streets of Singapore any hour of any night without thinking somebody's going to put a knife in your ribs. I like that more than I like protecting creeps. There's no drug problem here and everyone works, either privately or in government programs, so there is no homeless problem, no beggars on the street. The place has the highest per-capita income in Southeast Asia. It's an experiment that's working."

From 1819 to 1959, Singapore was a British colony important as an island seaport for trade in the Far East. Today it is a futuristic city-state which is Hong Kong's rival in banking, high-tech communications and beauty. Decorated by flowers and shining in the tropical sun, Singapore is a city, a park and a fruit basket filled with rambutan, nangka, jambu and mangosteen. Most important, the city has achieved harmony among distinct ethnic groups: Chinese (77.7 percent), Muslim Malays (14.1 percent) and Hindu Indians (7.1 percent), all speaking English as Singapore's official language.

"Cut it out," Callahan said when he heard these numbers. "You sound like you swallowed a Funk and Wagnall's encyclopedia."

Maybe today's Singapore of affluence and order is best appreciated by a person who knew yesterday's Singapore. After golf one afternoon, we sat with John Cheng, a fifty-six-year-old business executive. A son of first-generation Chinese immigrants, Cheng grew up on a small farm raising pineapple, bananas and jackfruit. His family had no money, he said. "But we were lucky. We had land. And in Singapore, everybody can get an education."

For $2.50 a month, he attended a Christian Brothers school before going on to the University of Malaysia in Kuala Lumpur, a boat ride across the bay from Singapore.

"So in 1959 we gained our independence from England," Cheng began his history of Singapore. "There were traumatic years because we were in union with Malaysia. But on August 9, 1963, we were separated from Malaysia. We were on our own. All of a sudden, Singapore is by itself. We said, 'Okay, now we got to go.'

"Understand, Singapore has no natural resources. Even today we buy two thirds of our water from Malaysia, and stones, and even our sand. Our leaders decided we must be multinational for business because without other nations coming in we would be helpless to help ourselves.

"We created favorable conditions for multinational companies to bring their money into our country. We had much to offer them. We speak

English, the world's language. We have good education. Our government is pro-development. And so Singapore changed from low-skill jobs to high-tech. Japanese brought shipbuilding. Americans brought oil rigs and steel foundries.

"IBM came. Caterpillar. Wells Fargo. Chase Manhattan. Allis-Chalmers. First Chicago.

"We built a nice hive and we brought in the honey."

With the honey came a set of draconian laws designed by Singapore's longtime Prime Minister, Lee Kuan Yew, first elected in 1959. Paul Theroux lived in Singapore three years. In his 1975 book, *The Great Railway Bazaar*, Theroux wrote: "Politically, Singapore is as primitive as Burundi, with repressive laws, paid informers, a dictatorial government, and jails full of political prisoners." The writer cited fines and jail sentences for crimes such as "mosquito breeding," "shouting in the lobby," "allowing insects to breed," and "throwing a piece of paper into a drain."

We met Don Kennedy, an American living in Singapore whose work took him throughout Southeast Asia. He loved the city: "The ban on the sale, manufacture and importation of chewing gum was done to stop people from disrupting the subway system doors, or that's what the government says. The toilet fine for not flushing makes you think about flushing, so you do. The littering fines and public embarrassment that go with getting caught—the local paper, the *Straits Times*, makes a point of bringing it to light so that others will condemn it and not do the same thing—make you think twice about littering."

To create the appearance of democracy, if not the reality, voting is compulsory by law. When Lee Kuan Yew decided the country was overpopulated, he instituted strict birth-control measures that in thirty years reduced the birth rate by half. To control traffic while raising money for government, Singapore allows its citizens to buy automobiles only after paying as much as $20,000 for a Certificate of Entitlement. With the COE, a person then has the privilege of buying a car at a price driven to exorbitant heights by government duties ($205,000 for a Mercedes 200E).

"After you buy one," said Don Kennedy, "you must pay a license fee every six months. And then, after ten years, you must dispose of the car or pay a very high renewal fee."

John Cheng submits to such laws because he sees Singapore as a small, isolated, vulnerable place.

"In the United States," he said, "you have missiles. You have antimissile missiles. You have millions of troops. We have none of this in Singapore. You understand our paranoia, then? We are fragile. We are vulnerable. So we do what keeps the boat afloat. It's a small boat, don't rock it. If it rocks too bad, we all sink."

Admiring the passion of our host, I yet had a question. In its shortest form, the question was: *"Chewing gum?"* The irrelevant thought occurred that, when chewing gum is outlawed, only outlaws will have chewing gum.

"Our trains in Singapore run on schedules that bring them to the stations every one and a half minutes," Cheng said. "They were discovering that the trains run late and they worked to discover why. They found that chewing gum had stopped up the doors. Gum interfered with the electronics that opened and shut the train doors. So. Interfering with the trains, is that worth chewing gum?"

Even the zealot Cheng laughed about the certain absurdity in such a solemn explanation. He said, "For gum, don't worry. They don't shoot you."

Singapore's contribution to golf came so indirectly as to be remembered late in the twentieth century only by readers of a book called *The Curious History of the Golf Ball.* It tells the story of hard times in Scotland during the 1840s. A divinity student, Rob Paterson, the son of a teacher, didn't have enough money to have his shoes cobbled, let alone buy feather golf balls.

"In its inscrutable way," the book reports, "Providence took a hand in 1843 by causing the arrival at Dr. Paterson's home of a large wooden box from Singapore. In it, sent by an older missionary son, was a statue of the Hindu deity Vishnu, goddess of fertility and preservation.

"The ornate and graceful four-armed figure in black marble came carefully packed in a mass of blackish-brown shavings. These the learned doctor recognized as gutta percha, dried gum of the Malaysian sapodilla tree.

"Since he knew the exotic material had some value—it was fashioned in those days into whip handles, papercutters, and other knicknacks—Dr. Paterson saw to it that the shavings were not thrown out."

As he had seen his mother roll dumplings, the young Paterson found a smooth board, heated the gutta percha until it was malleable and rolled the stuff under his palms until it took the shape of a ball.

It became the first gutta percha golf ball. "After it cooled," the book goes on, "he painted it white lest he lose it in the herbage of the Old Course. For that is where, early one April morning in 1845, he fearfully took his little creation to try hitting it with his golf clubs. After several strokes, the poor thing disintegrated. But the first few hits had felt and flown not badly at all."

The more durable guttie replaced the featheries of Scotland and the ball-making revolution was on. The things you learn going around the world.

Singapore's leaders once noticed an alarming number of single women over age thirty.

"Lee Kuan Yew wanted to remedy this," Dr. Un Hong Hin said. "So the government created SDU."

Perhaps the government thought of the program as the Social Development Unit, but those Singaporeans weary of government intrusion into their lives put another meaning on the initials. They decided SDU meant Single, Desperate & Ugly.

"SDU succeeded," the doctor said, "in persuading one in a hundred men to hold hands with an SDU woman."

The traveling Yanks found themselves again dragooned by cordial hosts and fed heaping quantities of delights followed by a Singaporean beer or three. The little doctor seemed to be the house radical. He said, "There is no freedom of expression here. *Cosmopolitan* and *Playboy* are not allowed here. If you write anything the government doesn't like, *Golf Digest* will not be for sale here. And even with total control of the media, the vote is only 60–40 in favor of the government. With free expression, the government wouldn't get twenty percent."

Singapore, in the summer of '93, joined China, Malaysia and Vietnam in prohibiting the purchase and installation of satellite dishes capable of receiving television signals from the Hong Kong-based Star-TV, a system reaching thirty-nine countries with Hindu, Chinese and English-language programming that includes news reports. One Singapore scholar called satellite TV "the newest hired gun of imperialism."

After three beers, or five, we had fallen in love with the decidedly not SD&U woman across the table, a willowy charmer named Kee Bee Khim who for twenty-one of the previous twenty-two years had been the club's women's champion. Good enough to play in Asian tournaments against the world's top players, she once met one of the best. "Oh, I forget her name, but you know her," Kee Bee Khim said, "that very nice Mexican girl with the big boobs," which is one way of remembering Nancy Lopez.

After five beers, or seven, we determined that Kee Bee Khim was married and to a man who didn't deserve her. She and her husband were separated. She said she still saw him around the club. "On *my* club membership," she said, "he brings his girl friend to the club to play tennis. *That* will end very soon."

We figured three or four strokes of the cane should serve the cad about right.

Callahan said, "JOHNNY TWO-THUMBS! OH, NO!"
He had forgotten.
The tattoo parlor closed at four.
I said, "We'll get it next time we're in town."

The Diabolical's Thirteenth Hole
487 Yards, Par 5

I have read about a golf course in Singapore said to sit by a jail, a lunatic asylum, a graveyard and a maternity home. Three of the four destinations would have served me well by day's end at Singapore Island's Bukit course.

Fred Couples, an American hero, once struck a drive from the high tee at the Bukit's par-5, 487-yard finishing hole that sailed so far right it landed on an adjoining course. It landed behind a line of mighty trees over which an approach to the eighteenth is impossible for anyone save an American hero. He promptly threw a high 5-iron draw toward the clubhouse, the ball describing a wide arc above a tennis court, a caddy-shack and putting green that all sit out of bounds. When finally the ball came to earth, Couples might have kicked in the eagle putt, it was so short.

Another American of my acquaintance stood on that tee looking across a wide valley to an uphill fairway making a left turn. This American saw the trees on the right as well as trees on the left. He saw all this trouble and he was, to be frank, a lesser hero than Fred Couples.

Which is to say, I whip-topped yet another worm-fright off the tee. Then I sclaffed a 5-wood to a spot two hundred yards from a green hidden by trees. To reach the green from there, a hero needed a powerful, low, running shot off a side-hill lie. It is a shot I could expect to pull off every other decade or so.

Meanwhile, Tom had taken the Couples route right and then popped a 5-wood back across the fairway into the left-side trees not much ahead of my position. Two holes down in this circumnavigational match with five to play after Bukit, I decided to go for the green from the awkward lie. No time to lay up after laying up into that Calcutta tank.

So I hero-topped a third shot, the ball skittering through leaves looking for a place to hide from the embarrassment. Ground balls for 18,000 miles now, on three continents and eleven countries—a pattern of misbehavior which provoked an interior monologue too adjective-rich to be reprinted. Just say it was followed by a fit of club-throwing or, more accurately, club-boinging. As my 3-wood boinged against Bukit's fairway, our host John Cheng said, "Dave's been on the road too long, I think." And he didn't even know about the Johnny Berardino dream.

Tom had his own problems, hacking a shot away from some tree roots before we both reached the green in four. Two putts each. Bogeys. Five holes to go and Tom remained two up.

I sent a postcard to Bud Shaw, a columnist at the *Cleveland Plain Dealer*:

Bud,
Numbers:
Of countries visited: 16.
Of diabolical holes played: 13.
Of times Tom has looked at the topless 'Liberté' on a French franc note and said, "Give me two pickets to Tittsburgh": 7.
Of rental cars abandoned: 3.
Of passports lost, found and replaced: 3.
Of monks in "For Buddhist Monks Only" seating section at Chiang Mai airport: 2.
Of monks waving wooden doves at speeding cars: 1.
Of actual fist-fights by travelers interacting with natives: 0 (so far).

Yours for better golfing,
Albert Schweitzer

CHAPTER 14

Beijing Golf Club

Beijing, China

**Where We Play Roadside 8-ball After
Airmailing the Great Wall**

HER REAL NAME was He Wei but she called herself Hilda. His real name was Jiawa Hong but his breastplate identified him as Hubert. The third desk clerk at the Palace Hotel, Lili Min, went by Nancy. This was all for the convenience of Western visitors. China is open for business.

"A More Open China Awaits 2000 Olympics," shouted a hundred billboards between the airport and midtown Beijing. The bad news had not been delivered yet. Meanwhile, the confession contained in the phrasing "*more* open China" just slipped out in translation. "A Billion Warm Hearts Welcome the World," other signs said. Still others: "Citius, Altius, Fortius." Faster, higher, stronger. "Peace, Progress, for a Better World." And, atop an advertising needle, a miniature of the Seattle landmark: "Around the World Golf."

"Do you suppose," Dave supposed, "that could be a welcoming banner for us?"

It turned out to be another project in the wishing stage, the promise of a coming reality, like the race track we passed along the highway that was built on the hope that someday the government will permit horse racing.

Thick as gnats, bicyclists buzzed the Beijing streets, never zooming, just sailing along, as coordinated as a migration. Almost to a woman and girl, the women and girls modeled knee-high or thigh-high nylon stockings that, in any case, didn't come up to their shorts or dresses. Only one man every few blocks, always an older man, still wore the gray Mao suit from the mind's memory of China.

By the time we had checked into the Palace, it was getting dark, and Tiananmen Square was just a half hour's walk away. We went there directly, hoping to find the equivalent of our Red Square teacher. But no one like that was around.

Standing in the spotlight of Mao Zedong's portrait at the entrance to the Forbidden City produces much the same sense of wonder as standing outside St. Basil's and gazing at the Kremlin fortress. Until the eighth year of Shunzhi in the Qing dynasty, the gate was known as Chengtianmen (Gate of Receiving Heaven Orders). It was long since Tiananmen by October 1, 1949, when Mao proclaimed the founding of the People's Republic of China from its rostrum. Mocking the events of 1989, Tiananmen means Gate of Heavenly Peace.

Across the road, the mammoth square, which sometimes accommodates 500,000 people, was lit like a park with globes, although standby klieg lights could turn the night into day at any hour. Kids had come there to kiss; littler kids to rollerblade and crash skateboards. Toward one boundary of the square, in the Chinese version of Lenin's Kremlin Kooler, the warty remains of Mao lounged in the Mao Zedong Memorial Hall. Just as in Russia, cynics suspect Madame Tussaud.

Alongside the Monument to the People's Heroes, where a uniformed sentry stood at ease, a specific warning was printed in English: "No spitting, throwing cigarette ends, waste paper, fruit skins and cores. No urination in the area." Could this really be the place where students stood up to tanks? "That one student at the tank," Dave said. "Where did he stand?"

We decided to save the Forbidden City for the next day, after our morning appointment with Zhou Minggong of the Beijing Olympic Committee.

A young cyclist talked us into hiring his rickshaw. He was drenched with sweat when we reached the Palace Hotel.

"Hi, I'm Annie," said a twenty-five-year-old Chinese Myrna Loy in black slacks and a white, long-sleeved blouse.

"Hello," I answered. "I'm Lin Phong."

"Is your name really Lin Phong?"

"Is your name really Annie?"

"I'm Xie Bin."

"I'm Tom Callahan. This is Dave Kindred. But you may call him Kubla Khan."

She smiled like a princess and we went into the conference room.

Fourteen easy chairs, each with a black lacquer table and a steaming teapot on a doily, were set up for the four of us. Zhou Minggong, Vice Chairman of the Media and Publicity Commission, wore a Slazenger golf shirt, a Gleneagles blazer and the look of a player. Xie Bin's title was Executive Secretary of the Commission, but her function here was as interpreter. Earlier, Dave and I had privately agreed to bring up Tiananmen last and to soft-pedal our opinion that, unless Olympic high pooh-bah Juan Antonio Samaranch was bucking for a Nobel Peace Prize, Beijing's chances for the 2000 Games were small. Tiananmen had pretty much settled that. All around the world, but particularly in the United States, editorial writers were drumming against China on human rights grounds.

We talked for a while about the Beijing Golf Club, where we had a tee time the next morning. Zhou explained that it had been constructed for the Asian Games in 1990 but really for the Olympics. He seemed not to have heard that Atlanta's plan to reinstate Olympic golf in 1996 had fallen through. But he knew 1900 and 1912 were the only previous Olympic tournaments, and it pleased him suddenly to think that China might have the opportunity to revive the sport.

"In 1991," he said through Xie, "a survey among Chinese people showed 91.6 percent supported Beijing's bid. In May this year, 98.7 percent supported the bid." (Here's to the 1.3 percent that still say no to government surveys.) "China is a special country. Very spaceful. Large population—22 percent of the world. Very kindhearted. Hospitable people. What better place to publicize the spirit of the Olympic movement? What better opportunity for the world to see us and know us, to share our long history of civilization and culture, to improve world peace? We need each other. Your technology. Our big market. It's something good."

Although Zhou was about to break into a patter on facilities and infrastructures, seventeen venues built and seven more to be built, Dave could resist no longer.

"What effect should the Tiananmen massacre have?"

"Since the Tiananmen accident in 1989," Xie translated carefully, "different people have different opinions. As time is passing, history itself will answer this problem. At the time, some Western media had exaggerated reports. I have some friends in the United States and France who tell me that, when the Tiananmen accident is talked about now, perceptions have already changed."

"So what is the truth?" Dave asked evenly. "Hundreds dead, thousands injured? How many pro-democracy demonstrators jailed? And how can it be reconciled with any ideal such as the Olympics?"

"But the Tiananmen accident," she continued to translate, "should be totally separate from Beijing's Olympic bid. Some people stick to the problem of the human record of China. They say one thousand are in prison because of the accident. This is not true."

"You keep saying 'accident,'" I interrupted. "Is this a difficulty of language? Do you mean 'incident'? You can't mean 'accident.'"

She didn't wait for Zhou to speak this time. "It's a difficulty of language," she said almost inaudibly, lowering her head and folding her hands into her lap.

For her sake, it seemed to me, Dave tried to think of something gentle to say. He mentioned the kindness of the people we had been encountering on the street, their curious eyes and ready laughter. "Yes," Zhou resumed with a sigh. "If you talk with the citizens, they do not talk too much about Tiananmen. What Chinese people are concerned with mostly these days is the economy. In the words of Den Xiaoping, China should adopt a policy of reform but base that reform on Chinese characteristics and Chinese realities. In a country so big, stability has to override everything else. It has to. China should go her own way in opening up to the world. China cannot fit everything of the Western style into her society."

We left it there. As "Annie" walked us out, I surmised, "If you were twenty-one in 1989, you must have been a student yourself."

"I was," she said, "at the Beijing Language Institute, an English student."

"And you didn't know or hear anything about Tiananmen?"

"I was too busy worrying about a job."

We parted at the elevator, but on the ground floor she came running out of the stairwell. This time, she wanted to speak for herself.

"If it's true," she said, "it's sad." As though this were costing her in some way, she added, "I think maybe something did happen." And she wanted us to know one other thing, about her Western name.

"I took 'Kathy' before 'Annie,'" she said. "We were permitted to choose for ourselves. But I decided I didn't like 'Kathy.' What does 'Annie' mean, do you know?"

"Yes," I lied. "It means 'Angel.'"

"Then it's a good name, isn't it?"

"For you, it is."

China's interest in the economy was evident both at the Forbidden City, where the back of the admission ticket was a Mitsubishi ad, and the Great Wall, where foreigners were charged a premium rate to enter an attraction originally designed to keep them out. China has two currencies, confusingly enough. You make your purchases with clean and crispy foreign exchange certificates (F.E.C.) and receive your change in oily renminbi (the "people's currency") as supple as chamois. Since we never ran across anybody who accepted renminbi, we were involuntarily cornering the renminbi market.

Allowing for a good deal of chipped and peeling red paint, the Forbidden City was almost as gilt and grand as it was portrayed in the movie *The Last Emperor.* The Chinese tourists ran their hands across the gold bumps on the red door with a special awe. Behind Mao's portrait, beyond the first of a domino line of palaces, hawkers peddled T-shirts while souvenir pavilions featured Qing gewgaws and Ming gimcracks. Past the second imperial palace, two full-size basketball courts appeared as out of a dream. In our world cavalcade of recurring American reference points, Michael Jordan had already left Mickey Mouse, Marilyn Monroe, Ronald Reagan and the Washington Redskins in the dust. These courts, however, were unsigned.

Two or three more palaces on, when we were stuffed to the panting gills with carved dragons and stone lions, we turned around and headed for the Wall, pausing only at Beiha Lake to watch an old man impersonating "a carp leaping over a gate." Once this was the "basin of heavenly water," where emperors prayed for longevity. Now it is the commoners' swimming hole, where amiable ancients like Wang Guiyuan, the "king of flotsam," celebrate the fact of it. "Give me food and a book and I can float for a day," said the king of flotsam.

Our section of the Wall was a less-traveled part at Mutian Valley about an hour's drive from Tiananmen. At the base of the mountain range at Mutianyu, a sign advised: "You will have greater pleasure and you will be a true hero if you take the cable car." Eying the burros grazing nearby, I told Dave, "You know, I always wanted to be a true hero." Noticing a camel among the burros, he nodded. "Yeah, me too." We heroically sprang for the cable car, this time a closed gondola.

Opposed to walking any time he can ride, Kindred came upon an unattended ski chair at the Sarajevo Winter Olympics in 1984 and offered me a lift up snowy Mount Bjelasnica. Those hatchet-faced birdmen were about to lean into the sky.

"Do you know what you're doing?" I inquired reasonably.

"Absolutely," he said.

Up into the frozen fog we floated, higher than either of us anticipated, until we felt like angels on grappling hooks. As we continued to climb, the chair gradually gave way beneath us, leaving us hanging by our respective poles with our legs dangling like deceased horse thieves.

"Is this more dangerous than you expected?" Dave asked cheerfully, hugging his pole.

I couldn't say. As a matter of fact, I couldn't speak.

It wasn't until a rider passed by going the opposite way that we simultaneously glanced up and pulled down the crossbar that locks the seat and holds you in.

A Mongol met us at the top in full battle regalia. For a small fee, he was available to appear menacing, even murderous, in a Polaroid. For just a pittance more, he would outfit us in our own cardboard armor and throw in stringy black beards on the pagoda. That is, on the house. If we were in a hurry, we could simply pop our heads into the face-holes of the plywood

Mongols he had lined up in a horde. I think I may owe St. Andrews an apology.

Some 1,500 miles of barricade, the only human installation detectable from outer space, rose and fell with the contours of the heavily wooded mountain pass as it wound its way magnificently out of sight. Sitting on a turret step, leaning on his fist like Dobie Gillis, Dave was worrying, "How are we going to hit a ball off this?" when a light went on over his covered head. "Wait a minute," he said, peeking up. "I got it."

At a relatively level stretch of the Great Wall of China, he doffed his precious "Wanderers" cap, fluffed it up on the rock ground and balanced a golf ball on the button. "Are you sure you want to do this?" I asked. He dialed his adjustable club to an 8-iron and said: "Keep an eye on it."

I have to admit, it flew majestically. Not the ball, the bill of his cap. Just the bill. The rest of the cap hit the side barrier and came back. He beheld it as a small boy might a Christmas puppy under a taxicab.

I shrugged fairly sensitively. Mumbling, "Since it's already dead . . . ," I bunched up a ball and took my own slash at history. Somewhere in the heavy undergrowth of Mutianyu, two dimpled orbs are waiting to drive the anthropologists nuts.

Back at the base of the mountain, where the T-shirt salesmen were once again in full voice, a kid pantomimed for permission to try Dave's club. Just as the kid was about to powder a rock, Dave dropped him a ball and, without even a practice swing, he slammed it straight into a cement drain for a hole in one. This is an easy game.

On the way there, we had swerved past a lot of open-air pool tables on a boulevard the driver identified as Singshun. On the way back, we pulled over at one of the busiest tables, wanting only to watch. But cue sticks were quickly extended and a new rack was drawn. Under a leafy tree, in a rustling breeze, on a lopsided table of frayed and faded felt, Dave proceeded to demonstrate his misspent youth.

I scarcely got off a shot. Dave called it in the corner, made it in the side, off this combination and that. All of the eyebrows around the table curled up. Then all of the grins came out. When he potted the final ball, they clapped warmly. He made a debonair bow and tossed the stick on the table like Willie Mosconi or Rudolph Wanderone.

That was the happiest I'd seen Dave look since long before he bludgeoned his hat to death. I had a bad feeling about the Diabolical hole coming up in the morning.

The Diabolical's Fourteenth Hole
437 Yards, Par 4

"Enjoy the beauty of semi-nature and semi-artificiality. Beijing International Golf Club."

This wasn't where we were going, but it was such an honest billboard that we stopped off anyway. We had heard a slander that the International (the *other* course) was a comical monstrosity, meticulously drawn up in yards but inadvertently carved out in meters (if not precisely a Frankenstein at least something of a pituitary case). Well, it looked nicely proportioned and ruggedly handsome to us. Regarding country club politics, capitalistic instincts may have already descended on China.

At Beijing Golf Club, the J. Michael Poellot course on our agenda, a nearsighted little gentleman in a club tie and navy blazer suggested: "Since golf began before the Industrial Revolution, and for that matter predates the concepts of either capitalism or socialism, perhaps we shouldn't think of its arrival in China as pertinent to any political circumstance. By the way, 'revival' would be a better word than 'arrival.' As you know, China invented golf. That is to say, a very similar game was played in the imperial court of China long before it was known in Scotland. China was the very first country to play a game using one club, one ball and one hole."

The speaker, Mashiko Kunihiro, was Japanese. He was the president of Beijing Golf Club, which figured. Ninety percent of its members and guests are Japanese businessmen stationed in Beijing. "The Chinese people will take their place quickly, though," he predicted. "Golf is an inner game. It's a fight within yourself. Like the Japanese, the Chinese revel in inner games. And they're even keener about winning. They're very concerned about that. If Mao were alive, he should start playing right away. Deng, I'm afraid, may not have quite enough time to learn. In any case, he would not wish to run into Zhao Ziyang on the golf course."

Mr. Kunihiro was obviously a scamp, but some of his humor needed translating. "You don't know Zhao?" he said, a little appalled. "He's the former Prime Minister of China. Deng fired him for splitting the leadership and necessitating the Tiananmen crackdown. He's our best Chinese player here at the club."

"What does he shoot?" Dave asked.

"Eighty-nine, fifteen more than his age."

"Let me at him," I said. "Does he take renminbi?"

Mashiko accompanied us to the first tee, where Dave topped his drive, clouted a mulligan into a fairway bunker and knocked a 5-wood out of the sand three inches from the hole. "Mark that, will you?" I said. "Never mind, it's good. Nice 5." The battle was joined.

Only because we were in China was the golf course notable. On the same plot in New Jersey, we would have said, "Nice course, lushly green, maybe a little undermowed." And rather long. Three of the par 3s were over 200 yards and three of the par 5s reached 575. The lady caddies, wimpled like flying nuns, recommended a lot of 3-woods.

When Arnold Palmer designed the first Chinese layout just across from Hong Kong, he claims in the latter stages of the project to have received a telegram from the Chinese investors, saying: "Money running scarce. Are greens absolutely necessary?"

These greens weren't only necessary but impeccable. And whoever cut the cups that morning knew what she or he was doing.

Our hole was the 437-yard par-4 fifth, straightaway but not really. A tall forest crowded the left perimeter adjacent to the landing area and, a little farther on, a single spreading tree stymied any second shots launched from the right side—even from the fairway. Just when I thought there was no place to drive it, Dave hit the perfect drive, long and snug to the left side of the fairway. I hit a 3-wood hard but just far enough right to have no second shot around the tree. After I hit a good 8-iron over it, I had fifty yards left.

Dave, meanwhile, hit a 4-iron dead on the flag but five yards short of the green. The pin was in front too, in a swirling little swale. It was better to be off the green than past the hole.

I missed the green to the right with a wedge, killing the suspense, and then chipped it strong to two feet above the hole. My hope now was for Dave to chip in or knock it close enough to tap in so at least my bogey could be conceded. Being careful to stay under the hole, he stubbed a pitching wedge to a foot. Good. A 4 and a 5. For the first time since way back at St. Andrews, the margin that twice had been three holes was down to a measly one with four to play. It was a match.

What we were playing for had long since been decided, but we'll get to that later. It's more than renminbi.

CHAPTER 15

CALEDONIAN
GOLF CLUB
Tokyo, Japan

Where R2D2 Tends Hayakawa-san's Small Gardens

THREE DAYS IN Japan reminded me that even a man who loves the pain of golf can get enough of Scotland's heather, gorse and whin. Those bushes with sweet names are the Devil's own bouquet. Those evil little spiny plants are grown in hell's hothouse and taken to linksland golf courses by the Prince of Darkness himself. There he waits, laughing.

I know this. Tom knows this. We have hit balls into heather, gorse and whin. There's no getting out once you get in. Your best prayer-slash leaves you with a wedge bent at the hosel, after which your wrists require medication, if not a siege of drunkenness. These weeds are part of a dark plan. The sage Alistair Cooke says the plan is based on Calvinist religious doctrine that man is meant to suffer here below and never more than when he goes out to enjoy himself. As the English golfing laureate Peter

Dobereiner told us before our journey, "The Scotch have much to answer for."

Peter's words came back to me on our first night in Japan. Two months
past Royal Portrush, I could feel Northern Ireland's murderous weeds
ripping the soles off my shoes. I could hear the roar of the devouring
Carnoustie beast, its hairy chest heaving under the tattoo: GODDAMMIT!
Leeches nibbling Tom's ankles at Major Sam's in Kathmandu and white-
throated vultures circling Tollygunge—these are the Devil's hired hands,
sent out to make a golfer's lot miserable.

Old Tom Morris had been sent to my room at the Caledonian Golf
Club. There he stood, about to hit a tee shot. In the portrait above my
bed, the St. Andrews hero stood as a bearded, unsmiling, miserable figure
stuffed into a tightly buttoned suit with the look of horsehair to it. The
temptation was to shout, "Get thee behind me, Old Tom." Instead, I went
to my bedroom window and drew back the curtains—to a revelation.

From the window I saw a landscape ghostly and beautiful. Caledonian's
eighteenth green was just beneath the window. The eighteenth's white-
sand bunkers glowed in a bright light which seemed to rise from the earth.
The light struck the green's ridges. Black shadows fell on the low spots.
The light danced on a lake and across the lake to the thirteenth green.
There I could see white sand from the green all the way to the water's
edge, the sands both bunker and beach.

It was midnight and I looked for the source of the light. It came from
behind the eighteenth green where someone with the soul of an artist had
planted a string of floodlights. As it happened, the someone had majored
in aesthetics at Keio University in the late 1950s. He had studied art,
music, design and philosophy as it related to physical beauty. After a turn
in Japan's steel-making industry, he found his proper place in golf. Since
1971, Haruyoshi Hayakawa had taken land and caused it to become art.

Every day on this happy voyage we learned again that we knew almost
nothing. The *Japan Times* reported that golf is the newest status symbol
in the Czech Republic's "rush to embrace every aspect of capitalism from
the mobile phone to BMWs. From a still-unbuilt club outside Prague that
charges more than $3,000 for membership to the 18-hole course in the
lush woods above the elegant spa town of Marianne Lazne, golf epito-
mizes the new challenge of capitalist self-improvement: getting, or at least
acting, rich.

" 'We want to move toward the West,' " Otakar Jurecka, vice chairman of Investicni Banka, the Czechs' third-biggest, said. 'We know it's not possible without golf.' "

Even in Vietnam, near Ho Chi Minh City, the Song Be Golf Club began construction with plans to charge $20,000 for memberships. The boss of the local Communist party, Do Muoi, a seventy-six-year-old duck hunter, "was very impressed and surprised by the beauty of the golf course that's taking shape," the *Japan Times* reported.

And Japan taught us more. I expected the golf to be crowded, slow and expensive. It was all of that. I didn't expect the extraordinary blend of order and beauty. Certainly, the Japanese are famous for just such precision. Yet, as in Calcutta, until you see it and feel it and smell it yourself, it's only a thought. Setting foot on Haruyoshi Hayakawa's golf courses made the thought real. These courses were delights to be savored by any golfer any time. Seeing his landscape at midnight, I made a note: "Golf in Scotland is punishment. In Japan it is pleasure."

Hayakawa built Caledonian from a design by Mike Poellot, the Californian whose work we first encountered at Beijing. The thirteenth, a par 4, and the long eighteenth are masterpieces. As you walk the fairways, the holes seem to be pastel paintings with every brush stroke important. They also test skill and nerve by asking: If you get to the right spot, can you fly a shot over that lake and over the beach bunkers to the green?

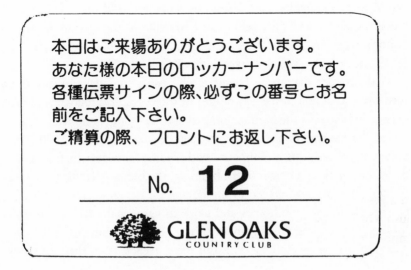

To sustain the pleasure of the thirteenth and eighteenth, Hayakawa set floodlights to burn all night. A Japanese course should have the feel of "a walk through small gardens," he said one afternoon at his Tomisato Golf Club. There Hayakawa's wife, Hatsue, almost holed a 4-iron tee shot, doing a little hop of her own as the ball bounced off the flagstick. Later she drifted away to inspect to inspect a riot of purple petunias planted according to her blueprint.

Dropping golf balls behind them, England's colonialists of the nineteenth century moved the game from Europe to Africa to Asia—but never to Japan, which was closed to imperialists because it was building an empire itself. In 1929, a century after Royal Calcutta's opening, Japan built its first world-class course, Kasumigaseki Golf Club, just outside Tokyo. That course and Torakichi (Pete) Nakamura's 1957 victory in the Canada Cup are the historical underpinnings of Japan's golf frenzy. By 1993 there were 1,934 golf courses in Japan (540 near Tokyo) with 116 being built.

The curious truth is that most Japanese golfers never set foot on a golf course. Of 12 million players, maybe 2 million play a real round. The others can't afford it. Instead, they pay $20 an hour to bat lopsided balls from the upper stories of Japan's ubiquitous multilevel driving ranges.

Because Japan is so small and mountainous, only five percent of its land can be used for agriculture. Land, then, is too precious to be used for much else. Golf courses are usually cut into hillsides where construction requires massive earth moving that drives costs to $30 million, six times the average U.S. cost. As a result, there are few public courses, and private-club memberships cost a fortune. They are sold on Tokyo's stock market, Caledonian's once selling for $600,000. At the time of our trip, a visitor's weekday greens fee at Caledonian was $200. Weekends were $300. Caddies cost $40 and taxes added $40.

Small wonder that those Japanese who can afford the pleasure often turn a round of golf into a way of life. At those prices, a fellow would not change his shoes in the parking lot, play a three-hour round with a candy bar at the halfway house and hurry back to the office. For $600,000, a Japanese golfer wants a clubhouse with ceilings fifty feet high and windows the length and height of the building, the better to frame the beauty of the golf course at his feet. (Mike Poellot on Japanese clubhouses: "As the people live in tiny homes and work in very small offices, they look forward to spending time in what really are huge monuments.")

In the end, a fellow expects a full day's escape from the real world.

Such a day might begin when you look out your Caledonian Club bedroom window at 6:30 A.M. You see the eighteenth. You see the lake. The sunlight is soft and warm already. You see women at work. They walk in the beach bunkers at the thirteenth hole. They pick up the night's fallen leaves.

Then:

8:15 A.M. — Breakfast.

9 A.M. — Hit balls.

9:37 A.M. — Tee time for first nine holes.

Noon — Full lunch in the club restaurant.

1:37 P.M. — Tee time for second nine.

4:33 P.M. — End of round, beginning of Japanese bath procedure. Shower in hot water, rinse in cold while sitting on a little stool, after which you throw your body into a hot tub twenty-five feet long. The tub is more a pool, really. With a third-story window running its full length, the pool seems to be part of the sky.

5:15 P.M. — Float in the sky pool of poaching waters. Close your eyes. Say, "Toto, I don't think we're in Kathmandu any more."

5:25 P.M. — Float some more, occasionally turning your head to admire the panorama of the golf course far below.

5:30 P.M. — Get help to lift your limp body out of the hot tub.

6 P.M. — Ask the Hayakawas if you can pay in installments, maybe a dollar a year for 600,000 years.

Spirited from our hotel near Narita International Airport by Hayakawa's relentlessly hospitable lieutenant, Minoru Sakamoto, we were taken to the Caledonian Club's guesthouse and shown to suites where my biggest problem was deciding which of the three beds to sleep in. Between the two bedrooms was a bath as large as most hotel rooms. A silk dressing robe had been placed just so on my bed pillow.

At dinner that night, Japan's Rising Sun flag shared the table's center with the Stars and Stripes of the United States. Women in silk kimonos glided around the room. They moved so silently as to arrive unseen. Toasts of welcome and thanks were made. Food was served: needlefish and crab, shrimp sushi, cooked sweetfish, gingko nuts, soup made of snapping turtle with spring onion and ginger.

As we removed our shoes and slid our legs under the polished table for dinner with the Hayakawas, Sakamoto and the club's senior manager, Kosuke Takasu, a woman in silk whispered into my ear, "Sake?" She was at my shoulder, unseen until that moment.

"Surely," I said.

"So," I thought, "this is how emperors lived."

"Dave-san, you like the sake?" Haruyoshi Hayakawa said.

"Surely," I said even as living flame licked against the sides of my throat.

More food appeared, delivered by silent women in stocking feet: turbot with seaweed and chrysanthemum, lily bulb cake, tilefish with beans, sea bream.

Hayakawa-san's son sat alongside the father. The son is a graduate of New York's Pace University, newly married to a New Jersey woman. "She is homesick a little," the son said. "Also culture-shocked a little. Our apartment is small and here we cannot have a car, it is so expensive both for the car and for the apartment parking permit which we must show to be allowed to buy a car."

Sake appeared, and whispers on stocking feet, and food was delivered: baked clam and matsutake mushroom, sea eel, shiitake mushroom and honewort, Japanese noodles with herring, pears.

In time, and not very much time, the sake began to speak. It was given voice by Tom. He was so charmed by the smiling Mrs. Hayakawa that he now said to her son, "Is she really your mother? Hatsue is not nearly old enough to be your mother."

From around the table came laughter and then Sakamoto made a gesture with his hands. He turned a crank above his left palm: the Japanese signal of excessive flattery. "We call it 'crushing the sesames,'" Sakamoto said.

Thousands of sesames were crushed into metaphorical powder before the sake ran dry that night. We all became handsomer and lovelier and cleverer by half. The Hayakawas declared they liked Americans most of all foreigners because they are so bright and so open-minded. Tom and I declared Caledonian Golf Club one of the absolute best golf courses in the world, certainly No. 1 on the Royal & Diabolical tour.

"When you come to America next, you must let us know," Tom said. "We must return your kindnesses and hospitalities."

Then the smiling Hayakawas led us from the dining table and outside, where under a sky full of stars we walked in the ghostly light and stood on the eighteenth green looking across the lake to the white beach bunkers at the thirteenth. And there I changed my mind about this being the way emperors lived. Emperors didn't have it so good.

The great Texas sports columnist Blackie Sherrod rode in the belly of a torpedo bomber over Hiroshima a few days after the atomic bomb. He saw the earth barren and covered with a dust the color of iron rust. A green city had been made into a pale red desert. There were skeletons of trees here and there. He saw a broken stone wall where a building used to be.

Blackie said that even through the turret of the plane he seemed to smell a strange, musty odor, "like of old houses, dark and shuttered against the outside." He never forgot what the United States did to Japan or what Japan did to the United States. All these years later, Blackie would not, I imagine, grind sesames at a dinner table where the Rising Sun shared space with the Stars and Stripes.

Minoru Sakamoto's eyebrows looked like white arcs above his wide eyes. The stocky little man, smiling and bowing, moved like a humming-bird, ready to dart in several directions simultaneously. He became friends with Hiroyushi Hayakawa when both men majored in aesthetics at Keio University. As Hayakawa's Tokyo Green Company grew, he reached out for his university friend. In the summer of 1993, Sakamoto was Hayaka-wa's general manager.

"Is there anything besides golf you would like to do in Japan?" Saka-moto asked us.

I said, "Not really. You've done too much already."

"Please say."

By now we had figured one thing out. We offended our Japanese hosts more by turning down invitations than by asking for them. So I said, "A baseball game, maybe?"

Whooooosh, the next afternoon we were on a train speeding from Nar-ita Airport to the downtown TokyoDome. Because the shiny ballpark's roof made it look like one, the place was known as Big Egg. That night we saw an important Pacific League game between the Seibu Lions and Nippon Ham Fighters.

Even before entering the Big Egg, we saw a T-shirt that told us we had moved from a Steinbrennerian culture to one allowing more possibilities. The T-shirt's legend read:

My Team Has Never Won,
But That's All Right.
I Love Baseball.

You can drop a buck or two in the Big Egg. Game tickets for our seats thirty rows up on the first base side cost $38. Japanese dinners in boxes with chopsticks cost $13, a beer $8, hot dogs $3.80. For $10 a minute a vendor passing through the aisles of the 40,000-seat palace would rent you a cellular telephone.

The baseball was very good. The scoreboard showed the velocity of every pitch, most in the 85-mph range. Good, but still a shade below American major league quality. Because Japanese players are smaller than Americans—a six-footer is a big man in Tokyo—the ball moves more slowly out of their hands and off their bats. Everything seemed a step slower than America's best.

At one point, three Japanese women in our section of seats put arms around each other and posed for a photograph. They all wore baseball jerseys: the Yankees, the Pirates and the Braves.

On the train back to Caledonian that night, Minoru Sakamoto, who himself had never been to the TokyoDome, took a nap. He woke up smiling after eight minutes.

There were the pop-up Panasonic television screens at each seat on the Japan Air Lines plane from Beijing to Tokyo. En route to the TokyoDome, we saw WELCOME projected in red blinking lights onto the tunnel wall from our train even as it sped toward the city.

So, as much as the Japanese love electronic gadgets, we shouldn't have been surprised at the golf course. But Tom said, "Dave, look at this. Our caddy's R2D2."

If not exactly the *Star Wars* little squawking robot, it was close enough. The $10,000 golf cart seemed to have a mind of its own. The thing carried your clubs. It rolled through the rough, around the greens and on to the next tee. It did this on narrow strips of concrete laid over wires which transmitted radio signals. R2D2 stopped and started on remote-control commands from a transmitter on the belt of your caddy.

(About Japan's women caddies: they were fabulous. Your caddy was likely to be a thirtysomething mother who put her children in the club's day-care program so she could earn $36,000 a year running R2D2 and telling you, "Keep it reft." In which case, you should keep it left because these women knew everything. With no more information than the sight of a broken-down sportswriter, my caddy knew about the seven thimbles of sake the night before. She knew the scribbler would hit a 5-iron 151 yards with a push-fade.)

Of Japan's gadgets, only one worried me.

It came with a label, HOW TO USE, but I was afraid to touch it.

I counted the lines of instruction on its use. There were thirteen lines of instruction. Then I counted the number of diagrams illustrating its use. There were twenty-seven diagrams. It had a red button here and a white button there. Hidden under a removable cover was a black lever to be used if all the buttons failed.

On the side of the thing, an arrow pointed to little holes called BEAM RECEPTOR WINDOWS. What beams, I wondered, and where would they come from? Why would they be received in my room? This was beginning to read like a Tom Clancy technobabble novel.

Users were told how to heat the seat. In capital letters, we were told about FACILITATING USE OF WATER FROM THE REAR.

These instructions and diagrams were written in English. Under those instructions were more instructions, only these were written in Japanese. There were thirteen more lines of how to do it and twenty-seven diagrams of where to do it along with all those arrows pointing to the beam receptor windows, not to mention the rear-water-facilitating options. This was Tom Clancy indecipherable in Japanese.

To read these instructions and to study the diagrams, I was on my knees in a very small room. I had never seen a toilet seat just like this one.

I have been in truck stops, biker bars and my grandmother's half-moon privy. Looking for friends of a dope dealer who turned up murdered/floating in the Kentucky River, I once frequented a pool hall where the man at the cash register had a pearl-handled revolver on his hip and slapped a log chain against his thigh. "Nice place," I said, "you got a men's room?"

Usually toilet seats are simple deals. You put the lid down, you sit

down. Not with this Japanese thing. It had red buttons and white buttons
and beam receptors and twenty-six lines of instruction and fifty-four diagrams in two languages. Moses coming off the mountain didn't carry so
many instructions.

The thing looked like a jet fighter's ejection seat.

You sit on this deal wrong and who knows? One bad flush and a guy
is history.

The writer James Fallows has said no one visits Japan and remains the
same person. If that's so in our case, it's because of the Hayakawas and
especially Minoru Sakamoto, who made Japan unforgettable for two Yank
sportswriters. The morning of our final day in Japan, when he had delivered us to another club that invited us in, he offered to confirm our airline reservations.

At the finish of our play that day, a fax message waited at a locker
assigned to us.

Dear Dave-san and Tom-san,

Your flight reservations of Delta Airlines #52 have been confirmed.

Please forgive me for not staying there with you until you depart
for the States. I think I should be reserved to do so, as you are Glen
Oaks' guests today.

I hope to see you again here in Japan or in the States someday in
the future.

Have a nice trip!

Sakamoto

The Diabolical's Fifteenth Hole
374 Yards, Par 4

From a high tee, Caledonian Golf Club's dogleg-right thirteenth plays
374 yards around the lake decorated with beach bunkers.

You have your choice. The nearer you drive it to the lake, the shorter
your second shot—albeit a second shot over water and sand to a shallow,
two-level green. On our day, the pin was all the way back on the upper

level. Oh, and you should know: drive it on the short-way line and a good one rolls into the lake.

On the other hand, driving left of those dangers created new dangers. The second shot is very long to a narrow opening of a green with water at its right edge.

The thirteenth, then, combined the elements that make Caledonian memorable. It delivered pleasure in the form of unblemished beauty. (Imagine Augusta National, only more carefully tended.) And it asked all the questions which reveal a player's game and character. Experts say Kasumigaseki Golf Club and Hirono Golf Club have Japan's best courses. Maybe they are as good as Caledonian. They can be no better. It is impossible to do the important things better than Caledonian does them.

If the reader heard in the previous paragraph the whispers of a lovestruck player, the reader perhaps guessed that the player liked his tee shot at the thirteenth. It works that way. Our life's vision often depends on how we hit our most recent shot. No one ever burned down an orphanage after breaking 80 for the first time. It would be no surprise to this reporter to learn that Lizzie Borden hit forty straight ground-ball tee shots before taking forty whacks with her ax.

So, yes, my drive on the thirteenth was a good one down the middle and left me 143 yards to the pin.

Tom's drive, popped up, came down on the fairway's left side. When he asked our caddy for a 5-iron, she said, "Two hundred yards, sir."

We had grown accustomed to being wrong while the caddy was always right. At Tomisato the day before, what do I hear when I'm about to hit a sixty-foot putt? I hear, "Hey, hey, hey." My caddy, in her pale green uniform, her face all but hidden under her bonnet, immaculate in her white gloves, is shouting, "Hey, hey, hey." She is pointing to a spot eight feet right of my chosen line. "That much break?" I say. She says, "Ya, ya." I take her advice. The ball stops two inches from the hole. I bow.

So at Caledonian, when the choice was trusting himself or the caddy, Tom put aside the 5-iron in favor of a 5-wood, which he hit very hard and very high, drawing it over the water and bouncing it off the green to a spot maybe thirty-five feet from the cup, altogether a sensational shot.

My second, a 6-iron, faded to the center of the green. I had a 10-footer for a birdie.

Tom hit a good pitch shot from heavy grass by a drain, dropping a wedge on the ball and popping it up so it rolled dead a foot away. An easy par.

My putt stayed out on the left. A happy par. Through fifteen holes, Tom stayed one up.

CHAPTER 16

PEBBLE BEACH

Pebble Beach, California

Where We Wanted to Shout, to Run Rather Than Walk

"Why so?"

"Because tomorrow — is Sunday!"

"Monday," replied Mr. Fogg.

"No — today — is Saturday."

"Saturday? Impossible!"

"Yes, yes, yes, yes!" cried Passepartout. "You have made a mistake of one day! We arrived twenty-four hours ahead of time; but there are only ten minutes left!"

THE INTERNATIONAL DATELINE that saved Phileas Fogg allowed us to rise on a Sunday morning, drive from the Caledonian to Glen Oaks, play golf, have lunch, play golf again, have a bath, drive to the airport, fly the Pacific from Tokyo to Oregon and arrive back in the

United States on the same Sunday morning. Could the whole journey have been just a dream?

In the middle of the crossing, in the dark of the cabin, the reverse culture shock began to assert itself when a Japanese traveler one row ahead asked permission to tilt back his seat. Where we were going, this is not the custom. We arrived in Portland to find the San Francisco connection delayed four hours. An officious Delta agent acted as if everyone's destination was out of his way. We were home.

From San Francisco finally, we drove to Monterey, a gleaming ride that repaired our hopes. As the "Duke of Del Monte," Samuel Finley Breese Morse, liked to say, "the effect of the Monterey Peninsula is to make one want to shout, to run rather than walk." If you can feel this way in an automobile, Dave and I did.

Morse, the dot-and-dash heir, a grandnephew actually, sired the Pebble Beach Golf Links in the early twenties. An attorney named David Jacks owned the property first. The city of Monterey had deeded it to him some fifty years earlier to settle an $1,100 legal bill. That surveyed out to about fifteen cents an acre. Shrewdly he sold to the railroads for $5.00 an acre. A young attorney, Morse, subsequently dispatched by the Southern Pacific and Central Pacific to liquidate an unprofitable holding, fell in love with it instead.

Particularly smitten with the seven miles of coastline (although it did set his new company back almost $185 an acre), he commissioned California amateur champion Jack Neville to codesign a golf course with God. Then, being an old Yale football captain, Morse spent half a century drop-kicking real estate developers off the cliffs.

Since 1978 the course has passed from Twentieth Century-Fox ($72 million) to Marvin Davis ($150 million) to Minoru Isutani ($841 million) to Masatsugu Takabayashi ($500 million—not so good, Mr. Isutani) and soared and swooped and soared again through various phases of glory and neglect and glory again, never losing its three essential charms: its public status, being the only U. S. Open course the people can play; its natural character, resisting the overdevelopers at every cove; and the sea.

This stop (and Augusta to come) was very much in the spirit of our paean to St. Andrews. Some churches simply require you to drop by and light a candle. In the case of Pebble Beach, our sole interest was the golf course. We stayed in the designer town of Carmel and thought of dining at Clint Eastwood's old Hog's Breath Inn. But there was a two-hour backup and that's just too long to wait for hog's breath. We ate at a pie house and ached for the morning.

Both of us had played Pebble before. Once, I competed in the AT & T Pro-Am, which spreads itself liberally over Spyglass Hill, Poppy Hills and Pebble Beach in a piny, deer-laden preserve called 17-Mile Drive. (Were Cypress Point still in the rota, we could say "spreads itself conservatively." Cypress was dropped because its black membership was holding so steadily at none.) By then, though, the tournament wasn't the Crosby any more, and it wasn't the same.

Bing Crosby died in 1977 on a golf course in Spain. Bobby Jones, Dwight Eisenhower, Arnold Palmer and Hope-and-Crosby probably represented the "first foursome" in the selling of American golf. One blowy January at the Crosby—just about the only kind Monterey has—Jack Murphy called to offer: "Would you like to go with me to see Bing?" Jack had arranged a private audience.

Crosby was a curious interview. While neither the complete De Sade of his first family's memory nor the grandfatherly sage of the second wave, Crosby alternated between both characters almost minute to minute. First he would be up, happy, loquacious—vain about his vocabulary. Then he would curse the minions who were screwing up his clambake and stare away for long, uncomfortable moments like the dipsomaniacal actor in *The Country Girl*. Only while discussing the grounds themselves was he Father O'Malley.

"This place isn't just the Louvre," he said. "It's everything that's in the Louvre too, with all the artists gathered round." He wrinkled his nose at Bob Hope's alternate description: "Alcatraz with grass." But he nearly smiled when Murphy repeated the remark of another celebrity in the Pro-Am ("I've never been so wet in all my life") and then identified the speaker as Johnny Weissmuller.

Golf was a prop to Hope, but a serious matter to Crosby, who didn't live to see his last son win the U. S. Amateur Championship. (In the gallery at the final match, Nathaniel Crosby's mother wore a man's hat, old and brown and strangely familiar.) Crosby last competed in his own tournament in 1956, when the weather was especially Icelandic. He and his pro partner were hopelessly over the 54-hole cut line by Saturday afternoon as they leaned into slanting sheets of freezing rain near Bing's home adjacent to the thirteenth fairway.

"Ben," Crosby said, "we can pack it in right here and have a drink in the house."

"If you don't mind," Hogan replied, "I'd rather play it out." That was Hogan's final round at the Crosby. He shot 81.

Pebble's famous gentle beginning was even more placid than usual. I hit the first three greens and two-putted them all for pars. Dave made a twelve-footer for par at No. 1 and then an eight-footer for birdie at two. Our hearts were singing.

We had fallen in with a genial pair of Los Angelenos, Rodney Scully (no kin to Vin) and Fred Meyer, whose attractive sidekicks, a pair of cheerleading wives, worked heroically to simulate a full gallery. Scully and Meyer played nicely but had hoped to play better than they can and establish a lasting memory. Under that kind of pressure, they naturally butchered a few shots. When they did, they moped more than a little, reminding us of less virulent cases of ourselves two months before.

Testing my new serenity (a bit too testily), I followed a perfect drive at the short No. 4 with a cold-shanked wedge and a triple-bogey 7. But, relatively unflustered, I hit a 4-iron into the middle of the next green for another par. For some reason, I was momentarily incapable of sustaining bitterness. The same could be said for Dave. Where had all our anger gone? The crystal day was part of it.

We bogeyed the sixth, the par 5 that starts Pebble's drama, where the world plunges away to the right and, on a rock island just offshore, seals slap their flippers deliriously while otters noisily shuck shells. Empty golf carts with the brakes unengaged are known to meander from as far away as the thirteenth hole, steal slowly across the sixth fairway and plummet— clubs, cigarettes, wristwatches and all—into the churning ocean.

A persistent Pebble Beach legend has it that two unobservant Japanese gentlemen drove blissfully down the middle of the eighth fairway and straight off the cliff to their deaths. Even their midair epithet has somehow been recorded for posterity (an obscene expression of abject betrayal always related in a combination English-Japanese tongue). After researching all of this thoroughly, R. J. Harper, the head pro, found no corpses at the foot of any Pebble Beach precipices, just one rather badly beaten-up survivor.

"There was a fellow once at No. 8 who, leaning over the cliff, retrieved his own ball but then spotted another one just a few inches farther down—"

Wouldn't Aesop be enjoying this?

"—and, holding on to a twig branch with one hand, he reached for it with the other. He fell about 150 feet, but only broke an arm and a leg. Carts roll off all the time, of course. Particularly, for some reason, at six."

The 107-yard seventh is a darling, obstreperous little downhill terrier. Connoisseurs are amused by its impertinence. Depending on the gale force, the tee shot may be a wedge, an 8-iron or a knockdown 4-iron. I hit a wedge into the crevice of a rock on the starboard side of the little green, thereby averting a swim to Ecuador. Dave hit the back of the green for a good par. Meyer almost hit the hole and blissfully made his 2 for that memory he was needing. The wives danced and clapped like leprechauns.

We'll come back to the eighth, the Diabolical hole. Our friend Peter Andrews fervently hoped we parred it. "I love reading about stuff like that," said the bright particular star of *American Heritage,* "just as I love reading about men who have won the favors of Catherine Deneuve. It may not be immediately useful to me, but it does have a certain anecdotal value and I am delighted to know that it can be done."

The pro Hubert Green, a Howdy Doody figure who speaks without moving his lips—and also won a U. S. Open—has concluded at nine (464-yard par 4) that "the farther you hit your drive, the worst shape you're in." Dave and I both hit respectable drives into complete misery. Ten, another tightrope along the escarpment, is quicker poison. I actually chipped in there for a par. I have no idea how.

A sand trap got in the way of Dave's pleasure at eleven, but he almost birdied the 202-yard par-3 twelfth, and I one-putted to par it. At thirteen, fourteen and fifteen, we contented ourselves with fighting off seagulls and looking for such famous landmarks as "the roots of Palmer's evil." In the process of making a quadruple-bogey 9, Arnold twice clunked the same tree at fourteen. Overnight, it was splintered into smithereens by lightning, appearing to establish definitively who was God's favorite golfer.

At sixteen, Scully hit a poem of a drive he could take home with him and keep forever. Basking in his glow, I had eight-footers for birdie at both sixteen and seventeen, missing first left and then right. One can no more stand on the seventeenth tee without imagining Jack Nicklaus in 1972 than stand on the seventeenth green without picturing Tom Watson in 1982.

While a psychology student at Stanford, Watson was given to rushing to Pebble after classes to play only the last few holes alone in the fading light. "All right," he'd say to himself at the seventeenth tee, "you have to birdie one of the last two to beat Nicklaus in the Open." When he chipped in at seventeen to do just that, and scored a birdie at eighteen for good measure, the point was made that God has more than one favorite.

At the par-5 eighteenth, the most recognizable of all finishing holes, the driving options are four: hook it into the ocean, draw it into the fairway, push it into the rough or slice it into the neighbors' backyard. During the AT & T, I had the benefit of a Texas teaching pro and Harvey Penick protégé named Chuck Cook, whose serious business that week was to tutor Tom Kite and Payne Stewart. On a lark, he also caddied for me. Standing on the eighteenth tee, I didn't know what to do.

"I'll give you $1,000," Cook whispered, "if you hook it big into the ocean."

"What?" I said.

"But it's got to be big, way by the rest of these bums."

That took all of my fear away. Plus, I suddenly noticed the wind was howling from the left. I couldn't hook it into the ocean if I tried. I drew it perfectly 283 yards to a little blue disk sunk in the fairway. As the disk proclaimed, exactly 265 yards remained to be navigated. I puffed my chest and reached for my 3-wood.

"Don't be ridiculous," Cook said.

I hit a 4-iron, a 9-iron and two-putted (from five feet) for par. But where, I've wondered, would I have been without Cook? Here, with Dave, I finally learned the answer: in the Pacific Ocean, twice. Between us, we had fifteen pars and a birdie at Pebble Beach and still we couldn't escape the shadow of 90. But we were happy and we were home.

The Diabolical's Sixteenth Hole
431 Yards, Par 4

After his man, Tom Kite, chipped in at seven, Mike Carrick, the Canadian caddy, secretly won his little piece of the United States Open.

"Do you like the 3 [iron]?" Kite asked.

"I like the 4," Carrick replied.

The wind was with them, strong. Pebble's par-4 eighth hole is really two par-3 holes. A half-blind tee shot to the edge of the cliff. Then a wide-eyed second shot over the cliff, the drop, the surf, the beach, the facing cliff, a stretch of grass and a bowl of sand to the green.

"How far to the rough?" Kite inquired, meaning the collar of the cliff.

"Two-fifty exactly," Carrick said.

"So you like the 3."

"The 4."

"Three, you mean."

"Four."

With the brute wind, Kite hit Carrick's 4-iron precisely 245 yards. If he had hit the 3, who knows what he would have shot that Sunday? But he hit the 4, and at long last, in his forty-third year, Kite won his first major championship.

"Nice call, Mike," he said softly to Carrick, whom no one has ever heard of.

The wind was against us, strong. I hit a driver—I thought, too good—at the picture window of the Firestone mansion on the hill. The ball stopped on Kite's spot, exactly five yards from oblivion, not far from the DANGER STEEP CLIFF sign that is usually pointed out during the retelling of the Japanese cart riders' demise. From thirty yards back on the right side of the fairway, Dave tried a 3-wood second shot that would have worked well in a lighter breeze. The wind swatted the ball straight right and it bounded farther right off the boulders toward the beach.

Being slightly thick, I put a 5-iron second shot into the same jet stream and the ball floated right of the green into a deep swell just this side of unplayable. With a sigh, I dropped another ball where I stood and hit a lower 5-iron onto the back of the green. The pin was in front. Walking up to where I stood, and where his ball had started across the gorge, Dave took a drop and hit a 3-iron onto the front.

Our caddy was a Scotsman named John Cowan. He knew Tip Anderson of St. Andrews and appeared to have had some of the same experiences. He looked clear-eyed and well barbered but not what you would call prosperous. Before the round, Cowan shifted our clubs from the light bags we presented to even lighter ones he maintained. He is not a man inclined toward unnecessary exertions.

My first ball was visible just below the green.

"Don't go down there," Cowan begged like a father trying to dissuade his son from war.

"I'm 4 otherwise," I said. "Maybe I'll get lucky."

"There's a snake down there," he said. His voice said "snake." His eyes said "dragon." "Your mate's 4 too," he said. "Make the putt."

"If it's playable, I have to play it, don't I?"

"It's unplayable."

"I can see it."

"That's an illusion."

"I can hit it."

"You can't."

"I've come almost 40,000 miles."

"The putt's only 40 feet."

I two-putted it for a double-bogey 6. Dave did the same. I was still one up with now two holes to go.

Our next stop wouldn't be a place but a man, a mood really, a dream. At a pay phone outside the Pebble Beach pro shop, Dave put in a call to the tour pro Mac O'Grady in Palm Springs. That charming eccentric once arrived at Ben Hogan's Fort Worth office completely unannounced, and for an hour sat cross-legged on the floor at the master's feet talking about the loops and logarithms of the golf swing. "Maybe Mac can help," Dave said.

We thought of calling Hogan directly, but that has never been a winning plan. Gary Player tried it once from Brazil. Player was fighting his lifelong hook and just wanted to talk about it for a few minutes with Ben, who had cured his own famous case of the bends. "Playing with a hook," Hogan once said, "is like playing with a pocketful of rattlesnakes."

After hearing Player out in silence, Hogan asked brusquely, his customary tone, "Are you affiliated with a club manufacturer?"

"Dunlop," Player replied, perplexed by the question.

"Call Mr. Dunlop," Hogan said, and hung up.

O'Grady offered to phone the pro shop at Shady Oaks and call us back, which he did. "When you get there, ask for the head pro," Mac instructed, "a young fellow named Mike Wright. He's expecting you. I told him the whole story. No promises, but he'll try to help." No promises, but Mac's voice was dancing. "You guys have got a real treat in store for you," he said merrily.

Taking a last soft glance at Pebble, we wondered what he meant exactly.

CHAPTER 17

SHADY OAKS COUNTRY CLUB

Fort Worth, Texas

Where Ben Hogan Is the Man in the Window

AS BEN HOGAN polished the silverware, I watched his hands. Tom and I waited at a nearby table. Hogan did each piece carefully, first the fork, then the knife and spoon. He rubbed each with his napkin and returned it to its proper place. He sat alone at a table for eight in a corner. Now and then the four other men in the room stole glances at Hogan's back. It was eleven o'clock in the morning.

Someone once asked Hogan how he would like to be remembered and he said, "As a gentleman." At eleven in the morning, he wore a gray sports coat, blue slacks, white shirt and blue tie. He smoked a cigarette, his lighter placed just so by the package. He sipped from a glass of white wine. His hands moved slowly and surely.

Ted Williams met Hogan late in Ben's prime. The man whose hands made him one of baseball's best hitters said, "I just shook a hand that felt like five bands of steel." Hogan's hands then were as brown as rawhide. Now they were an old man's blue. Only two weeks earlier, with no fanfare, he had turned eighty-one.

Every morning, Hogan came to his corner table in the grill room at Shady Oaks Country Club. He always sat in the same place. He faced the window through which he could see the eighteenth green and up the wide fairway. For years he had lunch and then carried a 5-iron a half mile to a spot hidden inside the course. There he hit balls. He might carry seven or eight balls and walk after them for the exercise. On the way, he said hello to everyone he passed.

At his practice spot, he liked silence. Mickey Wright was the best woman player ever and a fellow Texan. She often went to Fort Worth to watch Hogan hit balls. When she asked if he minded, Hogan said, "Not as long as you don't say anything."

Hogan last played competitively in 1968. His contemporary Sam Snead stayed out there by using unorthodox putting strokes, first croquet-style and later sidesaddle, dignity be damned. Not Hogan. If he couldn't be Hogan, he would become a ghost. He appeared only on his terms. He said no to Jack Nicklaus, whose Memorial Tournament honored the titans: Bobby Jones, Walter Hagen, Arnold Palmer.

When years passed and Hogan was not chosen, Callahan asked Nicklaus about it. "I'm not going to lie to you," Nicklaus said. "We invited Hogan our second year and he refused. He said, 'I don't want to be eulogized while I'm alive.'"

At Shady Oaks, in private, Hogan kept hitting balls because that's who he was, a man who hit balls. "Hogan invented practice," Jimmy Demaret said. A hard man who once heard a famous player ask for the secret to his swing, Hogan told him, "The secret's in the dirt. Dig it out, like I did."

Even at age seventy-seven he produced awe. "Fifty years older than me and hitting 4-irons 195 yards," said the Shady Oaks pro, Mike Wright, one of those kids Tommy Bolt called flat-bellied limberbacks. "One day a member playing with Mr. Hogan said, 'What'd you hit, Ben?' Mr. Hogan put his 7-iron back in the bag. He takes a 6 and hits it within three feet of the first one. He puts the 6 back and hits an 8-iron to six feet. He's got it surrounded. It doesn't take a genius to figure out the moral of that story."

Hogan quit hitting balls in 1991. He no longer could make a full swing that satisfied him. His friend Bolt had said of the young Hogan, "Ben applied himself to each and every shot completely. He never in his life took no ol' funky-butt swing." In his old age, Hogan said, "I could chip, but what fun is that?"

Still, if you went into the Shady Oaks bag room in the summer of 1993 and there went to space number 51, you found a Hogan bag, a deep burgundy, its label the Ravielli line drawing of Hogan at impact. There you found the bag filled with Hogan clubs, the forged beauties his company made at his command. He hadn't hit a ball in two years, but he left the clubs there. He paid for the space, the same as everyone else. He never asked any favors.

I watched Ben Hogan's hands because I had seen them in 1967 when they were sure and strong and looked like the hands of a man who had worked at life. I watched Ben Hogan light a cigarette and I thought of my father's Lucky Strikes. These men were born a month apart in the fall of 1912, Hogan and Dad.

An upset stomach sent Dad to a doctor. He came home and died in two weeks. With so far to go, we ran out of time. Seeing Hogan's hands again, I wanted to tell Dad about his grandson and great-grandsons. Jared and Jacob were four when Santa Claus brought them baseball gloves. Dad would have wanted to play catch.

A kid sportswriter at his first Masters in 1967 saw Red Smith roll three or four pieces of white paper into his upright Smith-Corona typewriter. "You know he's not a real newspaperman if he puts only one sheet of paper in the typewriter," Red liked to say. He sat three rows from the back of the Augusta press barn, the right side of the right-hand aisle. He used both hands to insert the paper into the typewriter. His hands trembled. Red was sixty-one years old.

The kid saw Hogan on the practice range, the third man from the right end. Every shot with every club flew two yards left of the target and then fell two yards right, a fade two decades in the making, the ball dropping in the caddy's shadow.

Hogan was fifty-four, soon to be fifty-five, and he had a bad knee, left over from the car wreck that nearly killed him in 1949. At every step there was an old man's hitch. Hogan. Ben Hogan. The Hawk. All those Aprils ago, he shot 66 the third day of the Masters. His 30 on the back nine tied the record. It left him two shots out of the lead. He last had won a major tournament in 1953, the year he dominated golf, winner at Augusta and in the U. S. Open as well as in the only British Open he ever played, bringing the Carnoustie beast to heel.

That third day in 1967, early in the afternoon, the kid sat in the press barn wondering what a real sportswriter would be doing—when Hogan began his run: four straight birdies around Amen Corner.

A 7-iron to seven feet at the tenth. A 6-iron to one foot at the eleventh. A 6-iron to the twelfth, leaving a fifteen-foot putt that caused him to say, "I am still embarrassed to get before people and putt. Hell, I'm even embarrassed to putt when I'm alone, but the only way to beat this thing is to play. I hear children and ladies saying, 'For God's sake, why doesn't he hit it faster?' So I say to myself, 'You idiot. You heard them. Why don't you hit it faster?' "

He made the putt at the twelfth. He reached both par 5s, the thirteenth and fifteenth, with 4-wood second shots for two-putt birdies. A kid's first Masters and Ben Hogan was on fire, his scoreboard numbers changing from black to the sub-par signal of red, a red 2. The kid heard someone say, "We better get out there."

The kid first saw Hogan coming up the ascending cathedral aisle that is Augusta National's eighteenth fairway. Hogan walked through applause, thousands of hands clapping, a waterfall's roar. He started the day as an heirloom on display; he became a contender. He became the Hogan who had survived the car wreck and won the U. S. Open the next summer. At every green the galleries recognized the Hawk in full flight. Even Hogan, who didn't hear Carnoustie's train, heard Augusta's worshipers.

"I'd had standing ovations before," he said, "but not nine holes in a row."

At the eighteenth, Hogan put a 5-iron second shot twenty feet above the hole. The kid sportswriter sat in press bleachers rising next to the green. He saw the little man in the white cap standing over the putt that day. He sees him still.

Embraced by cathedral silence, Hogan stood over the downhill putt. He stood over it and waited. And then he touched the ball gently, just started it rolling. Down the hill. Murmurs now. The ball near the hole. And then it dropped from our sight. Hogan had made the thing.

He made it for his 30, for the 66. Hurrahs raised the cathedral's roof then and Ben Hogan took the warmth of the people and thanked them by lifting high his flat white cap. It was late in the day and his shadow fell long on the green. The kid saw this, and he was glad, and he hoped the old man, a hard man, liked it.

Hogan loved it. In the clubhouse later, he told a dozen reporters, "There's a lot of fellas who have got to fall dead for me to win. But I don't mind telling you, I'll play just as hard as I've ever played in my life."

The young hero Arnold Palmer sat off in a corner. He changed his shoes and listened. Hogan sat under a sunlit window framed by lacy white curtains. He was balding, his hair gray and white at the fringes. His face was hard and dry as a Texas summer. He would shoot an aching 77 the next day and never again play in the Masters. Not that it mattered. All that mattered was this moment, Hogan again Hogan, a man telling us again who he was.

The twilight sun came through the white lace curtains. It fell soft and golden on Ben Hogan's face one more time.

Tom and I had come to Shady Oaks at the invitation of the club's pro, Mike Wright, who now reached behind his office door to an old box of golf clubs leaning in the corner. "These are Mr. Hogan's second-to-last set of clubs," he said. "He's got the last set at home. He says he's working on them. But here. I want you to look at this."

At the end of a pilgrimage, many a believer has picked up a holy relic as proof certain that his faith is well placed. I picked up Ben Hogan's 5-iron.

"How's it look?" Wright said.

The 5-iron's face looked all wrong. It looked as if someone had twisted the face to increase the loft while pulling the toe back from square. Someone, in fact, had done just that. The pro said, "Mr. Hogan did it. And feel the grip, too."

The grip was very thick and a ridge ran along its bottom side. The ridge forced my hands into a weak position on top of the shaft. Hogan had been very busy with these clubs.

"People forget how important equipment was to Mr. Hogan," Wright told us. "He thought of each club as a piece of jewelry. He designed this club face and grip over the years to help discourage the hook he'd had as a young player. I took this club to the range one day and I couldn't hit it. I hit every ball over the right-field fence."

I should pause here. Over the years, I tried many times to arrange interviews with Hogan. The best I did was a letter or call of thanks but no thanks. All that stuff was a long time ago, he said, and when you get to be an old man, you'll understand that memory fails. His secretary said, "You wouldn't want to embarrass Mr. Hogan," and I always said, "No, of course not, I'll write the piece without him."

In Calcutta when we decided to go to Fort Worth, Tom and I had no idea if we could meet Hogan. But we had to go. It would be good to shake his hand, maybe say a word or two, but if that couldn't be done, even if we couldn't even see him across the room, at the least we would walk the Texas ground he had walked. So from Pebble Beach we called Mac O'Grady.

When Mac explained to Mike Wright the journey we had made, the pro first hesitated—"I'm reluctant"—and then said to come ahead, he would introduce us to Hogan. Wright avoided writers because he respected Hogan's desire for privacy. Wright also said he wanted no publicity for himself. In the end, he agreed to help us for one reason alone: "I want people to know the Mr. Hogan I know."

Too young to have known Hogan as a player, the pro knew Hogan as a warm and kindly gentleman who once upon a time made history. Wright's cubbyhole office was a Hogan museum, its bookshelves heavy with Hogan theories and observations. On the wall, a 1955 *Life* magazine cover advertised Hogan revealing "The Secret" of his swing. The pro showed us a small "golfer's watch" made in the 1950s to be attached to the belt. It carried Hogan's name on the face.

Wright took us into the pro shop's workroom where he set up a television monitor. He wanted us to see his favorite videotape. It showed Hogan, maybe sixty-five years old, in his signature flat white cap and gray sweater, hitting balls at his Shady Oaks practice spot. Mike said, "I've talked a lot about the swing with Mr. Hogan. But he told me, 'Don't tell anybody. It's a secret.' And I never have."

We asked to go to Hogan's practice spot. On the way, the young pro parked the golf cart. If we wanted to know Mr. Hogan, we should hear this story.

"I was twenty-three years old, the assistant pro, when the Shady Oaks golf committee asked me to come to a meeting settling the head pro's estate. As far as I knew, it wasn't an interview for the head pro's job. But Mr. Hogan asked me if I had written a letter to the golf committee saying I was interested in the job. I said I had and he offered to proofread it for me.

"He said, 'Now, you know the committee is going to interview you for the job, don't you?' I said they just talked about a 'meeting,' but I assumed the job interview would be part of it. So Mr. Hogan asked me, 'What are you going to wear?'

" 'What I've got on,' I said. A nice golf shirt and slacks. I didn't want to go in there wearing a suit and have the committee think I was being presumptuous. I'd just go in the way I went to work every day. Mr. Hogan told me, 'No, go buy yourself some clothes and let me pay for it.' I said I wasn't comfortable doing that. So he took off his sport coat and handed it to me. 'Wear this,' he said.

"His coat was too small, though, and, with all due respect to Mr. Hogan, it smelled of smoke. So I went to Sears and bought a coat, shirt and tie, all for under $65. They even ironed it. Still, I took Mr. Hogan's coat with me to the 'meeting.' It was, in fact, an interview. When I got done, I went back to the shop. Mr. Hogan was still at the club, past the usual time when he left, and I gave him back his coat.

"I got the job the next day. I don't know if Mr. Hogan recommended me. I do know he supported me. And I also know he could have put an X on anybody he didn't want."

Grantland Rice called Hogan "soft as a fire hydrant." Henry Longhurst described him as "a small man, normal weight no more than 140 pounds, height about 5 feet 9 inches with smooth black hair, wide head, wide eyes and a wide mouth which tends, when the pressure is on, to contract into a thin, straight pencil-line. You could see him sitting at a poker table, saying, expressionless, 'Your thousand—and another five.' He might have four aces, or a pair of two's."

Sam Snead remembered Hogan's eyes. "Ben'd put those steely blues of his on you. Boy. That came from his days dealing cards. He dealt in Vegas or somewhere, to make ends meet. That's how he learned that stone face. He got so he wouldn't even let Jimmy Demaret play gin rummy 'cause Jimmy's eyes'd get real big if he got good cards. Not Ben's. No, sir-eee."

This was the Hogan who in eight years, 1946 to 1953, won four United

States Open championships, two Masters, two PGAs and one British Open. This was the Hogan who came back from that terrible auto accident, came back the next summer, limping in pain, to win the U. S. Open. In 1950 Gene Sarazen called Hogan "the most merciless player of all the modern players" and said, "His temperament may derive from the rough, anguishing years of his childhood or the hostility he encountered as a young and overdetermined circuit chaser. Whatever the reason, he is the type of golfer you would describe as perpetually hungry."

Hogan was nine when his blacksmith father had health and money troubles. One night in the family's Fort Worth living room, Chester Hogan rummaged through a valise. Another son, Royal, thirteen, watched his father search the case. The boy said, "Daddy, what are you going to do?" In answer, the blacksmith shot himself above the heart. He died the next day, Valentine's Day, 1922.

To help support his family—his mother, brother Royal and sister Princess, eleven—the little boy named just plain Ben peddled newspapers at a railroad station. Soon he heard of money to be made caddying at nearby Glen Garden Country Club. Some Saturday nights little Ben Hogan could be found asleep in a bunker at Glen Garden. The first caddies in line might carry twice on Sundays and earn an extra sixty-five cents.

As a teenager, Hogan three times was embittered by Glen Garden. At fifteen he seemed to have won a caddies' tournament in a sudden-death playoff, only to be told the playoff was a full nine holes. He then lost to the club prodigy, a skinny kid a foot taller by the name of Byron Nelson. The next year the club captain chose Nelson for a junior membership, saying, "Byron Nelson is the only caddy who doesn't drink, smoke, or curse." Without the membership, Hogan could enter no club tournaments. He could not even practice at the course where he had come to love the game. The club captain refused Hogan permission to hit balls in the caddy area. At sixteen Ben was too old for that, the man said.

By her account, Clara Hogan tried to warn her young son off golf, telling him he had no future in the game. "When I finished speaking my piece," the mother said, "Ben stood there and his eyes just blazed. He said, 'Momma, someday I'm gonna be the greatest golfer in the world.'"

He quit high school before graduation and turned pro at nineteen. In his first tournament, he tied for thirty-eighth and won $8.50. The year was 1932 and the Depression was on. While trying the golf tour, he also worked in oil fields, garages, a bank, a hotel and as a gambling house's dealer and croupier. Years of small successes and large failures led to a moment early in 1938 when golf didn't seem worth the effort any more.

Living on oranges and staying in cheap motels, Hogan came to the Oakland Open with $8.00 in his pocket. Sam Snead saw Hogan the morning of the tournament's final round and told the story in his autobiography:

"I remember Ben standing outside the Claremont Country Club beating his fists against a brick wall.

" 'What happened, boy?' " we other young pros asked.

" 'I can't go another inch,' " groaned Ben. He was as close to tears as that tough little guy can get. 'I'm finished. Some son of a bitch stole the tires off my car.' "

His Texas contemporaries had surpassed Hogan. Byron Nelson, out of the same caddy yard, won the New Jersey and Metropolitan Opens. Jimmy Demaret won the Texas PGA. Ralph Guldahl won the Western Open and the 1937 U. S. Open. Ben had told his wife, Valerie, that 1937 was the decision year. "Now or never," he said.

By January '38, with no money to get out of his Oakland motel, with his Buick jacked up by thieves, a man whose father killed himself in the family living room would have found sympathy if he said he'd felt enough pain, it was time to quit, his doubting mother had been right after all.

Instead, Oakland shaped Hogan's career. A Texas sportswriter wrote that Hogan played the Oakland final round "with a set jaw, lips locked into a tight smile that was not a smile, and eyes of steely intensity," a portrait of the Hogan the golf world would come to know.

He shot a 69 that day to finish second to Harry Cooper and earn $380. It was enough to put tires back on the car. It was enough to convince Hogan he could go on. He won his first tournament in March 1940. In 1959 he last won a tournament. In between, *whatever the reason,* Hogan became Hogan.

Tommy Bolt, Hogan's buddy, could play some himself. He won the 1958 U. S. Open. "Ben was the greatest golfer you ever dreamed of seeing," Bolt said. "Arnold Palmer and Jack Nicklaus are great. But listen, pal. They couldn't carry Ben's jockstrap. Only way you beat Ben was if God wanted you to."

———

We came to the place where Hogan hit balls. It was out of the way, but hidden only in the sense that people who saw Hogan there gave him those moments alone. He dropped balls and hit them from the crest of land rising gracefully from a narrow creek 200 yards away. There on the Hogan hill at Shady Oaks, Mike Wright felt as if he were not alone.

"Mr. Hogan is here somewhere, peering around a corner, watching," he said.

The young pro said someday it would be nice to put up a little statue on Hogan's hill.

Even with Mike's assurance of an introduction to Hogan, Tom and I didn't count on it. Things happen.

As we stopped for lunch after nine holes, we first went to the locker room. There we turned a corner toward the washbasins. And very nearly ran into the ghost.

In his coat and tie, Ben Hogan moved one hand across his thinning hair. He dropped a towel into a bin. He moved to his right a bit and passed these strangers coming in, all sweaty. Here's what Hogan said, and I know because I wrote it down. He said, "Hello."

Here's what Tom said after Hogan passed us, and I wrote it down because Tom, a hard case, is not easily impressed. (He once insulted Sonny Liston so spectacularly that he and the fearsome heavyweight champion of the world fell to wrestling around a hotel room, their nose-to-nose dance rearranging the furniture it didn't destroy.) Here is what Tom said in the Shady Oaks washroom: "Hogan. It's Hogan. It's like seeing Babe Ruth."

During lunch with Mike Wright, we watched Hogan polishing the silverware, smoking, asking for a second glass of wine. Then Mike took us to Hogan's table where the great man rose to greet us with a smile and a twinkle in eyes once thought of as steely. He looked trim, fit and lively. He couldn't have been more gracious to two reporters appearing at his table.

"Please, sit down, Mr. Hogan," I said. But he continued to stand by the table, the better, I supposed, to keep these things brief. Hogan always came to his work with a reason for everything he did, even for matters as simple as a cap. It was said he wore the white flat linen cap because it worried him less in the Texas wind than the wide-brimmed hats of the forties. Sounds right.

"Welcome, welcome," he said. "It's so nice to have you here."

I told him there were traces of Hogan all over the world. "So we had to come see you."

"It's good to see you," he said.

At a mention of the 1967 Masters, he nodded and smiled but said nothing. The walk up the eighteenth fairway would have been forgotten, too. We had walked the ground of Carnoustie's sixth hole, made famous by Hogan's work there, the work so well known that historians speak of Hogan's Alley. Tom began to tell about his eagle putt. "Mr. Hogan, your hole at Carnoustie, I almost . . ."

Only to be interrupted by Hogan. "I can't remember every hole. It was so long ago, you know."

"That's all right, Mr. Hogan," Tom said. "They all remember you."

Tom's favorite memory was Hogan's surprise appearance in the press barn during Masters week of 1977. "I asked you if you ever played the perfect round and you said you 'almost dreamed' it once: seventeen straight holes in one and then you lipped it out at the eighteenth." Tom looked at the smiling old man. "You said you were mad as hell."

Hogan laughed. "I think that's right."

As Red Smith used to say when he had the raw material for a column, we were rich by now. Hogan had been with us on this journey: his image on the Iceland pro shop's door . . . the Wee Icemon oblivious to the Carnoustie train . . . a French mademoiselle with a Hogan bag . . . a "Big Ben Hogan" driver for sale in Johannesburg . . . a turbaned Indian conjuring his name . . . my own bag of Hogan Radials, the clubs too good for their sorry owner . . . and now we had touched the ghost, made him real.

We would go play the back nine. Tom said, "You know, Mr. Hogan, playing the eighteenth hole here with you watching through this window, that's a lot of pressure."

"Aw," Ben Hogan said, "it's a baby golf course."

Weren't they all babies to Hogan? We said our thanks and good-byes and on the way out we shook hands. Hogan's hand was wide and strong. I wrote down his last words to us that afternoon. He said, "Enjoy your game. Come back."

We saw him one more time. We played the eighteenth. He was the man in the window. Smoke curled from a cigarette. We fairly well butchered the hole.

The Diabolical's Seventeenth Hole
208 Yards, Par 3

The short holes at the Royal & Diabolical Global Golf Club are mighty examples of the architect's imagination. One day soon we will go back to Calamity, eager to risk again the calamitous consequences of a shot that doesn't fly far and true. Lost City put crocodiles in our line of sight and Chiang Mai asked us to come out of our shoes if we would reach that green 235 yards away.

The fifth at Shady Oaks completed a set of par 3s as demanding as any a suffering wayfarer would hope to see. Played from an elevated tee— downtown Fort Worth sat below us on the horizon—the fifth would give up a par only to the player bold enough to strike a tee shot 208 yards, across a valley, to a wide but shallow green perched atop a steep mound. A baby golf course? Any shot headed even a touch left at the fifth hole, and the cup was far left on our day, would bounce off that mound and come to rest in pine needles behind 937 trees, give or take one or two.

Our momentous match remained in doubt. Tom was one up with two to play, a dire circumstance for your obedient servant. Not that a defeat would be my first. Years earlier I lost in the fifth-flight quarterfinals of a city tournament to a Cro-Magnon man: his brow was an offensive line-man's, his arms were furry, and his legs, bursting out of plaid Bermuda shorts, were parenthetical. C-M man hit the pill while walking toward it, never bothering with the formality of address. It was 5 and 4, I'm afraid.

A blind man has beaten me, as has a fifteen-year-old girl and a great-grandmother. I have never lost to a man with one leg, but I have lost to two men with one arm and to a one-eyed sportswriter who, when a buddy asked him to keep an eye on his beer, took out his glass eye and put it on the bottle's mouth.

Perhaps you have noticed. I have delayed my report on the fifth hole at Shady Oaks. I have done this for two reasons. One, to build unbearable suspense. Two, I want to tell you about the back nine.

Tom and I played well on the back nine after meeting Hogan at lunch. Infused with the master's mystique—how better to explain the inexplica-ble?—we 14-handicap tourists struck every shot on the club face for most of two hours. Our best ball on the back nine was four under par. The sixteenth hole is a 149-yarder over a deep creek to a tiny green under tall trees. There we had eight-foot birdie putts from opposite sides of the cup. We both made 2s.

We were heroes.

Alas, only one of us was heroic earlier on the fifth hole. There Tom hit a gorgeous shot, a 2-iron draw that flew high over downtown Fort Worth and screeched to a halt in the left fringe twenty feet from the cup.

My tee shot was a popped-up 5-wood headed left. The ball didn't bounce off that steep mound at first. It rocketed off a cart path. And then it bounced off the mound. And kicked left. And came to rest behind 937 trees, give or take one or two.

By the time I scraped it up the hill, Tom had a tap-in par. He closed me out. He won the global confrontation 2 and 1. O diary. Now I had lost to a fookin' Irishman.

CHAPTER 18

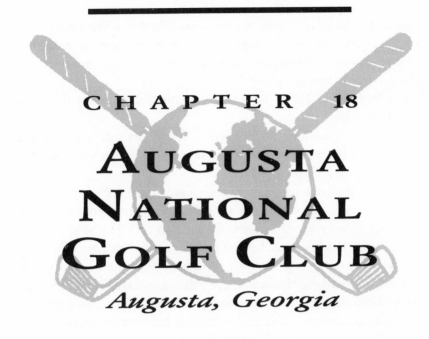

AUGUSTA NATIONAL GOLF CLUB

Augusta, Georgia

Where We Drive Down Magnolia Lane Without Once Getting Lost

Never to finish,
But to begin again.
Life is a circular thing.

FOR TWO MONTHS Tom and I had gone in circles. Some were the eccentric circles made of loops and squiggles traced by our rental cars while we wandered manfully rather than ask unmanly directions. Some circles were the circles of golf: standing on a round planet hitting a round ball into a round hole with a roundhouse swing, every circle designed to bring us back where we started. And these circles were inside the biggest circle of all, the journey itself, the beginning planned as the ending. William Least Heat Moon once wandered the edges of America and wrote, "Following a circle would give a purpose—to come around again—where taking a straight line would not."

Tom had asked, "Does Cheryl have even the slightest worry that you'll go and not come back?"

"Only if we crash into Mount Everest," I said. My wife hated the idea of flying across oceans and over mountains on God Knows What Airlines. "Otherwise, she knows I'll be home."

She knew the game had been running away from me. Newspapers had changed in ways that didn't suit my taste; they wanted sound bites on newsprint at the expense of stories well and fully told. *The National* experience left me disappointed. I didn't look for another newspaper job and no newspaper job came looking for me. Maybe that's the way it happens. One day you're young, the next you're a dinosaur. I said as much to Jane Leavy. We worked sports together in Washington. She became a novelist. She knew self-pity when she heard it. She said the sweetest, smartest thing. She said, "Get off your ass, Kindred. Go write."

Our only child and his sons moved a thousand miles away. Maybe only those of us who were too busy for their own children can understand our absolute and unconditional love of grandchildren. When Jeff, Jared and Jacob moved away, my depression was black. Cheryl shared the frustrations and anger. She hoped the trip would help. She said, "More than a lark, less than a crusade. A recess, maybe?" A sportswriter thought of it as a time out called to stop the bad guys' momentum.

Then, in my little Georgia town, at an antique sale on the courthouse square, I saw the wooden-block puzzle with the child's verse.

Ride, ride the carousel . . .

The lyrical words had the unexpected and salutary effect of confirming the need to go do it. Get on a plane with Callahan. What the hell, why not? Build your own carousel. It was time to move on. Let newspapers be what they would be. Maybe there would be a place for you at a newspaper someday, maybe not. Just let it go. Do the best you can at being a grandfather from a thousand miles away. Anger puts white hairs in your mustache. Ask for a recess, call a time out. Go ride the carousel.

Reach for the golden ring . . .

From Atlanta we had flown east two months to Atlanta. Back where we began, Tom and I drove another two hours. Around the world and then some to get to Augusta National. And, if necessary, we would have gone around twice. The best golf writer living, dead or Texan explained the place in nine words. Dan Jenkins wrote, "God must have been a 2-handicapper from Augusta."

Arriving an hour ahead of schedule, we had time for the traditional Gene Roswell breakfast at an International House of Pancakes restaurant. (Roswell, a New York sportswriter, gained fame by telling an IHOP waitress, "Gimme blueberry pancakes, and heavy with the ketchup and mustard.") Callahan and Kindred had spent sixty-nine days on planes, trains, dingmobiles, tuk-tuks and elephants. We had cursed in cow pastures and laughed in lagoons. Now we had come to the last stop. We would tee it up on God's own track, after a pancake or three.

We turned right leaving the IHOP parking lot and made a left off Washington Road into the club grounds where we told the gate guard we were to meet the member John Murray, Jr., an Augusta businessman. The guard said, "Mr. Murray is already here. Go right on down. Just turn right at the end of the lane and there is the parking lot."

We drove down Magnolia Lane toward a clubhouse done in the Southern plantation manner, white and glistening, the sort of place Scarlett O'Hara had in mind for her and Rhett. The lane passed under a canopy of branches put up by magnolias. It was just a skinny little road like every skinny little road—except for a few matters of history, such as: Bobby Jones came down it and Ben Hogan came down it and Sarazen and Nelson and Demaret and Ky Laffoon with his shotgun in the trunk and Sam Snead with hair and fat Jack Nicklaus and thin Jack Nicklaus and Tom Watson, Seve Ballesteros and hundreds of dreamers including Bert Yancey, who built clay models of Augusta's greens so he could run his hands over them in hopes of absorbing the feel necessary to play them well.

"This is the only course I know," the player Lionel Hebert said, "where you choke when you come in the gate."

In the spring of 1931, the greatest golfer who had ever lived drove down a skinny dirt lane between magnolia trees and stopped at a plantation manor house even then nearly a hundred years old. Once the crown jewel of an indigo plantation, the manor sat on land which belonged to the Cherokee Indians until U. S. General James Oglethorpe, a peace pipe in hand, did business with the chiefs in the eighteenth century.

That spring day in 1931 when Bobby Jones first saw the magnolias, he walked to the back of the manor house, past the oak trees hung with wisteria and past the enchanting azaleas of the place which had become a vast nursery. Years later Jones would say, ". . . when I walked out on the grass terrace under the big trees behind the house and looked down over the property, the experience was unforgettable. It seemed that this land had been lying here for years waiting for someone to lay a golf course upon it."

In that judgment as in so much, Robert Tyre Jones, Jr., came near perfection. To stand on that terrace of land more than a half century later is to go back in time. What Jones saw in 1931 is what the Cherokee saw before him and what we see at the end of the twentieth century: a broad sweep of land falling away from beneath our feet, the land soft and green, velvety, running to pines which seem placed so they cast shadow where shadow is needed to make the valley a piece of art.

This is what a golf course should be: an invitation to play. From Augusta National's terrace, you can see fairways as broad and smooth as country rivers. There is no rough. The deepest grass covers little more than the bottom half of a ball. Some courses by canyons and oceans make the heroic shot their signatures. At Augusta National, the signature is that of Bobby Jones, a subtle, sophisticated competitor who in 1934 invited the world's best players to the old Indian ground where he had caused a golf course to be laid upon the land.

Jones's signature is nowhere more beautifully done than at the thirteenth hole. Walk from the terrace behind the manor house, down into the valley of pines, out to the thirteenth green, as far as the property goes, out where the second shot over a brook to the short par 5 is Thursday's heaven and Sunday's hell. I once stood near the thirteenth with a retired Seattle stockbroker who had come to see the Masters for the first time.

"From here . . ." Ralph Preston began, stopping to look back to the corner of the fairway, seeing how the fairway narrows and tilts left toward the brook, all of it sidehill and indented with small troughs that test a player's balance, the green two-tiered and barely a step over that brook. "From here, it doesn't look as easy as it does on television."

"Not hardly," I said.

"Good," the stockbroker said.

The thirteenth hole at Augusta is a painting. It is a painting done by an eighteenth-century French impressionist whose palette weighed heavily with pinks. Look at it. Thousands of azaleas, millions of blooms dancing for hundreds of feet on a hillside. The painting has six shades of pink, the pinks running from a baby's blush to a purple so electric it must glow at midnight. Splotches of white, suggesting dogwood blooms, blur into the pinks and purples.

Whoa. Stop right there. A purple-prose alert: Right here and right now, we should stop.

The Masters is a *painting?*

Mac O'Grady shot an 82 in a Masters and then explained the inability to reason when confronted by Augusta National. He said, "I was overcome by the biophilia."

Several sportswriters scratched their haircuts. Mac went on: "It's the rolling fairways, it's the topography that's so beautiful, it's the feeling you get from all that. Biophilia is the effect experienced upon viewing a landscape. And the biophilia of Augusta is so beautiful in so many ways that you become entranced and you drift away from reality."

A cold critique of Augusta National and the Masters can be done. The flaws are plain. The Masters is a lesser championship test than the three other majors because its small field plays a course favoring long hitters who draw the ball. An agent for a prominent player once said, "The Masters is bogus, phony, pretentious and arrogant. It's the Old South at its worst, plantation masters keeping the low classes in their place."

It's that—and much more. The agent went on: "The Masters is an enigma and an anachronism, but it works. There's nothing in golf like it. It agitates, it motivates, it can't be duplicated. It's a heavyweight championship fight that lasts four days. It's the horses in the gates at the Kentucky Derby."

You know what else it is? It's a man on a mower. Looking for a column one April afternoon, this biophiliac found himself watching a worker cut the grass. Without knowing it had happened, mesmerized by the perfect nature of the man's work, I actually stood by the third fairway and actually watched a man cut grass. The man drove a big tractor, a Toro Reelmaster 450-D. The tractor had six grass-cutting rollers, three on each side. It was set to cut the grass to a height of one half inch. The driver's name was Ike Stokes and he had worked at the club for seventeen years.

On his Reelmaster, the cutters humming, not a clatter to any revolution, Ike Stokes drove up the fairway, made a left turn (but only after raising the cutters so he didn't leave a curving cut in the fairway) and came back. The soft spring sun of an April in the South kissed the grass. The grass became velvet, brushed to a gleam by Ike Stokes, who said, "Got no time to talk. Gotta hurry. Got all the fairways to do before dark."

"Hogan, in 1967, stood right there," I said.

We stood six feet from the spot on the practice tee at Augusta National. John Murray had a Hogan story, too. "This was in the days when players sent caddies out there with a shag bag and hit to them. Hogan was hitting 3-irons. His caddy had a towel in his left hand and the shag bag by his feet. Hogan's 3-irons would take one bounce and the caddy'd catch them, rub the dirt off in the towel and drop them in the bag. One bounce, every time."

Though Tom and I had come to Augusta for more than twenty years, we had never been there any time but Masters week. The place was quiet; a caddy said it was a normal day with a dozen foursomes out. We hit a few balls (no 3-irons for me), rolled a few putts and then it was time to do it. One of us remembered Major Sam Hamilton's injunction at Royal Nepal: "Always touch a cow on the way to the first tee."

No livestock allowed at Augusta National, sacred or otherwise, and we contented ourselves with approximations of nonchalance, as if every day we walked on the hallowed ground where Arnold Palmer invented himself and Dwight Eisenhower ran the country.

From that nervous tee, Tom hit a beautiful drive, long and down the middle just past the bunker. Mine was good enough, though it trickled into that bunker. And we had done it. A journey that began two months earlier on a shiny and chilly day at Royal Portrush would end on a shiny and steamy day at Augusta National. We were kids laughing on a merry-go-round of dreams. The golden ring, yes sir.

Even my caddy was perfect. Joe Collins had worked at Augusta National twenty-five years, since he was sixteen. He knew Palmer's original caddy, the one called Iron Man: "He got to be Iron Man because one day he tried to cut open a golf ball and show the insides. The knife cut off part of his finger. 'You ain't no iron man,' somebody said. So, Iron Man."

Where, I wondered, was Iron Man now?

"Cemetery," Joe said.

"Ike's caddy here was Cemetery Poteet," Callahan said. "They called him Cemetery because his heartbeat would get so faint that one night he woke up on a slab in the morgue."

We played with a young assistant pro. Eric Pedersen pointed out Augusta National's only palm tree (right of the fourth green). He also told a pro-shop story about the late Clifford Roberts, the dictatorial Wall Street stockbroker who helped Bobby Jones create the place: "Augusta's members have their own handicap system, just based on pars and birdies. Mr. Roberts would be partners with the assistant pros and count on them for birdies. One day Bobby Barrett hadn't made any birdies. So, at the turn, Mr. Roberts said, 'Bobby, you go on in the shop there and send out a pro.' And he did."

As big a drive as Tom hit at the first, he moved one farther at the second, maybe 300 yards. We were up for this. I made a six-foot par putt at the third and two more at the seventh and ninth. Tom knocked in a twenty-footer at the fifth and nearly holed a 6-iron tee shot at the sixth, the ball settling four feet away. At the ninth, another big drive left him less than ninety yards to the 380-yard hole.

I turned a big drive around ten's corner and clanged a sand shot off the flagstick at the twelfth. On that little hole, which Gary Player has called the best par-3 in the world, Tom dropped a 7-iron tee shot five feet left of the cup. At the seventeenth, he made a twenty-footer for par. For me it was fairways and greens coming home: pars at sixteen, seventeen, and eighteen.

Callahan an 89, Kindred 91. A point of comparison: at Pebble Beach we made fifteen pars and a birdie; at Augusta ten pars, no birdies.

Coming off the eighteenth, I thought of Charlie Yates. The Southern gentleman and 1938 British Amateur champion conducted press interviews each April in the old tin quonset hut put up for us scribblers. It wasn't much, but a rookie in 1967 figured if it was good enough for Red Smith it was good enough for him. In time the press barn became one of my favorite sportswriting venues. It was too small by half, smoky and dimly lit, and when rain rattled on the tin roof you might have been inside a barrel going over Niagara Falls. All the more reason to look forward to April in Augusta, when a guy could come off the course, pick up a barbecue sandwich and go to the press-barn interview room where one of the day's heroes was presented for our inspection. That's when good ol' Charlie Yates invariably asked the literati, "Gen'l'men, what's your pleasure? Birdies and bogeys, or jus' gen'ral comments?"

No birdies from Callahan or Kindred, though they had their chances. Lots of bogeys, all of them heroic. As for gen'ral comments, I have only one thing to say and Herman Keiser said it first. The winner of the 1946 Masters said, "I'll be back every year, if I have to walk fifteen hundred miles to do it."

The Diabolical's Eighteenth Hole
485 Yards, Par 5

Tom once played a round of golf with Jack Nicklaus, an experience that left him disoriented. "We spend our professional lives watching the world's greatest player," Tom said, "and suddenly the world's greatest player is watching you. It's like the world is upside down. I had the same feeling playing Augusta. We had gone through the looking glass. We were inside looking out. You see everything from other points of view."

Television has taught us about Augusta's thirteenth and fifteenth holes, small terrors of par 5s. But when your point of view is from the tee box, the eighth is the most difficult of Augusta's long holes. It's a long climb to an unseen green that dares the average guy to get a chip shot close enough for a par.

As for those simple little four-foot putts that everyone knocks straight in, I, to name one sufferer, saw no simple putts at Augusta. Every first putt on those fast and subtle greens had disastrous potential. At the sixth hole, Tom's four-footer for birdie looked easy: uphill, moving right an inch. But rather than be bold, Tom babied it and missed right. My four-footer there was pure fright: severely downhill, breaking eight inches right. My caddy Joe Collins said, "Out on the toe of your putter. Just touch it." I toe-touched it two feet past and missed the one coming back, too.

Look at the thirteenth hole. Harmless enough. You hit a drive down the middle, knock a shortish second shot onto the green and two-putt for a birdie. Only when you stand in the thirteenth fairway, only when you change your point of view, does the truth become apparent. The thirteenth can hurt you bad.

When you stand on the thirteenth fairway, you get a feeling. The feeling is of a sailboat's deck rolling in a storm's beginnings. The water swells

here and drops there. Even as wind moves the ship forward, it tilts it
sideways. Anyone waiting for the deck to come to dead level may be on
watch all night.

Not so dramatically but just as surely, Augusta's second fairway leaves
a 14-handicapper frustrated. Tom hit a big drive there leaving about two
hundred yards to the 505-yard hole. Only problem was, he didn't know
what to do next. Somehow, the ball came to rest on a downhill slope.
Tom's stance was uphill. The ball was below his feet. "It was kind of
okay," Tom said, "if I knew how to play." Instead, the awkward lie led to
a scuffed 5-wood shot.

At the thirteenth, Tom hit the tee shot of his dreams. "If you had told
me, 'Go place it anywhere you want,' that's where I'd have put it." It was
dead in the middle at the turn of the fairway toward the green—and again
an inconvenient lie for players of our persuasion. The rolling deck of the
fairway put the ball above Tom's feet this time and sitting down in a
tiny trough.

I had hit a 3-iron second shot ninety yards short of the green when Tom
said, "What do I do? I'm 210 yards to the green. The caddy says I'm
either in the best position or the worst, he doesn't know which. But he
thinks I ought to lay up."

"We didn't come all this way to lay up," I said. "Hit it."

We had seen a dozen Masters won and lost on such decisions. Curtis
Strange left it in the creek at the front of the thirteenth when a birdie
might have won it. Seve Ballesteros dumped one in the fifteenth's pond
to lose. We had wondered how great players could make such errors. Now
we were inside the looking glass. Now with 210 yards to the thirteenth
green, with that creek up there, with the lie awkward, knowing you had
to hit it perfectly—now we knew how a fellow might leave it in the creek.

But no way could Tom lay it up. One great shot and he had another
eagle putt. He had done it at Carnoustie. Now at Augusta he asked for a
3-wood. The TV commentators would have buzzed in anticipation of the
bold gamble: "Here's Tom Callahan, who had an eight-footer for eagle at
Hogan's Alley earlier in the round. An awkward lie, but that's a 3-wood
in his hands, I do believe. The Irishman is going for it. I think I heard him
say, 'It's the manly thing to do.'"

Tom's shot turned out to be a trying-too-hard line drive flying about
knee high and rolling to a stop near the creek bank. As for our third shots,
an electromagnetic charge surged through the Georgia air at the moment

of impact. The surge caused the laws of physics to be suspended. Our balls lost the power of flight. They went gloop in the soup at the bottom of the creek. From there, with some heroic work, Tom made bogey and I made double.

We were done with the Royal & Diabolical tour and all too soon. No more Kathmandu leeches? No more choking dogs in Mauritius? Please, let me hit one more ground ball to shortstop. And Tom needs another sidehill four-footer that he can leave on the amateur side. How unfair for the trip to be over just when we were loving/hating it the most. I think of a poem, "The True Golfer," by an F.J.G.:

> He topped the ball,
>   He sliced the ball,
> The divots flew aglee.
>   He damned the ball,
>   He cursed the ball,
> Then cried in agony.
>
> "I'd burn my sticks
>   and bag of tricks
> Without the least regret,
>   Were it not for . . ."
> (He shanked once more!)
> ". . . The pleasure that I get!"

AFTERWORD

PACKING UP

Christopher Columbus went around the world in 1492. That's not a lot of strokes when you consider the course.

I HAVE sportswriters' eyes. I first realized this in 1977 when the University of Evansville basketball team, the coach, the manager and everyone else aboard died in a small airplane that didn't quite lift off from Indiana. I had forgotten that. It's one of many things I relearned on this voyage with Dave.

Midwestern newspapers didn't seem to know how to cover the Evansville crash. Half of them dispatched cityside reporters. The *Chicago Sun-Times,* I remember, was one of those. The other half sent sportswriters, including the *Cincinnati Enquirer.* It was interesting. The cityside reporters hung around the airport talking to the Federal Aviation Administration investigators. The sportswriters hung around the chapel talking to the crying kids, who were stroking each other's hair.

In the morning, both divisions of chroniclers were loaded onto a boxcar in the rain and taken by rail to the muddy crash site on the rim of the airport. The cityside reporters wrote about the logistics: here was the fuselage, there was the wing. The sportswriters wrote about the Aqua Velva bottle that didn't break, about the unused salad dressing, the undisturbed suitcases and the desperate, overwhelming surprise that everything survives but the people.

One victim, the captain, was still in the wreckage.

"Did we have an Oriental pilot?" an FAA man called out matter-of-factly.

"Yeah, I think so," another answered in a drowsy voice.

"I got him."

Their colloquy felt colder than the rain, but it had the familiar timbre of the tough guys in the losing locker rooms declaring their uncaring hearts, thumping their bulletproof chests and trying not to weep. In any case, the cityside found this conversation irrelevant to the news.

Often, in sports, the news is scheduled. There will be news at the stadium at eight o'clock. It usually doesn't have to be sifted and reassembled. It can be described as it happens. And a catastrophe may be a fumble.

Meanwhile, on the other side of the paper, you can't finesse a rape or robbery. You have to tell it. Get the clips out of the library and you'll see how we do them. The address goes here. There we put the age.

I see things with sportswriters' eyes only because I landed on that side of it.

At school, I made a few teams but I wasn't a notable athlete. It's a matter of record that I did get carried off a lacrosse field once on the shoulders of my teammates. I was kind of a hero that day, but I don't like to talk about it. Falling into sportswriting was just a happy accident.

Near the end of my stay at *Time*, when the magazine was veering away from specialization in the direction of a repertory company, every fan in the building started chipping in sports pieces. A young woman wrote a charmingly breathless profile of Michael Jordan that discussed not only his desire but his "burning desire." Someone in the Washington bureau penned a tribute to Redskins quarterback Mark Rypien. Just as all of golf was starting to wonder what was missing in the Australian shark-killer Greg Norman, a Norman fan unaware even of the question wrote how fantastic Norman was.

I liked them all quite a lot. They almost made me think that anyone who has ever been close enough to the athletes to smell them should be disqualified from sportswriting, but that would eliminate Dave Kindred, Red Smith's truest heir.

Dave has decided to press on at the Super Bowl and World Series but to dabble elsewhere. I've decided to draw the line at twenty Super Bowls and World Series but to dabble in sports, maybe only at the oddest stops, hither and thither, where enough of my playmates still reside. Of course, whatever I write, I'm a sportswriter writing it. I can't help it.

It's a community of sojourners. Only the luckiest of us have families. For most of us, we're each other's families. To a number of us, golf has been a way of pausing, of getting out of the casino at the fight, of simply talking. That's all it was in this book.

I've never known the people who lived in the houses on either side of mine because I've really lived in a press box in the neighborhood of golf. There, my next-door neighbor has been Bob Verdi of the *Chicago Tribune.* Dave Anderson, a *New York Times*man, lived just across the street. Where haven't we been together, trying not to get too good at golf or too mad at each other?

Once, when the world was upside down, Jack Nicklaus stood behind a tee and watched Anderson hit a golf ball. As Dave swayed a smooth drive straight down the middle, Nicklaus murmured: "He not only can write, he can *play.*" Everyone should have a moment like that. I'm not sure Dave doesn't prefer it to his Pulitzer. "Put it on my tombstone," he said.

Verdi, Anderson, Dan Foster, Art Spander, Ira Miller, George Kimball, Hubert Mizell, Bill Nack, Hugh McIlvanney, Kenny Jones, Billy Reed, Tom McCollister, Ken Denlinger, Tony Kornheiser, Tom Boswell, Jim Murray, Furman Bisher, Shirley Povich—all of them were along on our trip. When Kindred fell back into formation at the World Series, the *Philadelphia Inquirer*'s Bill Lyon said from the next urinal, "I hope you guys really enjoyed it. Because we were all back here wishing we were you." Who else would they be?

"Everything written is part of the record of its time. Everyone who writes reflects the age in which he lives, and this is not less true of the sports reporter than of the dramatist, poet, novelist, essayist or historian. Games and the people who play them have had a place in every culture; of the ancient Roman monuments that still stand, the most impressive is the Colosseum."

Red wrote that. He has come up in this narrative with perhaps tiresome regularity. Dave and I apologize. It's just that any mention of his name makes both of us smile.

I would also like to offer a small apology to Ray Fitzgerald, the late, great columnist of the *Boston Globe.* He and I once forged a drunken pact that, if either of us ever wrote a book, we'd call it *The Bases Were Loaded and So Was I.* Doubleday demurred. On the same score, William Least Heat Moon will be relieved to know that we dodged the publisher's suggestion: *Blue Fairways.*

The *New York Times* once employed a hard-of-hearing baseball writer named John Drebinger, who had to turn up the volume on a breast-pocket gizmo whenever Casey Stengel lowered his voice. After a particularly cataclysmic game, while the Yankees manager stopped speaking entirely but continued moving his lips, Drebinger nearly tore off his shirt fiddling with the dials.

Unwittingly, he authored the ultimate title to the sportswriters' memoirs. It's just a punch line really. Nobody knows—or wishes to know—the story that led up to it. Drebinger must have thought he was keeping his voice down in the corner of a cocktail party when a lull hit the room and everyone heard him say:

"In all the confusion, I fucked the widow."

By Dave Kindred and Tom Callahan.

The final scores were 87 and 91, not so many strokes when you consider the course. The Royal & Diabolical played out to 7,266 yards, 37,319 miles, 69 days and, for those concerned with such things (like publishing houses and tax collectors), about $70,000. To be sure, we did not stay in hostels or eat at McDonald's. (Speak of the Devil, Dave's single day of food poisoning in Kathmandu constituted our sole malady.) Bill Corum captured the flavor of the newspaper profession in his declaration: "I don't want to be a millionaire, I just want to live like one." Typically, we deplored the poverty of Calcutta from the comfort of the Taj Bengal Hotel.

We made thirty-one take-offs and, symmetrically enough, thirty-one landings. In the upset of the year, we never lost a crumb of luggage, although in Bombay we were pulled off a plane a minute and a half from departure to identify our lumpy golf sacks on the tarmac. We patronized two kinds of boats, four kinds of trains and practically every kind of automobile, ranging from a Thai tuk-tuk to a KGB limo. We rode a cold-air elephant and a hot-air balloon. Still crinkling and jingling in our pockets are Irish pounds, Northern Irish pounds, Scottish pounds, French francs, Belgian francs, Swiss francs, Deutsche marks, old Soviet rubles, new Russian rubles, rand, Mauritian rupees, Nepalese rupees, Indian rupees, baht,

Singapore dollars, F.E.C., renminbi, yen and stacks of Icelandic 100s that might actually be worth something.

Gershwin was everywhere we went. So were Louis Armstrong, Fats Domino, Sammy Davis, Jr., Rodgers and Hammerstein and, believe it or not, Perry Como. You can't feel too far away from America when you see a guy walking down the street wearing a "Los Angeles 59ers" jacket. "He *almost* got it right," Dave said.

Over the sixty-nine days, we played thirty-six rounds of golf on thirty different courses, posting lows and highs of 74 (a hotel demitasse in Switzerland) and 104. We hung 118 U-turns. With the exception of one round in South Africa and another in Texas, we walked. We enjoyed that most of all. For whatever it says about us, we gathered almost no souvenirs along the trail, nothing at all for ourselves. Instead, we collected friends.

If they all show up on our doorstep at the same time, as we invited them all to do someday, it will be a strange convention indeed. I think of each of them as supplying an essential piece to a composite character who, when fully assembled, showed us the way home. Dave is less angry. I'm less disappointed. We're fifty-two and forty-seven and we're less than we hoped and more than we thought. It's not exactly a brick, but it's okay.

(I'm praying this wears off, but Dave came home actually in favor of the designated hitter and inter-league play. "To hell with the past," he said. "Bring on the future." Extraordinary.)

Louise Wakeman, the belle of Akureyri, lightly noted her sixty-ninth birthday in November. From the Arctic Open, she lowered herself into a volcano crater near Reykjavik, but could find no one else with the gumption to hit a golf ball. An 18 × 24-inch painting she has made of the clubhouse in Iceland is on its way there in a fancy frame. The "chocolate monkey" she won for finishing last turned out to be a luxurious blanket.

When he overheard us planning a Viking funeral for our lightweight but maddeningly unmanageable Sunday golf bags, Major Sam Hamilton said don't do that, send them to his lads. They're on their way to Nepal now filled with golf balls.

Roy Crawford is finally free on bond but may not get to trial before this book comes to print. In a warming voice, coming to hopeful, his wife explained they are waiting for a block of court time large enough to accommodate a most complicated case. In the last weeks, she used two of his three weekly visitor's passes while the third went to his closest golfing friend, who took him back to Portrush.

With Nicole's input but his own inspiration, the French architect Robert Berthet has begun a new creation in China. "I don't know what it is yet," he said. "It's still whispering to me. But it's a tremendous piece of ground, full of small mountains and millions of trees, a river, a valley, a big piece of luck. I'm open to it now." What did Patrick De La Chesnais say? "If you're open to things to happen to you, wonderful things will happen to you."

As South Africa is bearing down on its destiny, Moses Hadebe's words come back too: "Sports, especially golf, might seem to hold a low priority in our troubled country. But sports develop heroes, and heroes develop hope. I think it's important." One of the tableaus that has stayed with us is a man with a pistol in his belt hitting balls at a Johannesburg driving range.

Hogan said: "Enjoy your game." People used to think he didn't enjoy it; he couldn't. Maybe, at some point, he learned.

I came home to Washington after all, but not to stay. Angie, Becky and Tom hooted and clapped as I told my stories, the way they always have. I found a writing place by the water, where Becky bombarded me with greeting cards and love. She has a Masters degree now. Did I miss Girl Scouts?

Oh, our bet. By virtue of my victory, I claim the spoils we agreed on at the beginning. I get to choose the theaters of the rematch. I'm considering Brunei or Dubai or some other desert stop, where you carry the "course" with you in the form of a square of AstroTurf and pack your clubs on a camel caravan. There's a tournament in New Zealand where four-wheel-drive vehicles are essential and last year's winner lost only thirty-two balls. Then, what rhymes with Kathmandu? Why, Timbuktu, of course. And they say at the South Pole you can hit a ball on an ice field that spins for a mile and a half. "Sounds terribly appealing to me," Dave said.

We still haven't been to Tibet or South America or Australia. In 1987, Dave and I covered the America's Cup at Fremantle in Perth. That's where the last hole will be: Australia. I've decided that much. I can't say exactly where it is. In fact, I'm fairly certain it keeps hopping around.

Near the end of the regatta, it dawned on the Italian journalists that they hadn't seen a kangaroo. Well, nobody should leave Australia without seeing a kangaroo. So they rented a car and went helling into the outback looking for a skippy. Unfortunately, they didn't see him in time. They ran him over with a sickening thud.

After a funereal few moments, sighing and saying something in Italian that meant "What the hell," they propped the poor fellow up, put his lifeless arms into a silk Fila jacket and gathered around him for a class picture. At which point the kangaroo came to and went loping into the frontier—wearing the jacket—with the car keys—in the pocket.

Somewhere in the outback, there's a kangaroo in an Italian jacket with keys a-jingling. Those are the keys to the kingdom. His pouch is the eighteenth hole.

"I knew you'd get that story in somewhere," Dave said.

Everything fits eventually.

"Okay, let's get out."

And so we beat on, boats against the current, borne back ceaselessly into the past.

"I think we could end on a more novel note than that."

Yes, isn't it pretty to think so?

ACKNOWLEDGMENTS

Left to their own instincts, Kindred and Callahan might be lost in a jungle still. Happily, we had an army of helpers to whom we owe thanks for getting us around the world.

Thanks to the Callahans, Angie, Becky and young Tom. And thanks to Cheryl Kindred and her mother, Hazel Liesman. Dave's mother, Marie Cheek, and his sister, Sandra Litwiller, first tolerated and then encouraged the trip to Namur. Bless them both.

Thousands of logistical and philosophical puzzles were solved for us by Kathy Kelly, Bob Stroh, Nick Seitz, Jack McDermott, Bob Carney, Doug Hardy, John Huggan, Jack Stephens, Jim Armstrong, Katsumasa Miharu, Cheng Chunyu, Mahiko Kunihiro, Francis Gomes, Jim Anderson, Kirk Koning, Simone Anderson, Erin Kinder, Skuli Sveinsson, Nathan Knight and John Hewig.

Our agent, David Black, was helpful long before he sold the book to Doubleday. Amy Thomas, travel agent *extraordinaire,* did heavy lifting for months. With the exception of the Belgian horn-honker, the characters who breathe life into this book were gracious and generous to itinerant typists carrying golf clubs as passports.

Jerry Tarde, the gifted editor of *Golf Digest,* sustained us with his encouragement and enthusiasm from the start. As they say on the first tee, the man can play.

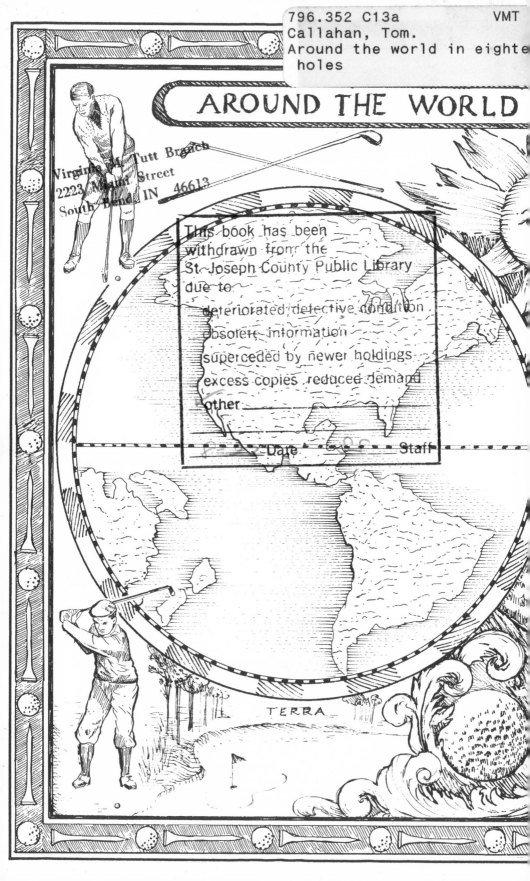

AROUND THE WORLD

TERRA